The Ultimate Secrets of Advertising

John Philip Jones
Syracuse University

The Ultimate Secrets of Advertising

Sage Publications
International Educational and Professional Publisher
Thousand Oaks ▪ London ▪ New Delhi

For information:

Sage Publications, Inc.
2455 Teller Road
Thousand Oaks, California 91320
E-mail: order@sagepub.com

Sage Publications Ltd.
6 Bonhill Street
London EC2A 4PU
United Kingdom

Sage Publications India Pvt. Ltd.
M-32 Market
Greater Kailash I
New Delhi 110 048 India

Printed in the United States of America

Library of Congress Cataloging-in-Publication Data

Jones, John Philip.
  The ultimate secrets of advertising / by John Philip Jones.
    p. cm.
  Includes index.
  ISBN 0-7619-2243-1 (cloth) — ISBN 0-7619-2244-X (pbk.)
  1. Advertising.   I. Title.
  HF5823 .J7174 2000
  659.1—dc21   2001001462

01 02 03 04 05 10 9 8 7 6 5 4 3 2 1

Acquiring Editor:	Marquita Flemming
Editorial Assistant:	MaryAnn Vail
Production Editor:	Diane S. Foster
Editorial Assistant:	Candice Crosetti
Copy Editor:	Joyce Kuhn
Typesetter/Designer:	Cristina Hill
Proofreader:	Scott Oney
Indexer:	Jeanne R. Busemeyer
Cover Designer:	Ravi Balasuriya

For W.M.H.J.

Contents

Epigraph

I learnt that what emerged from a dispassionate scientific
analysis of the confused events of war counted for no more in the
debates in which I became engaged than the in-built convictions
of various members of what were called the intelligence and
planning communities.

—Solly Zuckerman, 1978
(from his book *From Apes to Warlords*)

Zuckerman—empiricist and iconoclast—refers to a conflict that character-
izes all fields of activity: the conflict between unsupported convictions
and disinterested facts that contradict those convictions. Our knowledge of
how advertising works has until now been opaque, incomplete, and variable
in quality. And although some influential analysis remains bemused by the
difficulties, generations of practitioners and academics have developed un-
shakable (and often contridictory) views on the subject. This is a problem that
is addressed by this book.

List of Tables and Figures

Tables

Figures

Foreword: Red Threads

This ambitiously titled book tries to answer four questions:

- Does advertising work?
- How does advertising work?
- How much advertising works?
- How can advertising be measured and made accountable?

The last question effectively sums up the rest, and it can only be answered by our finding a way of calculating the financial return from advertising during a finite period (factoring out all other influences on the sales of a brand) and comparing this return to the dollar cost of the investment. Readers will be baptized in Chapter 7 with the method I recommend to do this difficult job, and Chapter 10 gives details of advertising accountability as it relates to 17 real brands.

The responsibility for the effectiveness of advertising is divided more-or-less equally between client and agency. Advertising cannot be successful unless the client markets a brand that will satisfy the consumer (normally well enough to encourage repeat purchase), and the brand must be sold at an acceptable price and be distributed widely throughout the retail trade. Besides these responsibilities, the client is an active partner in all matters concerning the advertising itself and takes the lead in determining the budget. The agency is totally committed to the advertising task. It writes the campaigns, assesses and endorses the budget, and plans the media (although this particular function is increasingly being done by outside organizations).

This book does not focus on how to write effective campaigns, nor how to arrive at the optimum advertising budget, nor how to phase this budget over time in the best media. These three matters—creative, budget, and media—are the most important operational concerns of advertising. I am, however, convinced that it is totally futile to plan such crucial contributions to the enterprise unless we are informed by knowledge of advertising effects. How can we talk about creative ideas without some degree of professional knowledge of the wide range of creative possibilities, and in particular, how specific creative ideas have performed in the real world? How can we propose an advertising budget without knowing about the effectiveness of similar (and also different) budgets? And how can we plan the details of media without knowing what specific media and media deployments have accomplished in the past?

My relatively brief discussions of the creative process, budgets, and media are therefore no more than extensions of this book's agenda, which is devoted essentially to the measurement of effects.

The book contains a good deal of information that has never before been published. This is important in itself. However, even more important is the fact that a good deal of time and effort has gone into analyzing and synthesizing—and generally thinking about—the data. Inhabitants of the world of information believe that everyone has an insatiable demand for facts. We are, in reality, drowning in them.[1] It is already exceptionally—and increasingly—difficult to select the relatively few facts that are important and to work out how to use them to our advantage. This is what I attempt to do in this book.

This volume is empirical, and the theory that it postulates is based on facts. The framework of how advertising works is described in Chapter 1 as the Gatekeeper model. Parts of this are repeated in subsequent chapters, where the elements of the model described in these extracts are examined with the use of marketplace data (and, in my judgment, confirmed).

The book is organized in a simple way. Chapters 1 through 5 are concerned with short-term and medium-term effects. Chapters 6 through 10 are devoted to advertising's long-term effects in all their complexity. The book concludes with two appendixes. Appendix A describes a wide range of tracking techniques by which the progress of advertising campaigns can be studied over time. The main part of this book does not study continuous advertising effects (for reasons given in Chapter 10). But tracking studies can represent an important way of looking at how the contribution of advertising develops, and readers should be made aware of their potential value. Appendix B is devoted to two supplementary methods of measuring the long-term effects of advertising. These are more theoretical than practical. However, given their potential importance, I believe that they should be used experimentally, and it is possible thereby that we will eventually be able to put flesh on their theoretical bones.

In Northern Europe, the local languages use a valuable metaphor, which can be translated into English as a red thread. It brings to mind a fabric, in which a red thread is a visible but not overly visible element of the weave. A red thread is used here to describe an underlying theme in a piece of writing—something that is constantly but not too aggressively evident. It is different from the structure or organization of a text, its basic blueprint. The structure of this book has just been described, but the writing itself contains a biblical total of seven red threads. These more than anything else reveal the underlying concepts to which the book is devoted. All parts of the book bear on them.

1. Behavioral Effects

Advertising works by influencing consumer behavior, and it does this in many ways. It can boost sales of a brand, thus increasing share of market in all circumstances except when the category is growing faster than the brand itself. It can defend a brand's sales. It can decelerate sales decline. It can increase penetration or purchase frequency or both. It can maintain sales in the event of a price increase.

Cognitive effects, which relate to consumers' awareness of brands, brand attributes and advertising campaigns, and also attitudes toward brands, are not much discussed here. Nor is the moot point of whether cognitive effects influence consumer behavior, or whether they are in turn influenced by it.

It is only by studying behavioral (and especially sales-related) effects that we can get close to the major topic addressed by this book, which is advertising accountability, the comparison of dollar return against dollar investment.

2. Advertising's Patchy but Multifaceted Effectiveness

There is not a scintilla of doubt that advertising *can* work and can influence consumer behavior. This does not mean that all advertising works. In fact, effective advertising represents no more than a substantial minority of all the advertising that is exposed.

How advertising works varies widely. Among the more important ways in which it can operate are (a) to build penetration (to bring in new users) or increase purchase frequency (to boost business from existing users); (b) to operate directly to stimulate brand trial by new users or work indirectly to reinforce existing users' inclination to buy the advertised brand repeatedly; and (c) to emphasize a brand's functional features or its added values—values that exist in the psyche of the consumer.

3. Three Orders of Advertising Effect

Advertising can produce a short-term effect, felt generally within 7 days of its appearance; a medium-term effect, measured over the course of a year; and long-term effects (in the plural), also measured over a year but representing effects that have built up over a number of years before this. The three effects are sequential, and each acts as gatekeeper to the one that follows. Most important, a short-term effect is a precondition for all other effects.

The shorter the period measured, the more the influence of advertising is felt on its own as an isolated stimulus. The longer the period, the more that advertising works in cooperation with other stimuli influencing sales.

Although this book is empirical, it aims to formulate an inductive (i.e., fact-based) theory. This theory aims to be general rather than specific, which means that *all important aspects* of advertising are covered by it. In a full sense, it tries to solve the very difficult problem of how advertising works.

4. Scale Economies

Large brands are generally strong brands (with few exceptions). Small brands are generally new or weak brands (with not quite such few exceptions). Large brands benefit from scale economies in all aspects of their manufacture and marketing.

Advertising-related scale economies are of cardinal importance. The best way to measure the long-term effects of advertising is via an advertising-related measure of these scale economies. The reasoning behind this is that large brands are indeed those that have benefited most from the long-term effects of previous advertising. These effects operate in conjunction with consumers' satisfaction with the functional delivery of these brands in a process of continuous mutual reinforcement.

5. Diminishing Returns

Surprisingly, incremental advertising pressure almost always yields diminishing returns when we measure carefully the sales that result progressively from increments of advertising. This is a short-term outcome, and it sets limits on how much we should concentrate advertising pressure, a matter of great importance in determining a brand's media strategy.

It seems paradoxical that although advertising works according to diminishing returns in the short term it can yield significant scale economies in the long term. This contradiction is best solved by focusing on the overall strength of the brand itself. Consumers will prefer a large brand over a small one on the basis of its performance. A large brand is likely to have a richer battery of added values in the minds of users. A large brand is probably in fuller retail distribution and carries greater influence with the retail trade. For those and other reasons, the *overall* response to advertising is likely to be greater for a large brand than for a small one. But even so, the pattern of incremental response for a large brand will still follow diminishing returns, as it does for a small brand. But for a large brand, the pattern of diminishing returns operates at a high absolute level; in contrast, for a small brand, it operates at a low absolute level. (This point is demonstrated diagrammatically in Appendix B, Figure B.5.)

6. A Snapshot of Accountability

To establish the measure of accountability for any advertising campaign, we must pick a finite period during which the dollar input and dollar output are measured. This process resembles taking a snapshot—a picture of advertising effect frozen in time. This is the reason why tracking studies—which are continuous and open-ended (like movies)—are not featured much in this book. The measurement of effectiveness in the short term, medium term, and long term is in every case discrete.

7. The Analytical Tools

This book is based on research that is state of the art. This includes pure single-source research; consumer panel research; a predictive technique to pretest television commercials; econometric evaluation; and studies of market and brand aggregates.

Although the data in the book are invariably based on sound samples and proven measurement techniques, I have tried very hard to explain them with the use of the simplest mathematics and (I hope) the clearest prose. I am not a supporter of the view that complicated research requires complicated exposition—in fact, just the opposite: Difficult concepts absolutely demand that they should be explained carefully and sequentially and in simple language. I have always been struck by the powerful image conjured up by Anatole France, who claimed that lucid prose is like white light; it is self-evidently simple, but its simplicity conceals great complexity.

What I find most frustrating about advertising evaluation is not the difficulty of the task, great though this is. It is that the plentiful discussion and controversy surrounding it are carried out exclusively among clever and well-informed technicians rather than by advertising decision makers. As a simple technician myself, I am happy in the company of my peers. But technicians are not the people who are in a position to implement the things I write about. I believe that people who are senior enough to make the decisions should be as passionately interested as I am in advertising evaluation in all its aspects. After all, it is their money that funds effective—or, more commonly, ineffective—advertising. But the issues have regrettably not penetrated either because they have not been presented with enough clarity or force or because senior decision makers have too many other priorities to spend much time engaged in discussions about advertising.

There is nothing new about this, and I have on many occasions addressed the upper echelons of management in large marketing companies on this topic.[2]

I have not achieved much success, but readers of this book can rest assured that I will not give up my efforts. Advertising evaluation really matters. And it matters most to advertisers who are interested in the profits earned by their brands. More accurate evaluation is the starting point to generating more effective advertising, and this is a *guaranteed* system for reducing the plentiful amount of waste. The result will, of course, be an inevitable increase in the manufacturer's profit. And profit is surely the most direct measure of the overall success of any business.

Notes

1. See Anonymous, "Quantifying Information: Byte Counters," *The Economist,* October 21, 2000, 96.
2. See John Philip Jones, "Advertising: The Cinderella of Business," *Market Leader: The Journal of the Marketing Society,* Summer 2000, 20-25. Also see John Philip Jones, "The Mismanagement of Advertising," *Harvard Business Review,* January/February 2000, 2-3.

Acknowledgments

My first thanks go, as always, to my wife, Wendy, to whom this book is dedicated. She has supervised the enterprise from first to last and carried out all the complex administration. She is my best (and toughest) critic. Not least, she has prepared an immaculate typescript for the publisher. She is one of the few people who can translate my handwriting into meaningful prose, and my multiple manuscript amendments are generally even more difficult to construe than my first drafts.

I am also extremely grateful to Media Marketing Assessment (MMA), which has made available to me a large battery of its most valuable data on the econometric analysis of advertising effects. This has formed the foundation for Chapters 6 through 10. Gerry Pollak has been the "point man" for MMA, and he not only presented me with large amounts of information in a form that I could understand completely, but he also took great pains to check all my calculations and test my interpretations of the figures. He was closely supported within MMA by two other experienced and talented analysts, its president Sunny Garga and its senior vice president Bob Wyman.

Another research organization, one with which I have worked extensively in the past, *rsc* THE QUALITY MEASUREMENT COMPANY, provided me with information of great depth and importance from which I constructed Chapter 3. They also deserve my gratitude.

I am equally grateful to the Institute of Practitioners in Advertising, the organization representing the advertising agencies in Great Britain, for giving me access to its incomparable collection of more than 600 rigorously evaluated case studies. I have selected from these the examples of tracking studies—all important cases of best professional practice—that appear in Appendix A.

The manuscript has been seen in whole or in part by a number of friends and professional associates, all experienced advertising practitioners and/or academics. In North America, these include George Black, Meg Blair, Erwin Ephron, Gary Gray, Allan Kuse, and Pam Shoemaker; and in Europe, Paul Feldwick, Robert Heath, and Nick Phillips. Despite the perceptive and constructive observations of these people, I must take the responsibility for all errors of commission and omission in this book.

Scott Bunting, of Industrial Color Labs in Syracuse, New York, produced all the superb computer-generated statistical diagrams not only on time but with his customary accuracy.

Big Ideas
and Good Ideas

M ost advertising practitioners are familiar with the phrase *big idea*, as used by David Ogilvy to describe the most important thing that goes into a successful advertisement:

> Unless your advertising contains a big idea, it will pass like a ship in the night. I doubt if more than one campaign in a hundred contains a big idea. I am supposed to be one of the more fertile inventors of big ideas, but in my long career as a copywriter I have not had more than 20, if that.[1]

Although Ogilvy's words give the strong immediate impression of informed and authoritative common sense, further thought suggests that something is missing from what he says. Ogilvy does not distinguish between *big* ideas and *good* ideas. Must a big idea also be good? And can a good idea be anything less than big? How do we explain the effectiveness of large numbers of unpretentious advertisements in fields such as direct response and retail? Such advertisements do not draw attention to themselves, but they work hard. Ogilvy's work was in highly competitive and advertising-intensive product categories, and in these, modest advertisements are generally invisible. It is the high profile of Bernbach's Volkswagen, Burnett's Marlboro, and Ogilvy's Rolls-Royce, Hathaway, Dove, and Pepperidge Farm that lingers in the mind. But I believe that big ideas *can* be less than good, and this chapter gives examples.

Like Ogilvy, I am concerned with big ideas. But I am going to use the phrase in a totally different sense from how it has been discussed so far. This book is devoted to explaining how advertising works. I am doing this, first, to help provide accountability for the large sums of money spent and, second, to help improve professional practice, thus diminishing the waste that comes from using ineffective advertising. The big ideas that I shall talk about are therefore those concerned with advertising strategy and tactics.

As I see them, big ideas are simple without being trite but dramatic enough to seize the imagination of the people who are going to use them. These are the business executives who are going to make major decisions under their influence: decisions such as whether or not to spend money on advertising a new brand; whether to increase, maintain, or reduce an advertising budget; and whether to continue with or cancel an advertising campaign.

The people who make such decisions are invariably senior executives— people at or near the summit of publicly owned organizations or who are the proprietors of privately owned firms. Decision makers are rarely advertising specialists or, even more rarely, advertising experts. They are general managers, and a good deal of their professional life is concerned with routine supervision, some of it extremely detailed depending on the personality of the manager. But very occasionally such people shake the status quo by directing major changes. Such changes are sometimes based on original ideas that have come out of the blue to the manager in question. More often, they are adaptations of big ideas offered by management consultants, or which are talked about in management circles and in business schools and discussed at industry conferences and in the more popular management journals, *Fortune, Forbes,* and *Business Week* in particular.

Consider the following: *Globalization, Outsourcing, Total Quality Management (TQM), The Paperless Office,* and three mutually related concepts, *Rationalization, Re-engineering,* and *Downsizing.* There is no doubt at all that these are big ideas, as evidenced by the extent to which they have influenced business practice during the past three decades.

However, it is fairly obvious to people familiar with the success or otherwise of business policies driven by such notions that although these are all big ideas they are not necessarily good ideas.[2] Their appeal to senior businesspeople is the way the ideas are rooted in common sense, plus the *réclame* that has surrounded them.

I am now going to look at a number of big ideas connected with advertising that have led to changes in the industry. These ideas are all concerned with the ways in which advertising is planned and written, matters best described as *advertising philosophy*.

This is separate from such things as the emergence of new media and organizational changes within agencies. Much upheaval has taken place in both media and agencies during the past 30 or 40 years: the fragmentation of the television audience as a result of cable stations; the birth of the Internet; the formation of creative teams within agencies; the introduction of qualitative research for advertising development; the birth of account planning; the separation of the media function from mainline agencies; new methods of agency remuneration; and the absorption of many prominent agency names into communications conglomerates. I shall not be much concerned with changes such as these because they are focused on the practical matters of producing advertising efficiently, smoothly, and reliably and augmenting the agencies' profitability and competitive position. They have been carried out to improve the *execution* of a basic philosophy.

I am concerned with the philosophy itself. As far as such advertising philosophy is concerned, I have been able to think of only four big ideas that have made an impact on the advertising profession as a whole since the emergence of full-service agencies at the beginning of the 20th century. This is a small number, and it confirms my belief that advertising people do not actually think much about their profession in any fundamental way. However, the following four are unquestionably big ideas, although not all of them are good ideas. I shall discuss each in turn.

- Scientific Advertising
- The Unique Selling Proposition
- Integrated Marketing Communications
- The Brand Image

Scientific Advertising

This is something indelibly associated with Claude C. Hopkins, the best-known advertising copywriter during the first three decades of the 20th century. He was a curious individual, but to David Ogilvy, he was technically "the supreme master."[3] Hopkins's work was based on direct response, and Scientific Advertising describes the simple technique of counting the number of sales orders generated by a coupon in a print advertisement and by simple arithmetic quantifying the cost per order.

Hopkins found it easy to demonstrate large differences in effectiveness between media vehicles, between different advertisements, and—most important—between relatively small variations of individual subjects. The actual advertisements that Hopkins wrote were full of copy, giving rich detail of why the reader should buy the brand. ("Reason why" copy was actually the norm for advertising of all types until the emergence of television in the years following World War II.)

Using the most extensive testing and quantifying the results according to cost per order, Hopkins was able to maximize the efficiency of an advertising budget in a surprisingly precise scientific fashion.

In 1923, Hopkins published a small book, inevitably titled *Scientific Advertising,* which sold in large numbers and is still in print.[4] As a scientific treatise this is a curious piece of work. It is full of generalizations (no doubt soundly based) but almost totally lacking in facts. It comes under the academic category of "relevancies without data"—an imperfect contribution to the literature but nevertheless preferable to the opposite, "data without relevancies"!

The deficiencies of this book aside, Hopkins's idea is relevant only to the minority of advertising that works by direct response—perhaps 20% of the total. For this specialist type of advertising, Hopkins's methods are widely used to this day. However, it is difficult to see how his technique of continuous detailed experimentation could ever be applied to general advertising except in a very rough-and-ready form. We must therefore conclude that Scientific Advertising, although it is a big idea, is not necessarily a good one; perhaps, like the curate's egg, it is good in parts.[5]

The Unique Selling Proposition (USP)

Rosser Reeves, the quintessential proponent of remorselessly hard-selling advertising, developed the idea of the Unique Selling Proposition during the 1950s and described it in a widely selling book published in 1960.[6] This led to the adoption of the USP at least in some form by a wide spectrum of agencies.

Although the acronym USP has been imprecisely used as a catchphrase—and is sometimes so used today—the original meaning was specific:

- "Each advertisement must say to each reader: 'Buy *this* product, and you will get *this* specific benefit.'
- "The proposition must be one that the competition either cannot, or does not, offer.
- "This proposition must be so strong that it can move the mass millions, i.e., pull over new customers to your product."[7]

The USP is certainly a big idea. It governed the thinking behind a number of powerful campaigns during its early years and thereby made a major impact on the growth of the Ted Bates agency when Rosser Reeves was its head. Nevertheless, I am compelled to call the USP a big idea but not a very good one because it has three flaws.

First, it is based on a functional differentiation between the advertised brand and the competition. It is generally unwise to base advertising on this type of argument because functional differentiation is easily copied, thus leaving the original brand's advertising campaign like the Emperor's new clothes. The USP closes the door against the brand's nonfunctional features—its added values or personality—features that underscore the functional differentiation and which provide the most deeply etched and durable way of distinguishing one brand from another.

Second, the supposed proof of effectiveness provided by Reeves is based on a fallacy. His research technique Usage-Pull shows that the consumers familiar with a brand's campaign tend to be brand users, while those unfamiliar tend to be nonusers. The tacit assumption is that familiarity with the campaign pulls over new customers. However, the reverse is at least equally true: The fact that a person uses a brand is likely to create awareness of the campaign as a result of the known psychological phenomenon of Selective Perception.

The third point about the USP is that it ignores the importance of repetition of purchase by existing users of a brand. This method of developing a brand's sales—boosting purchase frequency rather than penetration—is the most important objective for large brands of repeat-purchase packaged goods.

The problems of the Unique Selling Proposition were responsible for its virtual disappearance from professional practice, despite unsuccessful attempts by Ted Bates to resurrect it. Nevertheless, the USP remains a genuine piece of advertising archaeology.

Integrated Marketing Communications (IMC)

This idea has an academic *provenance*. It originated in the early 1980s and is closely associated with Don E. Schultz of the Medill School at Northwestern University.[8] IMC is based on the sensible notion that all components of a brand's communications should march to the same drum beat. They should all follow a common strategy and be planned to work cooperatively.

The main communications elements that should be integrated in the common plan are advertising (defined as "highly selective" advertising), direct marketing, public relations, selling to the retail trade, sales promotions directed to the consumer, in-store activities, packaging, and word-of-mouth (including influencing opinion leaders).[9] IMC is based on the targeting of heavy users of a brand (normally 20% of all buyers account for half its volume).

IMC is a big idea and is also, with qualifications, a good idea. However, there is a practical limitation on how efficiently it can be executed. It is in fact extremely difficult to use advertising media to target the heavy users of any specific brand. Different mass media offer various degrees of demographic concentration, but they cannot offer much beyond that to target brand users efficiently (i.e., without a good deal of waste). Direct mail is theoretically more efficient, but for both creative and cost-efficiency reasons it is generally more suitable for "high-involvement" goods and services than it is for "low-involvement" ones. High involvement is a phrase used to describe expensive items about which there is a complicated story to communicate and which are bought infrequently. Low involvement refers to routine purchases of goods bought in food stores and drugstores; for these, direct mail is hardly suitable except for the distribution of coupons.

It must also be remembered that, of the various communications activities associated with the brand, advertising is by far the most important. Since the IMC approach lumps advertising together with the other communication channels, it is not given the primary attention it deserves. In fact, in virtually all circumstances, the first and most important communication task is to get the consumer advertising right. All the other activities should fall into place as extensions of this.

Because the limitations of IMC are less apparent with higher-priced goods and services than with repeat-purchase packaged goods, IMC has had more scope to develop in high-involvement fields (e.g., banks, hotels, airlines, and automobiles) than with low-priced, regularly purchased goods, which nevertheless account for the majority of consumer expenditure.

Many agencies today pay lip service to Integrated Marketing Communications, and some make a serious effort to put it into practice. To some extent, the formation of large communications conglomerates, an important development of the 1980s, represented an attempt to provide "one-stop shopping" for clients who wish to coordinate their different communications activities.

The Brand Image

Brand Image is a concept closely associated with David Ogilvy, although as with IMC, academia made a contribution during the very early stages.[10] Ogilvy used Brand Image as a device to identify—almost to trademark—the work of his agency. This philosophy helps us understand why advertisements written by Ogilvy himself have such style and elegance, as if the very presentation of the advertising is saying something important about the brand (which indeed it might be). Ogilvy & Mather did not manage to maintain Brand Image as its exclusive property. The device is used today virtually universally, although agencies vary a good deal in the amount of emphasis they place on it.

> Every advertisement should be thought of as a contribution to the complex symbol which is the *brand image*. If you take that long view, a great many day-to-day problems solve themselves.[11]

> The manufacturer who dedicates his advertising to building the most sharply defined *personality* for his brand will get the largest share of the market at the highest profit.[12]

Is Brand Image a big idea? I think unquestionably yes. Is it also a good idea? I am much less certain, because Brand Image contains within it a dangerous distraction which can actually be counterproductive. The very act of concentrating advertising planning on brand values and therefore on the long term has led to a perilous neglect of the short term. British advertising, with its use of account planning and its fixation on brand values, is particularly culpable in this regard. Planning for the long term without cognizance of the short term can lead us to run ineffective advertising and waste our advertising investments. If we do not look for a short-term effect, we will miss our first opportunity to judge whether or not our campaign is working.

Concentration on the brand image thus leads us to take the second advertising step before attempting the first. This has provided the genesis of the analysis of how advertising works to which this book is devoted. I have tried very hard to build this analysis into a big idea about how advertising can be used reliably to build both sales and brand values.

My idea is called quite simply the Gatekeeper. At the heart of it is the notion that advertising must have a demonstrable short-term effect before it can be expected to benefit the brand in the long term. I believe that this is true and demonstrable. We *must* indeed be able to demonstrate short-term effect. If there is no such effect, the campaign should be stopped immediately. The gate should be shut.

There is nothing in my doctrine that takes issue with the possibility of advertising having perhaps powerful long-term effects. Half of this book is devoted to what advertising contributes to brands in the period beyond the present and the medium term. I simply take issue with the Brand Image school because I insist that advertising has vital preliminary work to do before it can begin to be focused on the long term.

The Gatekeeper

Every well-informed book or article about the measurement of advertising effects spells out in the most discouraging detail the difficulties of the undertaking, and in particular the problems of untangling the effects of advertising from those of the other marketing stimuli that are always in operation.

This repeated emphasis on the difficulties creates the inevitable although unintended impression that advertising makes only a small and rather uncertain contribution to the marketplace. The nervous approach of many analysts underplays what we actually know about advertising's effects, things we know firmly from both aggregated data and case-by-case evidence. In this book, I intend to take a more positive line and am prepared to defend my position, since I am more optimistic than many of my peers about our ability to demonstrate what advertising can do. I would not publish my data unless I had faith in their validity. And I can only remind those who disagree with me that truth is more often advanced by the clash of strong views than by the conflict of weak ones.

I am now going to summarize the theoretical framework of the argument spelled out in this book. This argument describes a model that has been constructed from a number of different *tranches* of evidence. At the same time, this summary provides signposts to chapters in the book where the individual parts of my model are more fully discussed and empirically supported.

The word *Gatekeeper* highlights the most important and identifiable element in the model. However, the full story covers much more ground. It proceeds in 10 steps, each of which is discrete yet together follow a sequence:

1. Advertising is capable of producing a pronounced effect on consumer purchases of a brand within a short period (generally measured as 7 days) after its exposure. In about 30% of cases, this effect is very large; all types of advertising can do this (e.g., rationally based and emotionally based). See Chapters 2 and 3.
2. Since more than one advertising exposure before the brand is bought has little more effect than a single exposure, budgetary and media factors are not very influential in determining advertising effectiveness. Because one advertisement does most of the work, the effect must come substantially from the advertisement itself, that is, from the creative idea within it. See Chapter 2.
3. This short-term effect varies a great deal according to the advertising used. It can be predicted before the event and also measured post hoc. See Chapters 2 and 3.
4. The short-term effect of an advertisement determines whether or not that advertisement will have a medium-term effect, and this medium-term effect will determine whether or not it will have a subsequent long-term effect. If there is no short-term effect, the advertisement will have no delayed effect. See Chapter 4. **THE MEASURED SHORT-TERM EFFECT OF AN ADVERTISEMENT IS THE GATEKEEPER. IN ITS ABSENCE THE GATE MUST BE CLOSED. A NEW CAMPAIGN MUST BE USED.**
5. A repetition of short-term effects over a period (normally 12 months)—effects felt exclusively during the periods when the brand is advertised—adds up to a medium-term effect. This is defined as the aggregate effect of advertising on consumer purchases of the brand across the course (normally) of a year. See Chapter 4.
6. The medium-term effect is a net effect—sales gains from our brand's campaign minus sales losses to competitive brands advertised during the gaps in our brand's schedule. Because such gaps are normally inevitable, the medium-term effect of advertising is virtually always smaller than the short-term effect. See Chapter 4.
7. The size of the medium-term effect is determined not only by the creative content of the campaign but also by the brand's budget and its media strategy. Budget and media are devices to engineer the advertising continuity needed to protect the brand from competitive assaults. Sales promotions can add to the effect of advertising; such synergy is strongest when promotions coincide with the most powerful advertising campaigns. See Chapters 4 and 5.
8. Econometric analysis can quantify approximately the size of the medium-term effect of advertising by estimating the value of the sales during a year that can be

directly attributed to the campaign. Econometric analysis is also able to quantify in round terms the effect on sales of individual doses of advertising. This is expressed by a small number, described technically as a coefficient of advertising elasticity. See Chapters 6 and 9. Although econometric estimates show that the medium-term effect of advertising is generally uneconomic (with costs greater than receipts), elasticity calculations often demonstrate that advertising can pay for itself in the very short term. This confirms the value of planning media to achieve a repetition of short-term effects, with maximum continuity. See Chapter 9.

9. Advertising can also have long-term effects that operate beyond a year and into the future. This process is cumulative (unlike the short-term and medium-term effects). A brand initially grows as a result of expanding penetration—an increase in the number of users—a process that gives a brand breadth and which is influenced by advertising in its short-term role. The long-term effects of advertising work by adding to this a depth of repeat purchase, an increased perception of value, and a boosted salience. See Chapters 7, 8, 9, and 10.

10. The long-term effects of advertising take the form of an enrichment of the brand and a strengthening of its relationship with the consumer. There are at least six ways in which this enrichment can be evaluated. The most important of them is a measure specific to the advertising itself. See Chapter 7.

In the chapters where the different parts of the model are discussed, relevant extracts from this 10-point description are repeated *in italics*.

The reason why the model was constructed was to enable advertisers to use it operationally. This book describes and discusses four specific practical applications.

First, clients must address the creative content that is at the heart of all successful advertising. The characteristics of successful campaigns are these:

- They offer a reward from the intrinsic properties of the advertisement itself, a reward to viewers for spending 30 seconds in the advertiser's company.
- They communicate visually rather than verbally.
- They surround the advertisement with an emotional envelope, within which is a nugget of rational differentiation for the brand. This does not mean that the advertising needs to browbeat the viewer with rational arguments.

I believe that these qualities, especially the last, are what enable a campaign to do the difficult job of augmenting the psychological added values embedded in the brand *while at the same time stimulating immediate sales.*

Second, because the initial effect of a campaign is all-important, every effort must be made to ensure and to demonstrate that it achieves such an effect. All advertisements should be pretested. There is good evidence that the short-term effect of advertising can be reliably predicted, given that the system used is not biased toward either rationally based or emotionally based copy. And although this short-term effect should also be measured after the event, it is too time-consuming and expensive to wait until the campaign has been run to find out whether or not it is working.

Third, the media for a brand should be directed at exposing the campaign at a minimal acceptable weight every week, and it should then be run for as many weeks as the budget will allow. Any inevitable remaining gaps in the schedule should take place during the low season.

Fourth, a research budget should be allocated to measure the short-term, medium-term, and long-term effects of an advertising campaign. The estimate of the sales value of the long-term effect can be added to the estimate of the sales value of the medium-term effect to provide a measure of advertising accountability, a calculation of how close the campaign comes to paying its way. The estimate does this by comparing the total value of sales generated with the cost of the advertising. Accountability, embracing both medium-term and long-term effects, *is the ultimate objective of all attempts to measure advertising effects.*

As mentioned, the calculation of medium-term effect can also normally yield an estimate of a brand's advertising elasticity, the sensitivity of sales to incremental changes in the advertising budget. This, together with a realistic measure of advertising accountability, provides the best possible combination of data to help determine a brand's optimum media budget.

The research budget for all these things will always be significant, but relative to the sales value of a substantial brand, and in particular in view of *the large opportunity-cost of running ineffective advertising,* this expenditure on research will be economic.

Market Research and How to Interpret It

Before I describe the research used in this book, I must mention the types *not* used.

First, no attempt is made to discuss the processes by which advertising operates on the human mind. This is a topic not susceptible to empirical examination and is a field in which investigators use their informed judgment supported by experiments in the psychological laboratory. This type of inquiry can provide flashes of enlightenment, although some analysts are skeptical. Noted physical scientist Solly Zuckerman once unkindly described this type of exploration as not research in the customary sense of an examination of the real world but, rather, something "mainly concerned with conjecture and speculation."[13]

Second, continuous consumer tracking is not used in this book in the primary role of measuring advertising effects. The technique follows trends in consumers' awareness and knowledge of brands and advertising campaigns and their perceptions of brand attributes and their attitudes toward them. This type of research is not sensitive enough to measure the short-term effect of advertising, which is the starting point of all the research in this book. Furthermore, it leaves open whether the consumer-based measures are driven by the advertising for a brand or by consumers' use of the brand itself. For an unambiguous measurement of advertising effects, we must of course be sure that we are measuring the former and not the latter. Nevertheless, consumer tracking is very useful for a secondary purpose—diagnosis, to help us understand *why* some advertising works as it does—and this aspect is discussed in Chapter 10 and in Appendix A.

Finally, qualitative evaluation of individual advertisements plays no part in this volume. Such research has much value in a different context—advertising development—but it cannot fit into my framework because it is sometimes ambiguous, often cloudy, and can never be quantified. This is due both to the technique itself and to the small size of the samples employed.

The model described in this book is, however, supported by extensive quantitative research, which is discussed in later chapters and is interpreted in a very conservative fashion. There are a number of reasons for doing this.

In the hard sciences, researchers use precisely calibrated instruments so that small variations in the readings are both accurate and significant. For example, there is a highly meaningful difference between one individual's body temperature of 98.6° Fahrenheit and another person's 100.6°.

In contrast to this type of measurement, the tools used for evaluating advertising are based on sampling, a device borrowed from the social sciences. We employ sampling for consumer surveys, product testing, retail sales measurement, counting the size of media audiences, and much else. The technique examines closely a relatively small number of people or homes or stores, and if the sample is correctly drawn, the answers from the sample are reasonably representative of the total population of such people, homes, or stores.

But it must be emphasized that the estimation is never more than a good (or sometimes less good) approximation. This is because of three imperfections in the research procedure.

First, there is the basic sampling error, a subject about which we have good knowledge. To illustrate this, consider an estimate, made by the optimum size and best type of sample survey, of an immediate 40% sales increase from exposing an advertisement. From this, we *know* that there is a 95% probability that the true answer will lie in the range of 42% to 38%. This represents a span stretching from 5% above to 5% below our estimate, or a total range of inaccuracy of 10%.[14]

The second problem emerges when we compare subsamples. This is a device we employ to calculate the immediate effect of exposing an advertisement, by comparing purchases in "ad households" and "adless households."[15] Subsamples are always different from one another in small ways, and this difference is enough to introduce a bias and thus cause some distortion in our figures.

The third problem is often the most serious one. It is the questions we ask of our respondents. When experiments are carried out asking different types of question to elicit the same information from people, consistent differences will always emerge in our findings. The only rule we can follow in drawing up questions is to frame them in as neutral a way as possible and make a conscious effort to avoid implicit bias. This is not as easy as it sounds. It is far better to collect data mechanically (e.g., from scanners and meters) so that we minimize the active intervention of human beings. This is the system mostly used for the quantitative research used in this book.

As a result of these three problems, I am adopting a rule of thumb based on doubling the minimum sampling error and therefore imposing an automatic and arbitrary range of error of 10% either side of any statistical estimate, or a total band of inaccuracy of 20%. An illustration of the practical application of this, using again as an example a hypothesized sales increase from the exposure of an advertisement, is presented in Table 1.1, which also lists a number of levels of sales increase and sets out the band of inaccuracy relating to each estimate, based on my rule of thumb of "10% up and 10% down."

Examine the four bands of inaccuracy. In cases where any bands overlap, there is in effect nothing to choose between the estimated sales responses which produce these particular bands. Thus, there is no difference between an estimated sales increase of 50.0% and 45.0% nor between 45.0% and 40.0% nor between 40.0% and 35.0%. We can, however, accept as significant a difference between 50.0% and 40.0% and between 45.0% and 35.0%. In these cases, the

TABLE 1.1 Alternative Levels of Estimated Sales Response to an Advertisement
Exposure

% Sales Response Estimate	% Band of Inaccuracy
50.0	55.0–45.0
45.0	49.5–40.5
40.0	44.0–36.0
35.0	38.5–31.5

bands do not overlap. This type of interpretation is simple enough, and in the
first statistical analysis in this book (Table 2.1 in Chapter 2), the actual bands of
inaccuracy are set out alongside the other figures.

What this comes down to is that although I am employing what I consider
high-quality data I am only prepared to accept as significant really substantial
differences in the individual statistical readings. I have limited myself in this
way in the belief that large differences are likely to be real and that conclusions
drawn from them will be credible. In addition, of course, this procedure is totally harmonious with the concept of the *big idea* which was the starting point
of this chapter and of this book.

Notes

1. David Ogilvy, *Ogilvy on Advertising* (New York: Crown Publishers, 1983), 16.
2. See, for example, a rather discouraging article: Anonymous, "Change Management: An Inside Job," *The Economist,* July 15, 2000, 61: "Two-thirds of re-engineering projects seem to fail; and, in Britain, less than half of all 'Total Quality Management' programs show any demonstrable results at all."
3. David Ogilvy, *Confessions of an Advertising Man* (New York: Atheneum, 1984), 114.
4. Claude C. Hopkins, *Scientific Advertising* (Chicago: Crain Books, 1966).
5. For non-British readers, the curate's egg refers to a famous cartoon that appeared in the English journal *Punch* during the middle of the 19th century. In it, a young clergyman is shown as the guest of his bishop and is eating a boiled egg. The curate is extremely sensitive to his own insignificance compared with the vast importance of the bishop. When the latter notices that the curate is eating a bad egg, the curate hastens to explain that, indeed no, parts of it are good.
6. Rosser Reeves, *Reality in Advertising* (New York: Alfred A. Knopf, 1960).
7. Ibid., 47-48.
8. Don E. Schultz, Stanley J. Tannenbaum, and Robert F. Lauterborn, *Integrated Marketing Communications* (Chicago: NTC Business Books, 1993).
9. Ibid., 69.

10. Burleigh B. Gardner and Sidney J. Levy, "The Product and the Brand," *Harvard Business Review,* March-April 1955, 33-39.

11. Ogilvy, *Confessions of an Advertising Man,* 100.

12. Ibid., 102.

13. Solly Zuckerman, *From Apes to Warlords* (New York: Harper & Row, 1978), 14.

14. Jeffrey L. Pope, *Practical Marketing Research* (New York: AMACOM, American Management Association, 1981), 207.

15. "Ad households" and "adless households" describe two groups of buyers of an identified brand during any particular week: those who have, and those who have not, received advertising for the brand during the period of 7 days before the purchase. This concept is explained in Chapter 2.

2

Passing Through the Gate

Advertising is capable of producing a pronounced effect on consumer purchases of a brand within a short period (generally measured as 7 days) after its exposure. This short-term effect varies a great deal according to the advertising used. It can be measured post hoc. Because one advertisement does most of the work, the effect must come substantially from the advertisement itself, from the creative idea within it.

Claude Hopkins would not have been in any way surprised by the above extract from the description of the Gatekeeper model. Direct response advertising works in no other fashion, and it is the immediate measurable response from such advertising that made possible Hopkins's technique of Scientific Advertising.

There is, however, much less agreement that the same principles and methods of operation apply to advertising for other types of goods and services, and in particular that for repeat-purchase packaged goods. The problem was and is measurability. These types of products are not sold by the manufacturer off the page and delivered to the consumer by mail order. They are distributed through third parties: in some cases, both wholesalers and retailers, and in other cases, retailers alone. With this indirect relationship between the advertiser and the end consumer, it has always been difficult to establish a clear link between the exposure of an advertisement and the purchase of a brand across the checkout at the store—and no link, no measurability.

Difficulty of measurement is an important background reason for the way in which the Brand Image doctrine has been so strongly supported over the years by many thoughtful advertising people. Their thinking is that, since it is virtually impossible to see any change in sales immediately after advertising appears, something else must be taking place. In fact, it is optimistically assumed that the advertising is working indirectly—and perhaps also powerfully—to strengthen the image attributes and associations of the brand and that the benefit will be seen in the long term. This idea remains strong today. It plays an important role in reassuring many advertisers who are running ineffective campaigns.

Some analysts still believe that all advertising effects are no more than the accumulated delayed effects of advertisements that have been exposed weeks, months, and years before. I believe this doctrine is wrong, or at the very least gravely incomplete, and I shall return to it in this chapter.

Paradoxically, David Ogilvy, the arch-proponent of the brand image, was the only noted writer of well-esteemed and successful campaigns for large consumer brands who declared his belief that the methods of direct response are totally relevant to general practice. In discussing where he went for guidance in the arduous job of giving birth to "great campaigns," the first two sources of valuable experience that Ogilvy described were leading mail order advertisers and the department stores, whose advertising also generally works directly. He then went on to talk about the generalized findings of the better-known copy researchers and the inspiration he received from the work of the more charismatic writers of general advertising.[1]

Ogilvy had a clear vision that both direct and general advertising follow the same underlying principles. In this, some of the creative men and women of the old school might have agreed with him, admittedly with qualifications. I believe, however, that his view would receive no support at all from the major creative figures of the recent past and today. The intransigent opposition by contemporary industry leaders to the idea of learning lessons from direct response is based on prejudice, as direct response is considered to be at the lower end of the advertising business.

What makes this prejudice so remarkable is a discovery made more than 30 years ago: a persuasive and widely published piece of evidence that advertising, in particular television advertising, is capable of producing an immediate and measurable effect on the sales of many brands of repeat-purchase packaged goods. This piece of work dates from 1966 and was carried out in Great Britain by Colin McDonald, who is still active in the research field.[2]

Let me return to the difficulty of establishing a link between the exposure of an advertisement and the purchase of a brand across the checkout counter. McDonald found this link in the hands of the consumer herself. The connection was demonstrated in an *apparently* simple way by calculating the difference in purchases of an identified brand by (a) individual consumers who bought it after they had received advertising for it and (b) those who had bought without such advertising. Because the individual consumer was identified as the single source of the two types of information—advertising received and brand buying—this type of research came to be known as Single-Source. It is a system that has become very important in the research world, despite the fact that carrying it out is much more difficult than it at first appears.

McDonald measured the buying of all brands in nine categories of repeat-purchase packaged goods in 255 households in the London area. The housewives recorded their buying and also the household's television viewing and the names of the magazines and newspapers read in the house. The homemakers did this by filling in diaries in longhand. McDonald planned and supervised the laborious calculations separating purchases preceded by advertising and purchases not preceded by advertising. The "window"—the period during which the advertising-buying relationship was measured—was the purchase interval, the time since the last brand in the category was bought.

An important feature of McDonald's research was that it was pure in the sense that brand buying was related to advertising for identified brands coming into the household, so the research connected *each brand bought to whether or not advertising for that same brand had come into the home before the purchase.* In a number of research studies carried out after McDonald's work, weaker types of data collection related advertising to buying. I have called these systems Diluted Single-Source research. In general, the findings from these studies have never been as clear or positive as those from the Pure Single-Source method.

McDonald surprised the professional world by the strength of the advertising effects that he demonstrated. It is therefore astonishing that a quarter-century passed before Pure Single-Source research was extended on a major scale and with the use of advanced technology. But eventually a large piece of such research was carried out in the United States in 1991 and 1992 by the A. C. Nielsen Company. My contribution to the enterprise was partly in the planning of the research method and more especially in interpreting the findings, which were released in a book published in 1995 and also in many journal articles.[3] Like McDonald, I found powerful effects immediately after the advertising.

Short-Term Advertising Strength (STAS)

The Nielsen system of Single-Source research was based on Nielsen's ongoing Household Panel, a properly drawn sample of 40,000 households across the United States, in which every purchase of regularly bought brands is logged with handheld scanners. In each home, the shopper uses the scanner to read the Universal Product Code (UPC) on each pack bought and thus records details of brand name, variety, and pack size. The shopper also punches in manually the date, the price, simple details of any promotional offers, the name of the store, and the identity of the individual doing the shopping. The information that has been fed into the scanner is sent to Nielsen by a simple automatic process over the public telephone lines. The data gathering is continuous—longitudinal, to use the technical language of statistics. The scanner system was data collection of a highly sophisticated type. Nevertheless, it represented only one of three pieces of information needed for Pure Single-Source research.

The second process of data collection covered television viewing. This initial Nielsen study concentrated on television alone, although later studies by other research organizations also covered magazines. (These are discussed later in this chapter.) Nielsen selected a representative subset of 2,000 homes from its Household Panel and attached a meter to every television set in each home to record when it was switched on and to which channel. The viewing of individual family members was not recorded, but "People Meters" enabled this to be done for the A. C. Nielsen Single-Source research in Germany (also discussed later).

The third piece of research tackled the immense diversity of television viewing patterns: the large number of different channels viewed in each of 150 cities and regions in the United States. Nielsen used a system called Monitor Plus, which employs a series of television receiving stations that log all the advertising that appears, at 15-second intervals, in the 23 largest Designated Market Areas (DMAs) in the United States, covering more than half the total population. Information is collected from all the main stations, both network and cable, in these areas.

Purchases in ad households *minus* purchases in adless
households = purchases driven by advertising.

Figure 2.1. Ad Households and Adless Households

There were thus three different streams of information: household purchasing, television viewing, and the identities of the advertised brands. I decided on a "window" of 7 days as the period during which a short-term advertising effect is assumed to be felt. Because the date when the brand was purchased was collected in the scanner, a way could be found to identify whether advertising for that same brand had entered—or had *not* entered—the household during the preceding 7 days. Nielsen took immense pains to devise the computer programs to generate the information that I specified.

The basic idea behind the research was the concept of "ad households" and "adless households," illustrated in Figure 2.1.

A subtle but important characteristic of these two collections of households is that the groups were different *for every single purchase occasion.* With each purchase of any brand, the 2,000 households on the panel formed themselves into unique combinations of ad households and adless households, plus a third group who had not purchased the brand at all at this time. For the next purchase of a brand, the groups were mixed totally differently.

The tabulation of the data was extremely complicated, but this was a vital part of the process. We were examining constantly changing combinations of the same collection of 2,000 households. The advantage of this system was that it guaranteed the homogeneity of the subsamples. The presence or absence of advertising was the sole variable distinguishing the subsamples on every occasion the brand was bought. Here are examples of what this meant in practice.

Buying took place at different times of the year during various seasonal highs and lows depending on the product category. In the high season, both the ad households and the adless households were buying a lot, and the only difference between them was, respectively, the presence or absence of advertising beforehand. It worked in a similar way in the low season when people were buying less. Buying also took place accompanied by sales promotions and un-accompanied by sales promotions. When promotions were in operation, they attracted both ad and adless households, and again the only difference between them was, respectively, the presence or absence of advertising before the purchase. The same was true of purchases unaccompanied by sales promotions.

The constantly changing grouping of ad and adless households was a totally different system from one based on a matched pair of permanent, geographically separated subpanels: the method used by the American research company Information Resources, Inc. (IRI) for its BehaviorScan panels. The research in France, discussed later, employed this latter method.[4]

The measure of advertising effect I developed was based on a brand's market share *measured in purchase occasions* and not purchase volume. The former is a sharper way of signaling advertising effects. The name I gave the system is Short-Term Advertising Strength (abbreviated to STAS), and it has three elements:

1. *Baseline STAS* is the brand's market share in the households that had received no television advertising for it during the 7 days before the purchase took place.
2. *Stimulated STAS* is the brand's market share in the households that had received at least one television advertisement for it during these previous 7 days.
3. *STAS Differential* is the difference between Baseline STAS and Stimulated STAS; this is normally indexed on the Baseline, which has a value of 100. The STAS Differential Index is the measure of the short-term sales gain (or loss) generated by a brand's advertising. It is a mathematical expression of the diagram, Figure 2.1, that demonstrates the difference between the ad households and the adless households.

A brand's STAS Differential is an average for all a brand's separate purchases across a year; my research was mostly based on the 12 months of 1991. The research measured a total of 78 advertised brands (with purchasing data for an additional 64 unadvertised ones). I covered 12 product categories, with a total of 110,000 purchase occasions: an average of about 1,400 per brand. The STAS measures are described in Figure 2.2.

The simplest way to show the sharp and wide-ranging effects of advertising is by dividing the 78 brands into a number of more-or-less equal groups and calculating the average STAS Differential for each. I ranked all the brands by the size of their individual STAS, then divided them into 10 separate blocks (of 7-8-8-8-8-8-8-8-8-7 brands), known technically as deciles. I then averaged the

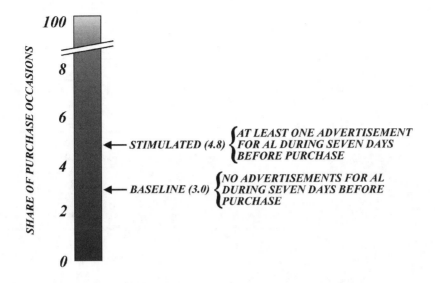

Figure 2.2. STAS Measures for Brand AL

STAS for each decile, with the results shown in Table 2.1. The bands of inaccuracy (described in Chapter 1) are also set out.[5]

Table 2.1 does not need much comment. At the top end of my sample of brands, the effect of advertising is very powerful, the most effective 10% of advertisements boosting sales by an average of 136% (or 150% at the extreme of the band of inaccuracy); 70% of advertisements cause some immediate sales increase, and 30% of advertisements are associated with a *reduction* in sales. I do not believe that these advertisements at the bottom end actually cause sales to go down because they are so positively awful. The better explanation is that the advertising is not strong enough to protect the brands from the more powerful campaigns of competition when the brand and the competition are advertised at the same time.

Research From Germany and Great Britain

Immediately after the findings of the American research were published, I was commissioned by the German advertising agencies' association, Gesamtver-

TABLE 2.1 Decile Analysis of STAS (78 Nielsen Brands)

Rank	Average STAS Differential	Band of Inaccuracy
Top	236	250–222
9th	164	170–158
8th	139	143–135
7th	121	123–119
6th	116	118–114
5th	108	109–107
4th	103	104–102
3rd	97	98–96
2nd	89	90–88
Bottom	73	76–70
Average	124	126–122

band Werbeagenturen (GWA), to carry out a similar piece of work in cooperation with the A. C. Nielsen Company in Germany. We used data from 1993 and
1994, and although the statistical foundation was substantial, the overall scale
of the research was about half that of the American study. However, the use of
"People Meters," identifying viewing by housewives, represented an advance
on the technique used in the American investigation.[6]

After another short interval, Colin McDonald, the pioneer of Pure Single-
Source research, gained access to the British Adlab database, which covered
four and a half years' experience of 5 important product categories. Overall, the
size of the Adlab investigation was larger than my American study by a factor of
more than 2 to 1.[7] McDonald tabulated and interpreted his Adlab data in the
same way as I had carried out the original American study.

It is instructive to compare the distribution of STAS effects in Germany and
Great Britain with the original work in the United States. We see this comparison in Table 2.2.

The distribution of the figures has approximately the same shape in the three
countries; certainly, the similarities are greater than the differences. The range
of advertising effects from Germany is more compact than that in the United
States, with less extremes at top and bottom. The British figures fall somewhere
between the American and the German. However, in all three countries the immediate effect of advertising on sales is shown to be very large, certainly in the
top deciles, and in all three countries there is a wide range of variation. Significantly, in all three countries, 30% of campaigns are ineffective.

TABLE 2.2 3-Country Decile Analysis of STAS Differentials

Rank	United States, 1991 78 Brands (Nielsen)	Germany, 1993 28 Brands (Nielsen)	Great Britain, 1986–1990 67 Brands (Adlab)
Top	236	154	184
9th	164	127	129
8th	139	116	119
7th	121	108	114
6th	116	106	110
5th	108	101	107
4th	103	100	102
3rd	97	98	98
2nd	89	92	93
Bottom	73	83	73

More Countries, More Replication

I have referred to IRI's BehaviorScan system, which differs from my own research in that BehaviorScan uses permanent and geographically separated household panels whereas I use a single national panel in which the ad households, adless households, and nonbuying households change with every purchase occasion and in this represent different groupings of the same basic panel of 2,000 homes.

IRI has never taken kindly to my system, claiming its own to have greater scientific purity.[8] I was nevertheless very surprised to see that when IRI published a range of STAS Differentials, its findings were close to mine. The published BehaviorScan research comes from France.[9]

The data in Table 2.3 were analyzed into quintiles (in which the STAS figures are ranked from highest to lowest and then broken down into five blocks). I recomputed the American data from Table 2.1 in the same way.

In the Scandinavian countries, market analysts have been both energetic and imaginative in making STAS calculations on the basis of relatively simple and inexpensive data-collection systems. Since the Scandinavian markets are small in absolute terms—although not in marketing sophistication—research companies are unable to afford the high cost of the technical equipment used for collecting data electronically, as can be done in countries as large as the United States, Germany, and Great Britain.

TABLE 2.3 First 2-Country Quintile Analysis of STAS Differentials

Rank	United States, 1991 78 Brands (Nielsen)	France, 1996 144 Brands (BehaviorScan)
Top	198	200
4th	130	139
3rd	112	117
2nd	100	99
Bottom	82	77

In Denmark, Flemming Hansen of Copenhagen Business School, working with the research organization TNS Gallup, developed a system using 6,700 personal interviews to measure both brand purchasing and advertising exposure signaled by awareness of advertising for a brand. Hansen found an ingenious way of eliminating "phantom awareness" (i.e., imaginary awareness of advertising that had not actually appeared).[10] He calls his measure Attitudinal STAS, or ASTAS. His range of quintiles, shown in Table 2.4, describes 23 Danish brands and is another example of broad similarity to the findings of the original American research. The slightly higher Danish readings are a result of the different method of data collection.

Hansen provided ASTAS figures for each brand from television and magazine advertising separately. The magazine figures are based on small samples, which may account for the fact that they are nearly all higher than those from television. Nevertheless, magazines are a powerful advertising medium in Denmark, and Danish society is highly literate.

In Norway, Thorolf Helgesen of the Norwegian School of Management, with Morten Micalsen of the Norwegian Gallup Research Institute, decided to revisit Colin McDonald's 1966 method of collecting data with the use of paper-and-pencil diaries filled in by homemakers. Using this technique, researchers carried out a study of 860 Norwegian households over a 2-month period at the end of 1997.[11]

The analysts examined 33 brands and found the STAS Differential for each to range between the two extremes of 329 and 55. Five of the 33 scores were negative. Again, there is similarity to the range of the American data, although the findings from Norway show stronger advertising effects—almost certainly a result of the different method of data collection.

TABLE 2.4 Second 2-Country Quintile Analysis of STAS Differentials

Rank	United States, 1991 78 Brands (Nielsen)	Denmark, 1999 23 Brands (Gallup)
Top	198	246
4th	130	196
3rd	112	154
2nd	100	122
Bottom	82	91

Like Hansen in Denmark, Helgesen and Micalsen also measured the STAS from magazine advertising and found results that were even more positive. As in Denmark, Norway has a powerful magazine press; also as in Denmark, the population is highly literate.

At the time when the Norwegians were getting their research under way, I fortuitously gained access to a large historical American database, from which I was able to calculate STAS figures from magazine advertising. This information came from Starch, a company that has been exploring the readership of print advertising since the 1920s. The data I received were derived from studies of 45,000 advertisements in *Saturday Evening Post* and *Life* over the years from 1944 through 1960.

With each of the journals in the study and immediately after each issue appeared, Starch measured the household purchasing of specific brands. This was done both in households that had received the issues of these journals in which the brands were advertised and in households that had not been exposed to the advertisements. This made it possible to connect the reception of the advertisements to the purchase of the same brands—in effect, Pure Single-Source research.

Using the arithmetic of my STAS system, with the Baseline indexed at 100, the average STAS Differential for all the measured magazine advertisements was 119 (a finding significant at the 99% probability level). This figure was calculated from all the brands in the sample for which suitable information was available—73 brands that had appeared in 707 different advertisements.[12]

Remember that in my original American research into television viewing and brand buying, the STAS figure for all the brands together averaged 124 (see Table 2.1). This average measured all amounts of advertising received before the brand was bought. As I shortly discuss, most of the effect of advertising comes from households that have received only a single advertisement. For these single-advertisement households, the STAS Differential averaged 118. The Starch magazine data are based on single-advertisement measures. This means that the average responsiveness of consumer purchasing to a single advertisement on television (measured by Nielsen) *is virtually the same* as the average responsiveness to a single magazine advertisement (measured by Starch).

The seven studies I have just discussed were all based on Pure Single-Source research. This review of immediate effects of advertising concludes with mentioning the work of Michael von Gonten and James Donius, who used the same Nielsen Household Panel as I did, but they analyzed the information in a totally different way. They did, however, produce conclusions similar to my own.

Von Gonten and Donius used as their main measure a brand's penetration: the percentage of households buying it during a defined period.[13] Their research tracks penetration growth from a selected starting point (e.g., January 1) measured at zero. This nil-penetration refers only to the beginning of the research period. The new buyers in the period will only rarely be true first-time buyers; they will be mostly repeat buyers from earlier periods, but this is ignored because the research concept is based on *penetration growth,* and to do this it is best to start at zero.

From this starting point, penetration for an established brand increases in a relatively smooth upward path, or trajectory. This trajectory serves as the baseline used by von Gonten and Donius when they measure the boosts or "upticks" that result from various marketing activities, notably media advertising and sales promotions.

The effect of these stimuli is measured as an upward step in the trajectory above the established trend. In any week, this trend is measured as 1 (a number chosen simply for purposes of comparison). The analysts' conclusions from the research are as follows, and each point is important to the present discussion:

- "Effective commercials average around 1.85 times as much (increase in) penetration as would be achieved if off-air during that specific week. The high end of the observed range is around 4 to 5 times."
- "Specific executions have the capacity to differ in effect, even when they are simple 'pool-outs.' "
- "The effect is observed in the week in which advertising airs and is absent in off-air weeks."[14]

Von Gonten and Donius also reveal interesting data on repeat purchase and subsequent additional purchase. These have some relevance to discussion of the long-term effects of advertising in Chapter 8.

All the evidence described so far comes from the various categories of repeat-purchase packaged goods. In the past, what has been learned about advertising in these tough, advertising-intensive, highly competitive product fields has been applied in a general fashion to many other advertised categories. There is no reason to doubt that the lessons from the research described here can also be applied widely. But this assumption should not be taken as an excuse for not carrying out parallel investigations in such important fields as travel, financial services, telecommunication, and the many and varied types of goods with a high ticket price, notably automobiles. Some work has been done, but it is unpublished.

How Many Brands Pass Through?

I have produced evidence supporting the proposition that *advertising is capable of producing a pronounced effect on consumer purchases of a brand within a short period (generally measured as 7 days) after its exposure. This short-term effect varies a great deal according to the advertising used. It can be measured post hoc.*

This evidence comes from six different countries and seven separate investigations. Six of these are based on Pure Single-Source research, conducted longitudinally. These studies examined a total of 446 separate brands and related household buying to advertising received immediately beforehand. Each brand study was derived from (plus or minus) 1,000 statistical observations. The statistical foundation for my conclusions is a total not far short of half a million separate pieces of data.

I believe that the strength and consistency of this battery of mutually supporting evidence has now pulled the rug from under the once-prevalent view that advertising cannot yield substantial immediate effects and that its only influence comes from the accumulation of multitudes of tiny effects that eventually produces something significant, or in the words from a well-known monograph republished in 1998,

TABLE 2.5 Quintile Analysis of STAS Differentials and Average Size of Brand:
United States, 78 Brands (Jones)

Rank	STAS Differential	% Average Share of Market
Top	198	3.6
4th	130	6.9
3rd	112	10.2
2nd	110	12.1
Bottom	82	7.9

> Advertising works over a period of time as a part of the gradual evolution of the
> individual's perceptions of a brand and its relations to other brands. The effect of
> a single isolated advertising exposure is likely to be minimal in most markets.[15]

I am convinced that this hypothesis is based on very little truth and that what
truth it contains is misleading.

The next question raised by all the research summarized here is *what is the
level of immediate effect that should qualify an advertising campaign to pass
through the gate* to be exposed further, with the aim of achieving a medium-
term effect, possibly building up to a long-term effect?

Bearing in mind my caution, flagged in Chapter 1, about the way in which
data should be interpreted, I believe that the initial cutoff level should be 120 on
the STAS Differential Index and that campaigns achieving STAS levels of 120
and more should be passed through the gate. There are, however, also a few
worthwhile campaigns that achieve a positive STAS Differential in the barely
positive 105 to 119 range. Which of these should we also choose?

Table 2.5 helps us make this decision. It contains a quintile analysis of the
STAS Differential for each of my original 78 American brands. These are compared with the share of market of the average brand in each quintile.

The lower levels of positive STAS Differentials are clearly associated with
larger brands. This is a manifestation of a general characteristic of such brands:
that they generally tend to perform rather sluggishly in the marketplace. But
they nevertheless make an above-average contribution to a manufacturer's general overhead and also often yield above-average profit because they command
an above-average consumer price (more precisely, an above-average *effective*
consumer price because they are promoted at a below-average rate). Bearing in

mind these special characteristics of large brands, I believe that the brands with a STAS Differential in the 105 to 119 range should be scrutinized and those that command a significantly above-average consumer price be allowed through the gate. We are looking here at advertising in its supportive/defensive role.

In my original study of 78 American brands, 31 have a STAS Differential Index of 120 and above. These should all go through. Of the 19 brands with a Differential in the 105 to 119 range, 7 sell at a consumer price more than 20% above their category average. I judge these also to be successful. Thus, 31 brands plus 7 brands, a total of 38—or about half my total of 78—should pass through the gate. The other pieces of Pure Single-Source research described in this chapter tend to follow a broadly similar pattern. And we should remind ourselves of the words attributed variously to William Hesketh Lever and John Wanamaker that half his advertising was wasted but he did not know which half. It seems that this generalization still holds, except that we *can* now identify which half work and which half do not.

In Chapter 4, I return to the 38 campaigns that pass through the gate and the 40 that do not.

An additional aspect of the measurement of short-term effect is described in Chapter 9, where it is shown that advertising is capable not only of producing substantial immediate increases in sales volume but that the advertising investment to achieve this can often be profitable.

The Key to the Gate

Before describing the key to the gate—the type of advertising that can achieve an immediate response—I must try to explain why the creative content of an advertisement is so important. In the words of the Gatekeeper model, *because one advertisement does most of the work, the effect must come substantially from the advertisement itself, from the creative idea within it.*

My original Pure Single-Source research revealed something that startled the advertising profession and immediately began to influence one aspect of professional practice: the deployment of media budgets over time. (This is discussed in Chapter 5.)

My discovery stemmed from a way that was found of analyzing advertising reception according to how many advertisements were received by different households before the purchase of a brand. Because it was possible to isolate the influence of advertising in homes that had received either a single exposure or multiple repetition of a brand's campaign during the 7 days before the brand was bought, Nielsen was able to pay special attention to the households that the purchase level in these households was three-quarters of the level in the households that had received much more advertising. This led to the discovery that these households accounted for three-quarters of all purchases. This point was also examined in a number of other Single-Source studies reported in this chapter, and the strong effect of a single advertisement exposure was confirmed with few exceptions.

This important evidence from my research led to two conclusions. First, with the 78 brands I initially examined, the number of successes confirmed that the weight of advertising was enough to cover a substantial number of potential buyers at least once. This means that the vast majority of media schedules for national brands will be heavy enough to give a single shot to enough buyers to cause a rise in sales, provided that the advertising is right. The second conclusion was that a strong effect from *a single advertisement* obviously meant that the budget and the media—the engines to achieve additional exposure—were less important (and from my original American findings *much* less important) than the intrinsic properties of the advertisement itself as causes of a sales increase.

What sort of advertising can do this? Some lessons are to be drawn from studying the successful *and unsuccessful* campaigns of the 78 brands in my original study. I was not aware of every one of the campaigns, but I was familiar with enough of them to draw some firm, albeit impressionistic, conclusions, although I am not of course able to reveal brand names. The campaigns differed greatly from one another despite the fact that the successful ones shared certain common characteristics. However, I urge caution against the notion that advertising can be created by formula. Formulas deaden originality and therefore remove the first important property of successful advertising—likability. But an awareness of the three qualities of successful campaigns is excellent learning material for sharpening our judgment of whether or not an advertising idea is likely to succeed in the marketplace.

Successful and Unsuccessful Advertising

The qualities of successful campaigns are not themselves totally unexpected. Indeed, a review of the wisdom of several generations of advertising gurus shows that these qualities have been widely described and discussed in the past, although the gurus said many other things and we must be selective in separating the wheat from the chaff. The campaigns are intrinsically *likable*. They are *visual* rather than verbal. And they encourage engagement by communicating their promise in terms *relevant to consumers, by offering a balance of the emotional and the rational.*

These points are more tactical than strategic; they are more concerned with the creative idea than with the creative objectives. Nevertheless, because a well-constructed strategy gives direction to the campaign itself, I am fairly certain that the three characteristics all originated in embryo in the brands' strategies and were laid down before the campaigns themselves were written.

To put these points in focus, we should appreciate the features that the campaigns did *not* possess. The campaigns were not hard-selling: They did not make strong, direct, and reiterated product claims. There were no "Slices of Life," no men in white coats making product demonstrations, no happy families—in fact, none of the widely used, and tiresome, advertising clichés. There was no attempt at all to persuade, in the sense of trying to overcome resistant attitudes. The campaigns were not didactic and verbal. They were characterized by the relatively small number of words on their sound tracks—well below the normally agreed maximum of 60 to 70 words—although this does not detract from the strength of their visual demonstrations. In general, the campaigns were concerned with consumer benefits rather than with product features.

The characteristics of successful advertisements are now discussed in a generalized way, and the points I make are offered as advice to future practice.

Intrinsically Likable

Advertising is totally ineffective unless some people, at least, are prepared to look at it. This is one of the reasons why advertising communication is such a difficult art. All viewers, listeners, and readers can recognize what advertising is, and most people turn away from it as an immediate and automatic reaction. The advertising writer's first task is therefore to think of a message compelling enough—or friendly and intriguing and involving enough—to cause some consumers to pause before they switch off their mental engagement and then to stimulate some of the people who pause to go on further.

There is no formula for doing this, but it is a striking feature of successful campaigns that the advertisers in every case manage to hold viewers' attention by giving a reward *for watching*. This is done by making the commercials engaging, entertaining, light-hearted, and amusing to look at. The advertisers address viewers as their equals and do not talk down to them. They respect the public's intelligence.

In some cases, the commercial is slightly incomplete, and the viewer is encouraged to take a modest step to understand what it is all about. In other cases, the commercial springs a surprise—there is something unexpected that slightly startles the person looking at it. A few of these successful commercials are both incomplete and unexpected (the qualities have a natural affinity).

The commercials are often amusing, but they tend not to employ broad humor. A striking characteristic of the sound tracks of successful commercials is their generally understated tone of voice. This is often slightly ironic, as if the advertiser does not take him- or herself too seriously. This is appealing to viewers and persuades them to form a bond with the advertiser, based on the relevance of the brand and how it is presented. Music also plays an important role in many cases.

The ability of a commercial to entertain is occasionally at odds with how strongly it can sell (and vice versa). A commercial is nothing more than a piece of paid-for communication with a behavioral objective. With the most effective commercials, the entertainment is embedded in the brand. If the entertainment in the commercial generates a warm glow, this glow is directed toward the brand, and with the most successful campaigns, it can actually surround it.

The reward for looking at an advertisement is a very subtle quality. In many types of communication including advertising, a single word can make a difference. When Groucho Marx was perfecting a wisecrack for the film *A Day at the Races,* he experimented with slightly different versions of the joke in front of different live audiences. In particular, he tested alternatives for one important word: He tried *obnoxious, revolting, disgusting, offensive, repulsive, disagreeable,* and *distasteful.* The last two words raised a titter. The other words got a more positive reaction. Finally, a new alternative, the word *nauseating,* drew roars of laughter. The wisecrack became a comic legend: "That's the most nauseating proposition I ever had."[16]

Small differences are, if anything, more important in the visual of a commercial, a point made succinctly by Bill Bernbach: "How do you storyboard a smile? Yet the quality of that smile may make the difference between a commercial that works and one that doesn't work."[17]

Important as likability is, it should never be seen as sufficient in itself. One of the most interesting campaigns examined in my original American research was for a newly introduced food brand. The advertising was characterized by stunning attention-value; the commercials were a joy to watch, and won many advertising industry awards. But the campaign was totally unsuccessful in the marketplace because it made no explicit claim or promise for the brand. It devoted so much attention to taking possession of the viewer's eyeballs that it forgot to mention what the brand was promising.

Visual Communication

The most powerful cultural trend during the past half-century has been the development of visual literacy—the growth in communication by images and symbols. This is true of all societies, from the most educated to the least, and it is, of course, a direct result of the growth of television. The accompanying decline in verbal literacy is an even more important—and totally deplorable— phenomenon, but this is not the place to discuss and lament it.

Television, the main engine driving the growth of visual communication, is also the main medium for the advertising in many product categories, in particular, packaged goods. Advertisers would be acting against their self-interest if they did not exploit television's potential, especially its power to demonstrate and its ability to generate mood and emotion.

Emotions and Rationality— and Their Relevance

Consumers buy brands for the benefits those brands give them. But a manufacturer should not believe that, given our highly competitive world, success will result if he only communicates a bald functional advantage, even if his brand is the only one to offer it. Functional benefits are very important, but advertising claims about these are processed in two ways in the consumer's psyche.

First, a functional advantage is often broadened in the consumer's mind into something much more emotional. This has a stronger effect than functional claims on their own, and the resulting amalgam is unique to the brand. The manufacturer's prospects are improved to the extent that this happens. A statement in an advertisement for a food brand that it has no cholesterol or sugar or salt releases a torrent of emotional signals about health and long life. The click of a camera shutter in a commercial can be transformed in the viewer's mind into a highly charged message: This click records—and in effect, freezes—the high points in the viewer's life.

The second way in which claims are processed is that the functional (or the functional-*cum*-emotional) qualities of a brand are perceived as having value to the consumer solely to the extent that they relate to his or her day-to-day life. Unless a brand has functional features superior to the competition in at least some respects, it will not be bought repeatedly. But these alone are not enough. The consumer must find the brand's functional features *more relevant* than the advantages offered by any competitive brands the consumer may be considering at the time.

It follows that unless the consumer is shown a brand's qualities in highly personal and relevant terms, it will have no appeal. Advertisers do this by studying their buyers. The positioning of their brand (determining where their brand fits into a competitive marketplace) plus the creative idea are both the direct result of advertisers' knowledge of their consumers.

One rather obvious (but sometimes forgotten) point is that advertising that shows people is likely to be more successful than advertising that does not. Qualitative research has shown that advertising about products on their own can generate cold, impersonal image associations.

The positioning of the brand in relation to its competitors must be thought out with agonizing precision. This positioning embraces both the brand's functional and nonfunctional features. When an important brand of which I have firsthand knowledge was first introduced, its selected positioning was the end product of an extraordinary process of experimentation. This involved writing and evaluating 19 alternative positionings, which were tested in the form of more-or-less finished films. The cost of this film production was prodigious, and perhaps more seriously, the procedure took more than two years to complete. But the result repaid the cost and trouble because the brand was—and still is—a triumph in the marketplace. It is no coincidence that it had one of the highest STAS Differentials measured by Nielsen.

An even more important point about functional features is that advertising that sells them successfully must be based on an idea that embraces both the rational and the emotional: the rational idea enclosed as it were in an emotional envelope. But if the idea is going to work at all, this envelope must contain something important to the consumer. The commercials should be likable—but the selling message must be unmistakable.

In successful campaigns, the rational features of the brand are almost invariably demonstrated. The purpose of this is partly to provide a rational selling argument. Just as commonly, it is aimed at providing the consumer with a postpurchase rationalization, a justification for a preference that may have been totally nonrational. Psychologists have a name for this curious effect; they call it Reduction of Cognitive Dissonance.

Notes

1. David Ogilvy, *Confessions of an Advertising Man* (New York: Atheneum, 1984), 91-93.

2. John Philip Jones, *When Ads Work: New Proof That Advertising Triggers Sales* (New York: Simon & Schuster/Lexington Books, 1995), 177-187.

3. Ibid. Also see the following by John Philip Jones: "Advertising's Woes and Advertising Accountability," *Admap,* September 1994, 24-77; "Advertising Exposure Effects Under a Microscope," *Admap,* February 1995, 28-31; "Single-Source Research Begins to Fulfill Its Promise," *Journal of Advertising Research,* May/June 1995, 9-16; "Single-Source Is the Key to Proving Advertising's Short-Term Effects," *Admap,* June 1995, 33-34; and "Is Advertising Still Salesmanship?" *Journal of Advertising Research,* May/June 1997, 9-15.

4. IRI was critical of my method because I did *not* use permanent and separate matched samples. From our published exchanges, I am not totally sure that IRI understands how my system works. See articles in *Journal of Advertising Research* by the following: Gary Schroeder, Bruce C. Richardson, and Avu Sankaralingam, "Validating STAS Using BehaviorScan," July/August 1997, 33-43; Leonard M. Lodish, "Point of View: J. P. Jones and M. H. Blair on Measuring Advertising Effects—Another Point of View," September/October 1997, 75-79; John Philip Jones, "Point of View: STAS and BehaviorScan—Yet Another View," March/April 1998, 51-53; and Leonard M. Lodish, "STAS and BehaviorScan—It's Just Not That Simple," March/April 1998, 54-56.

5. The band of inaccuracy is calculated from the increase over the index of 100 or the decrease below it. For example, the range from a STAS Differential *increase* of 136 is in the band 150-122. When indexed, the figures become, respectively, 236 and 250-222.

6. John Philip Jones, *When Ads Work: The German Version* (Frankfurt-am-Main, Germany: Gesamtverband Werbeagenturen GWAeV, 1995).

7. Colin McDonald, "How Frequently Should You Advertise?" *Admap,* July/August 1996, 22-25.

8. See the references in Note 4.

9. Pascale Merzereau, Laurent Battais, and Laurent Spitzer, *Flighting Versus Pulsing Strategies on TV: Some BehaviorScan Findings* (Madrid, Spain: *asi* European Advertising Effectiveness Symposium, 1999). asi@dial.pipex.com

10. Flemming Hansen and Charlotte Madsen, *Awareness and Attitudinal Sales Effects of TV Campaigns* (Copenhagen, Denmark: Copenhagen Business School, 2000).

11. Thorolf Helgesen and Morten Micalsen, "Short-Term Advertising Strength: New Empirical Evidence From Norway," in *International Advertising: Realities and Myths,* ed. John Philip Jones (Thousand Oaks, CA: Sage, 2000), 299-309.

12. John Philip Jones, "Consumer Purchasing, Starch, and STAS: Does Magazine Advertising Produce an Immediate Effect?" in *How Advertising Works: The Role of Research,* ed. John Philip Jones (Thousand Oaks, CA: Sage, 1998), 203-214.

13. Michael F. von Gonten and James F. Donius, "Advertising Exposure and Advertising Effects: New Panel-Based Findings," *Journal of Advertising Research,* July/August 1997, 51-60.

14. Ibid., 59.

15. Alan Hedges, *Testing to Destruction* (London: Institute of Practitioners in Advertising, 1998), 26.

16. Geoffrey O'Brien, "The Triumph of Marxism," *New York Review of Books,* July 20, 2000, 10.

17. William Bernbach, *Beware of Arithmetic* (New York: Association of National Advertisers, 1973), 5-6.

3

Getting It Right
the First Time

This chapter, like Chapter 2, is devoted to the immediate, short-term effect of advertising. The evidence in Chapter 2 leaves no doubt that advertising is capable of such an effect, although only 30% of campaigns do this strongly, with 40% working much less well and 30% being associated with declining sales. This information comes from a number of pieces of good research, each based on data collected over a long period of time—mostly 12 months.

But 12 months is a very long time in the world of business, and many an advertiser would see the post hoc analysis of sales as imposing an unconscionable delay in finding out whether or not the right decision has been made about spending the annual advertising budget. If the advertiser has made the *wrong* decision, 12 months will have passed and a year's budget been squandered. And in less than a third of cases will the decision have been a demonstrably correct one. These are not very good odds.

Is there any way that advertisers can learn much sooner whether or not to proceed with a good hope of success? This question explains the genesis of pretesting, a procedure that researches advertising by showing it to a sample of the public before it is shown to the public as a whole. There are various techniques available, ranging from qualitative evaluation using individual interviews and/ or focus groups, to quantitative testing in a laboratory setting or screening the commercial on-air. Advertisements are normally researched one at a time.

Print advertisements are normally tested in a different way from television commercials. But in view of the prime importance of television as an advertising medium for repeat-purchase packaged goods, this chapter is devoted exclusively to television.

It is not difficult to research at least one thing about a commercial. Using qualitative techniques, we can detect problems and screen the commercial for negatives by investigating clarity of communication and overall likability. However, getting rid of negatives is not at all the same as guaranteeing positive success. Predicting marketplace performance is difficult, but this is the topic that I must address specifically.

This chapter is therefore less concerned with correcting imperfections than it is with helping us make the heavy-duty decision about whether or not to spend our advertising budget on a campaign, remembering that when we commit our budget we are committing much of the money irrevocably. I devote what follows to discussing our ability to predict the selling power of the campaign and, in general, to supporting the words of the Gatekeeper model: *The short-term effect varies a great deal according to the advertising used. It can be predicted before the event.*

During the half-century since television advertising was first used, the research industry has untiringly invented new pretesting techniques. Their very number is evidence of a lack of universal agreement that a definitive method has been found. Perhaps the protagonists of the different techniques, being interested parties, have found their objective judgment to be, to some extent, at odds with their self-interest.

No one has attempted to use qualitative advertising for prediction, and I shall work on the realistic assumption that only quantitative systems are able to predict marketplace success with any degree of reliability. Most quantitative methods produce, as the central (although not sole) research finding, a single simple score. This is a number indicating how well the commercial performed in testing. Some pretesting services have tested hundreds, even thousands, of advertisements, so the score for an individual commercial can be compared with both the general average and the average for the product category.

If the test score shows reasonably substantial differences from the averages, these differences can provide support for a "go"/"no go" decision about whether or not to air the commercial. If it is very close to the average, the decision to run is a nice question of judgment, governed essentially by the competitive situation of the brand. If the competition is fierce, the decision will probably be "no go" but will likely be "go" if the competition is relatively light.

The simplicity of the scores makes them easy to use operationally. However, the disadvantages of this simplicity are seen by many practitioners—agencies, in particular—to outweigh the advantages. There have at times been scornful references to the way in which pretest findings supposedly oversimplify complex matters, reducing them all to a single number.

This issue does not brook any compromise. Opponents of quantitative pretesting should be reminded that in other fields—the hard sciences and medicine, in particular—a single number often establishes the difference between what is important and what is not. A diastolic blood pressure of 90mm is normal, but a reading of 100mm calls for treatment.

However, everything naturally depends on the reliability of the single numbers and the relevance of what they are measuring to the problem in hand.

The most common pretesting technique was for 30 years based on recall. It aimed to determine whether the public could recollect the advertisement under test and which specific copy claims in it could be remembered.[1] The system was eventually abandoned, although not without heart-searching, because of a decisive, albeit tacit, agreement within the advertising industry that the system was, in the last analysis, nonpredictive. It has not been used much since the late 1980s. No one has, however, expressed regret over the vast waste engendered through the long popularity of this research method: waste from the ineffective advertising screened in and, perhaps worse, waste from the potentially effective advertising screened out.

Recall is, of course, a cognitive not a behavioral measure. It is no more than a surrogate—and an inefficient one—for a measure of an advertisement's selling ability. If a pretesting method is to be any good at predicting the latter, it should have three characteristics:

1. It must be based on a robust but *indirect* method of measuring what it aims to measure, which is behavior. Bald questions (e.g., "Are you likely to buy?") are not only valueless but also dangerous.

2. It is an advantage to *conceal* the fact that it is the commercial that is being tested. Low-involvement communication must not be treated as if it were high involvement: Viewers must not be given instructions to "watch this," for this does not happen when commercials are viewed in the real world.

3. It must rely on a single screening of a commercial. Thus, if the communication is incomplete, we should be able to find this out easily by the commercial achieving a low pretest score.

Points 1 and 2 are based on common sense. Point 3 reflects the ability of a successful commercial to work on a one-exposure basis (as discussed in Chapters 2 and 5).

Not all pretesting systems follow these three rules. But some do, and some techniques are better than others. In this chapter, I discuss a single method: the Advertising Research Systems technique (the acronym ARS is trademarked), offered by a company based in Evansville, Indiana, called *rsc* THE QUALITY MEASUREMENT COMPANY.[2] The ARS system cannot claim a monopoly on accurate prediction. Nevertheless, it has a longer history than any other firm and, in my opinion, has a better track record of producing results that forecast the eventual sales performance of advertising. The company also has an impressive battery of evidence, much of which is described in this chapter.

The ARS system is derived from the one set up in the 1950s by Horace Schwerin, an unusual behavioral psychologist who deserves to be included in the pantheon of seminal market researchers. This is what Martin Mayer wrote about Schwerin in *Madison Avenue, USA,* an accurate journalistic exposé of the American advertising industry during the late 1950s. Mayer explains that during World War II Schwerin was a temporary army officer engaged in studying the morale of soldiers in training. One of the things he actually did was described as follows by Henry Newell, who became one of Schwerin's senior colleagues in the Schwerin Research Organization:

> They would broadcast a message to all the men at breakfast, urging them to change to their other pair of shoes when they returned to barracks. Meanwhile, Horace's people were putting chalk marks on everybody's second pair of shoes. When the men went out again for the morning's work, Horace's people would go back and find out how many of the shoes in the barracks had chalk marks on them, and he knew exactly how effective the broadcast argument had been.[3]

This was an early example of the trademark of Schwerin's research: an ingenious and oblique method of providing behavioral evidence—which *can* be measured—to demonstrate the effect of a psychological stimulus—which itself cannot be measured at all easily.

Schwerin's television commercial testing system was popular in the United States and Europe during the 1950s and 1960s, despite the sometimes ferocious antagonism expressed by agencies. This was partly because, as discussed, the system was thought to oversimplify and also because it introduced an outside party in addition to the client to pass judgment on the agency's work. To make matters worse, it was thought—without justification—that the system dictated a specific style of advertising (a point discussed later in this chapter).

These and other controversies, namely about Schwerin's reliability and the accuracy of the sampling, caused some loss of faith among users.[4] The method was improved in technical detail though not in fundamentals, since the structure of the system remained strong. The equity of the Schwerin organization was acquired by *rsc* in 1968, and the improved ARS method was launched in 1972. Since then, *rsc* has made continuous and healthy progress in the research field in the United States. In Great Britain, an influential country in the world of advertising, Schwerin ceased operations, and for more than a quarter-century, advertising planning there has been guided virtually exclusively by soft qualitative research.[5] This is valuable, but it also—rather significantly—does little damage to the *amour propre* of the agencies.

The ARS research system is proprietary and is described technically as a laboratory method, which means that typical consumers are invited to view a 1-hour entertainment program in a cinema. There are also commercials for various brands, including one for the brand being tested (although the audience is not told this). The program is preceded and also followed by a lottery for a quantity of brand-name goods, in which the brand whose commercial is being tested is included.

The ARS measure is based on a pre/post shift in brand choice obtained in a secure, off-air environment where it is possible to simulate purchase. The measure is calculated by subtracting the percentage of respondents choosing the advertised brand over the competition *before* exposure to the television material from the percentage choosing it *after* exposure. This captures the net effect of retention and attraction as a result of the advertising stimulus. In the United States, the ARS sample consists of 800 to 1,000 respondents, aged 16 or older, randomly recruited by mail from four geographically dispersed markets.[6]

What is being measured is the effect of the advertising stimulus on its own. Testing on the basis of a single exposure means that media weight and advertising repetition play no part in boosting the strictly creative power of the advertising itself.

The method can be described, rather cumbrously, as one based on a "pre/post preference shift." With most repeat-purchase packaged goods, the stimulus to buy is no more than a reminder—an evocation of previous brand experience—which triggers the purchase of a brand that in most cases is already in the consumer's repertoire. But although the purchase is a low-involvement decision and little thought goes into it, the advertising simply does not work unless it says something important about the brand. As discussed in Chapters 1 and 2, the most effective advertising maintains a subtle balance between the rational and the emotional. This enables it to resonate with what the consumer believes and feels about the brand advertised.

What matters most when evaluating all pretesting systems is, of course, how well they predict. I relate this primary issue to the ARS procedure in the form of answers to these three questions:

1. How consistent are the ARS scores?
2. What is the system's overall track record?
3. Are there biases toward any particular type of advertising?

How Consistent Are the ARS Scores?

Consistency goes to the heart of pretesting, just as it does to most types of research, for two specific reasons. The first and most obvious one is that consistency bears directly on the statistical reliability of the research itself. If there is any fuzziness in the questioning or imperfection in the sampling, then repeated tests of the same commercial are almost certain to show different results—which would of course destroy the fundamental basis of the research. This is not the case with the ARS system. The company defuses any possible objections by conducting duplicate tests of many commercials. Table 3.1 shows the results of such duplicate tests of 1,320 television advertisements involving 6 countries. Differences between the test and retest scores are statistically not significant.[7]

The second reason why consistency is important is more subtle. The value of the ARS testing lies not only in its capacity to predict marketplace performance but also in its ability to nurture an advertising campaign and build a brand's franchise and sales. Consistent results from advertising pretests can be tracked longitudinally, and the creative content of the campaign can be planned in such a way that it builds on success to produce gradual and incremental improvements. These can, in turn, also be monitored by pretesting conducted on a continuous basis. This process in operation can be seen in three cases described later in this chapter.

TABLE 3.1 Test and Retest of Individual Commercials

Market	Number of Commercials	Differences in Test/Retest
United States	1,005	Not significant
Canada	112	Not significant
Mexico	74	Not significant
United Kingdom	48	Not significant
Germany	47	Not significant
Netherlands	34	Not significant

What Is the System's Overall Track Record?

It has for a long time been obvious to *rsc* that a research system planned to predict what will happen in the marketplace can only be validated through a comparison between the pretest scores, collected before the advertising is exposed, and what happens when the advertising has actually been transmitted on television. The research company has therefore continuously collected sales data relating to the advertisements it has tested. The number of cases collected to date is more than 2,000, although *rsc* has not been able to get the clients' permission to publish large numbers of these, even in a disguised or aggregated form. The clients consider the information totally proprietary.

There is also a serious methodological problem in measuring sales effects. If the sales data are to be compared with the pretest scores, they must measure accurately a true short-term effect from the advertising. The importance of this point only became apparent in recent years with the advent of scanners in the home and in retail stores to measure sales week by week. Such research has shown how *short* a short-term effect really is. In the early 1960s, an attempt had been made to compare Schwerin pretest scores with sales measured over *4-month* intervals. This was a totally futile endeavor.[8]

Since 1996, *rsc* has been collecting cases based on scanner data.[9] Information has been and is still being collected in seven countries, although 87% of the figures come from the United States. The rules governing the inclusion of U.S. cases in the data set are as follows:

- The advertising had been tested before exposure.
- The advertising had run for at least two consecutive 4-week periods.

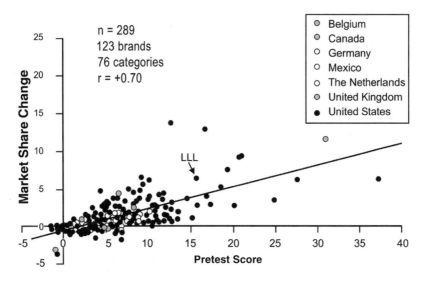

Figure 3.1. Year 2000 Global Scanner Validity Study of 289 Campaigns

- Scanner data were available, measuring sales over a period of 1 to 4 weeks.
- There was no distribution of free packs or bonus quantities of the advertised brand during the analysis period.
- Retail distribution data were available for new brands so that their sales could be weighted according to the level of distribution achieved.
- Finally—*and most important*—all brands for which pretest scores and scanner sales data were available had to be included, thus eliminating any question of skimming off successes and ignoring failures.

Figure 3.1 is based on data from the United States and six other countries (Belgium, Canada, Germany, Mexico, The Netherlands, and the United Kingdom). The diagram compares the pretest score (plotted on the horizontal axis) with the change in market share (plotted on the vertical axis) and is easily read. For example, Brand LLL (marked with an arrow) had a pretest score of about 15 and a market share improvement of about 5%. Here, as with most other cases plotted in Figure 3.1, the prediction predicts.

The diagonal line shown in Figure 3.1, which could be described technically as "best fit," represents the average connection between the pretest scores and sales and shows a positive relationship between the two variables. An important

TABLE 3.2 Pretest Score and Market Share Change

Degree of Elasticity	Score	Average Market Share Change
Very high	12.0 or more	Plus 4.6
	9.0–11.9	Plus 2.5
	7.0–8.9	Plus 1.6
	4.0–6.9	Plus 1.0
	3.0–3.9	Plus 0.4
	2.0–2.9	No change
Inelastic	Below 2.0	Minus 0.2

component of Figure 3.1 is that not only will a positive pretest score achieve a positive sales outturn, but a higher score will achieve a better sales result than a lower score will. This is illustrated in Table 3.2.

In Figure 3.1, the average line cuts the horizontal a little to the east of zero, showing that a small positive pretest score (under 3.0) is not strong enough to generate a significant sales change. This has an important practical implication. In a competitive marketplace, an advertisement must achieve at least a slightly positive score to maintain sales at current levels even without boosting them. Much advertising is, in fact, defensive. Lewis Carroll made the point in *Through the Looking-Glass* a long time ago: "It takes all the running you can do to keep in the same place."

But taking a modestly positive score as the starting point for advertising that has a marketplace effect, small increments beyond this can produce surprisingly strong sales effects. An improvement at the threshold level of 4.0 in the pretest score can boost a brand's share of market by half a point, which could mean hundreds of thousands of dollars of net incremental sales value. And because the airtime cost for a strong commercial is no greater than that for a weak commercial, this additional sales value will have a significant influence on the bottom line.

The most important single number in Figure 3.1 is $r = 0.70$, which is the correlation coefficient between the pretest scores and sales. It is a mathematical average of how closely knitted the two sets of data are over their complete range. A perfect fit would be described by a coefficient of 1.0. How should the figure 0.70 be interpreted?

It is a fairly strong correlation, despite the fact that a number of factors unconnected with the creative content of the advertising may have some influence

on sales (e.g., trade promotions, consumer promotions, pricing, and competitive advertising). The overall correlation coefficient of .70 is robust enough to
provide an endorsement of the ARS system, especially since additional ARS
cases, as they are released, are consistent with what has gone before. (The correlation coefficient for the first 155 cases was .71.)

The system can be used quite confidently to guide advertising decision making, and I have not the slightest doubt that reliance on the ARS procedure represents a major improvement over the use of subjective judgment—no matter
how experienced that judgment may be. In fact, we *know* on the basis of good
evidence that experienced judgment is an inadequate tool for making advertising decisions.[10]

The research company continues energetically to gather validating material,
seeing this—quite correctly—as the best way to build its business. But I must
also repeat what I said at the beginning of this chapter: that other research firms
also do good work in the field and a number of these are following *rsc*'s lead in
providing empirical validation for what they do.

Are There Biases Toward Particular Types of Advertising?

A persistent objection to all quantitative pretesting is that certain types of advertising are thought to get better scores than others. Most important, such testing has been—and sometimes still is—thought to discriminate in favor of rational, factual copy and against emotional, mood-engendering advertising.

The best way to examine this dangerous but important hypothesis is, again,
by comparing pretest scores with marketplace performance. Such an examination was made of the 289 campaigns described in Figure 3.1. The research company took these campaigns and subdivided them five ways. What emerged were
five separate tabulations of different groupings of the 289 campaigns.

The data, presented in Table 3.3, show remarkable consistency. Among the
12 subgroups analyzed, only the 1 examining large brands and the 1 measuring
15-second commercials show a correlation coefficient a little below the strong
overall average.

The examination of rational and emotional advertising was carried out on
the basis of a careful content analysis of the tested advertisements. The findings
in Table 3.3 answer any fear that the ARS system is biased toward rational copy.
There is, however, plentiful evidence that recall testing discriminates in favor of

TABLE 3.3 Year 2000 Global Scanner Validity Study: Correlation Coefficients of Various Subcategories of Advertising

Type of Advertising	Number of Brands	Correlation Coefficient
All brands	289	0.70
Established brands	227	0.62
New brands	62	0.68
Large brands	83	0.58
Small brands	144	0.67
Food brands	70	0.78
Household brands	70	0.63
Over-the-counter brands	26	0.82
Personal care products	123	0.71
30-second ads	207	0.72
15-second ads	53	0.53
Mainly rational ads	123	0.65
Mainly emotional ads	166	0.76

factual copy, and this is one of the reasons why recall testing is so little used today.[11]

Using Pretesting to Build Brands

The technique described here uses pretesting repeatedly and continuously to build on a brand's success to boost its sales on a long-term basis. When brands are demonstrably successful, they generally employ an unchanging advertising strategy, and the campaign itself is just as often made up of variations ("pool-outs") on a common theme.

However, some variations on the theme are more effective than others, and pretesting can be used to screen all commercials to ensure that each new one maintains the standard, and if possible, improves on it. Some advertisers have followed this policy for many years, and what follows are three examples, each illustrated with a chart showing the development of the brand's sales over

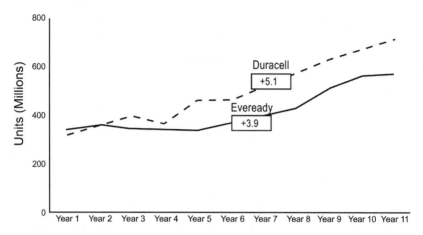

Figure 3.2. Sales of Duracell and Eveready Energizer
NOTE: Boxed numbers are brands' average pretest scores.

time together with data on the pretest scores of the commercials used during that period.[12]

The first example is *Duracell Batteries,* a brand that competes with Eveready's Energizer, the two forming in effect a duopoly that dominates the category. Duracell used ARS pretesting over a period of 11 years, during which time the advertising strategy consistently emphasized the battery's dual bene- fits: the functional property of its long life and the emotional associations of Duracell's high quality and trustworthiness. During the years of Duracell's growing sales, the campaign for Eveready's Energizer was the high-profile "Pink Bunny." The latter commercials were pretested by ARS and produced consistently lower scores than the Duracell campaign. The progress of the two brands, with the stronger sales trend for Duracell, can be seen in Figure 3.2.

The second case examines in more detail the pretest scores for the individual commercials in a campaign. This is for SmithKline Beecham's *Os-Cal,* an over-the-counter calcium supplement sold in a product category in which there is a good deal of direct and indirect competition.

Note two characteristics of this brand's progress, shown in Figure 3.3. The first is the large number of commercials used—20 over the three years of ad- vertising—and the consistency of their pretest scores: 13 with scores exceeding +10.0, with the lowest score +7.0. The months in which advertising took place are represented by the darker bars. The second feature of the sales increase is

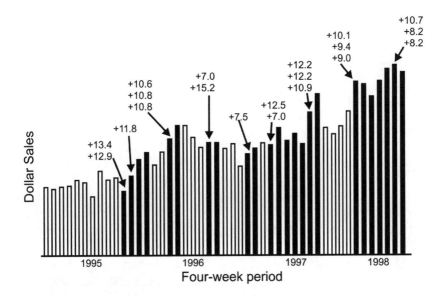

Figure 3.3. Sales of Os-Cal
NOTE: Numbers with arrows directed at darkened areas of the chart are pretest scores.

the solidity of the trend, with advertising making an obvious contribution. This is seen most dramatically when we compare the brand's static sales during 1995, when it was unadvertised, with what happened in the subsequent three years. The sales value of the brand, measured over 4-week periods, more than doubled between early 1995 and late 1998.

The third case described here is a classic study that has been published more than once in the professional press: Campbell's *Prego Spaghetti Sauce.*

Prego is a brand whose success can be attributed to a long-lasting advertising campaign based on Prego's thicker consistency than that of its larger-selling competitor Ragu, which is manufactured by Unilever. During Prego's long period of double-digit growth every year, Ragu outgunned Prego in every aspect of marketing policy, *with the single exception of the size of the ARS pretest scores.* The two brands are compared in Table 3.4.[13]

The sales progress of Prego over a 9-year period is shown in Figure 3.4. Halfway through this period, a change of strategy caused a reversal of the sales trend. In fact, the group responsible for marketing the brand drifted away from

TABLE 3.4 Prego and Ragu: Marketing Inputs, 1988-1992

Marketing Measure	Prego	Ragu
Advertising weight index	74	100
In-store display index	51	100
Retail advertising index	78	100
Average retail price index	110	100
Number of commercials aired	11	31
Average ARS pretest score	7.2	2.0

both the successful campaign proposition (the thickness of the sauce) and the ARS pretesting system. ARS nevertheless tested the new commercials that were used, and the weakening of Prego's sales coincided with a lower level of pretest scores.

These three cases are persuasive, and they are by no means isolated or exceptional. It must, of course, be emphasized that the strength of the success of these brands was in large measure due to the effectiveness of their advertising campaigns and the way in which these were refreshed continuously with new advertisements, albeit within a constant strategy. However, the success was also in small measure due to the way in which ARS pretesting was used as a monitoring device to make sure that everything was proceeding on the right track.

The cases illustrate the practical value of using pretesting longitudinally to help build brands.

There is also the negative lesson from the Prego case of the dangers of abandoning pretesting as a means of keeping a finger on the pulse. When a campaign comes to the end of its useful life—often a longer period than some marketing people believe, as evidenced by the plentiful examples of campaigns that have worked for decades—the signs are not always easy to detect. Tracking studies of consumer perceptions can often uncover a weakening of the brand's perceived attributes and associations before these work their way through to an actual sales decline. Collecting and interpreting tracking data is expensive and difficult, but the process can provide advance intelligence of priceless value.[14]

It is very likely that regular pretesting, by providing important advance warning of changes in the behavioral impact of the advertising—data which can be compared with the scores achieved by commercials that have gone before—can add another arrow to the quiver of the sophisticated marketing practitioner.

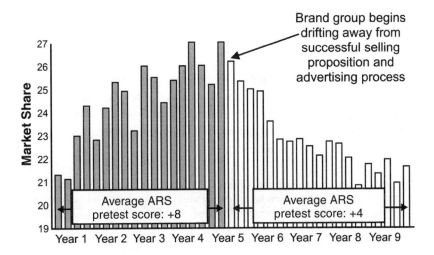

Figure 3.4. Sales of Prego Spaghetti Sauce

An Endnote From the World of Physical Science

Chapter 1 contains a quotation from Solly Zuckerman (1904-1993), a physician and anatomist who ended his career in the unlikely position as Chief Scientific Adviser to the British Government.

During World War II, he worked as a civilian attached to the Royal Air Force. At first, he was an analyst of the damage to the human body caused by aerial bombing; later, he was the main scientific adviser in the planning of targets for the huge Anglo-American bombing campaign at the time of the invasion of France. He participated at the highest level in discussions about bombing policy between the air force leaders of both countries, and in these interchanges the gloves were always off.

Zuckerman's large-scale and scientifically planned research on the ground in Great Britain, Africa, and Italy had demonstrated that the most militarily productive targets were rail communication centers in enemy territory. The British and American "Bomber Barons" had other views, which were derived from their own deeply rooted instinct supported by selective evidence. The air chiefs carried great political influence within the counsels of the allies. But despite this, the policy that Zuckerman recommended was implemented widely enough for the results to be measured after the fighting had come to an end.

Evidence collected after the war by British and American bombing survey organizations totally vindicated Zuckerman. It demonstrated that the strategy favored by the air chiefs—much of it indiscriminate bombardment—was not only horrific to the civilian population being attacked but also relatively uneconomic in comparison with its cost in human life and treasure. This prompted Zuckerman to make the following trenchant observation (which has already appeared as the Epigraph to this book):

> I learnt that what emerged from a dispassionate scientific analysis of the confused events of war counted for no more in the debates in which I became engaged than the in-built convictions of various members of what were called the intelligence and planning communities.[15]

Do these weighty matters of public policy operate also at a micro level? Should they influence decision making by an individual organization—even a manufacturing firm formulating its advertising policy? I see no reason at all why they should not.

The men and women at the summit of corporations, the executives who take direct responsibility for making the *financial* decisions regarding advertising, generally are less committed—even if they are involved at all—in deciding the *content* of the campaigns that will be run.[16] This is paradoxical, as it is essentially impossible to separate the campaign decisions from the financial ones. Whether or not top business people have the time, or feel qualified, to involve themselves in the former, their responsibility for the latter requires them to interfere enough in campaign decisions to rule that such decisions must be guided by the best objective quantitative research that the ingenuity of the market research industry can devise. This might—or might not—include measures of pre/post preference shift. The directive to use good research should concentrate on the principle of the procedure and not on details of its technical execution.

People at the summit of corporations should be made aware of the truly alarming statistic that (as explained at the beginning of this chapter) the odds are 2 to 1 *against* campaigns succeeding. In such circumstances, how can they fail to question "the in-built convictions" of their advertising experts and to demand something better?[17]

Notes

1. Recall Testing is discussed, with much skepticism, in John Philip Jones, *What's in a Name? Advertising and the Concept of Brands* (New York: Simon & Schuster-Lexington Books, 1986), 131-155.

2. *rsc* is an acronym for *research systems corporation*. The organization eschews capital letters.

3. Martin Mayer, *Madison Avenue, USA* (New York: Harper & Brothers, 1958), 269.

4. John Philip Jones, *Getting It Right the First Time: Can We Eliminate Ineffective Advertising Before It Is Run? Admap* Monograph No. 3 (Henley-on-Thames, UK: *Admap* Publications, 1996), 34-36.

5. Background to this is provided by a published exchange of papers dating from the mid-1960s. Robert Buzzell, an academic, tried to demonstrate the predictive power of the Schwerin technique with the use of sales audits every 4 months: a hopelessly inadequate measurement procedure. In response, Fothergill and Ehrenberg, a practitioner and an academic, respectively, destroyed the technical analysis made in the earlier paper without mentioning the inadequacy of the data! See Robert J. Buzzell, "Predicting the Short-Term Changes in Market Share as a Function of Marketing Strategy," *Journal of Marketing Research,* August 1964, 27-31; and J. E. Fothergill and A. S. C. Ehrenberg, "On the Schwerin Analysis of Advertising Effectiveness," *Journal of Marketing Research,* August 1965, 298-306.

6. John Philip Jones and Margaret H. Blair, "Examining 'Conventional Wisdoms' About Advertising Effects With Evidence From Independent Sources," *Journal of Advertising Research,* November/December 1996, 56.

7. Information from *rsc*.

8. See Note 5 (Buzzell).

9. All the validating data that follow were made available by *rsc*.

10. Leo Bogart, B. Stuart Tolley, and Frank Orenstein, "What One Little Ad Can Do," *Journal of Advertising Research,* August 1970, 3-13.

11. See, among others, Shirley Young, "Copy Testing Without Magic Numbers," *Journal of Advertising Research,* February 1972, 3-12; also Mayer, *Madison Avenue, USA,* 274.

12. The data on these three cases come from Margaret H. Blair and Hans-Willi Schroiff, "Advertising: Today's Sale or Brand-Building for Tomorrow?" *Quirk's Marketing Research Review,* 2000.

13. Jones, *Getting It Right the First Time,* 18.

14. See the Oxo case in John Philip Jones, *Does It Pay to Advertise? Cases Illustrating Successful Brand Advertising* (New York: Simon & Schuster-Lexington Books, 1989), 113-128.

15. Solly Zuckerman, *From Apes to Warlords* (New York: Harper & Row, 1978), 340.

16. The lack of commitment of business leaders to important details of their advertising is addressed by John Philip Jones, "Advertising: The Cinderella of Business," *Market Leader,* June 2000, 20-25.

17. See also Note 10.

4

Repetition, Competition, and the Growth (or Decline) of Brands

The most pervasive characteristic of human societies is that their fabric is permeated by the rough yet beneficial abrasive of competition. International *Realpolitik,* domestic politics, and the confrontations of the legal system are all based on it. In a subdued way it is even apparent in such socially desirable enterprises as religion, philanthropy, medicine, and education.

The most important and permanent feature of every type of commercial business is, not surprisingly, direct and indirect engagement with competitors. This makes itself felt both in preemptive activity and in responses to competitors' actions. And although there is nothing new about all this, competition provides the technical explanation for why the immediate effect of an advertising campaign sometimes can—but sometimes cannot—be extended into the medium term.

The STAS Differential itself, being a measure of market share, is totally based on competition. If any campaign achieves a high STAS score, then it can be assumed that its behavioral effect is greater than that of campaigns for competitive brands that appeared more or less at the same time. Competition is an even more important factor over the medium term because virtually every brand will have gaps in its media schedule, during which it will be vulnerable to competitors' advertising because it has been left unprotected. This is directly relevant to the deployment of an advertising budget over time, a matter discussed in Chapter 5.

These concepts, which are discussed in this chapter, are summarized in the Gatekeeper Model as follows:

> *The short-term effect of an advertisement determines whether or not that advertisement will have a medium-term effect. A repetition of short-term effects over a period (normally 12 months)—effects felt exclusively during the periods when the brand is advertised—adds up to a medium-term effect. The medium-term effect is a net effect—sales gains from our brand's campaign minus sales losses to competitive brands advertised during the gaps in our brand's schedule. Because such gaps are normally inevitable, the medium-term effect of advertising is virtually always smaller that the short-term effect. The size of the medium-term effect is determined not only by the creative content of the campaign but also by the brand's budget and its media strategy. Sales promotions can add to the effect of advertising; such synergy is strongest when promotions coincide with the most powerful advertising campaigns.*

Brands grow for at least eight reasons:

1. The quality and substance of the creative element in the advertising, generally considered the most important single factor influencing a brand's progress.
2. The size of the advertising budget.
3. The continuity provided by the brand's media schedule.
4. The number and value of consumer promotions. These are normally devices to reduce temporarily the consumer price of the brand, coupons being the most prevalent type of promotion used in the United States.
5. The number and value of trade promotions, all of which are price-related and, in effect, discounts to the retail trade. Trade promotions, despite the fact that they cost a manufacturer much more money than either media advertising or consumer promotions, have little direct effect on the consumer.[1] Such consumer effects as they have are felt through (a) extending the range of a brand's retail distribution; (b) increasing display at point of sale; (c) the occasions on which a manufacturer's brand appears in the retailer's own advertising; and (d) strengthening a consumer promotion by the retailer doubling or tripling the face value of a manufacturer's coupons.

6. A significant improvement in the functional efficiency of the brand itself.
7. Favorable publicity and word-of-mouth about the brand because it has in some way become a source of news.
8. Troubles afflicting the brand's competitors.

Brands decline for similar reasons, and here competition takes first place in importance. We must regard our brand from the point of view of the competition. Our strengths become their weaknesses, and vice versa. All the reasons listed above will now apply to competitive brands and will thus impinge unfavorably upon our own brand.

By far the most important factors are Numbers 1 through 4 on the list. Number 1—the quality of the advertising—invariably embraces Number 6—significant improvements in a brand's functional efficiency. In fact, Number 6 is part of Number 1 because a functional improvement will be the basis of a brand restage/relaunch, and hence announcement of the improvement becomes the most important task for the advertising. If it is not communicated speedily and efficiently, its value will be catastrophically reduced. My own experience of this type of failure comes from laundry detergents, a field in which it is particularly difficult to interest homemakers in product innovation.

This chapter is concerned with Numbers 1, 2, and 4: the content of the campaign, the size of the advertising investment, and the amount of consumer promotion. Number 3, media continuity, is discussed in Chapter 5.

I examine these marketing inputs with the use of data from the 78 advertised brands from my original Pure Single-Source study of American Nielsen data. Readers should remember the solid statistical basis of this work. It was derived from 110,000 statistical calculations, or an average of 1,400 readings per brand. The research therefore stands up to a substantial degree of generalization.[2]

In this chapter, the data are analyzed in three ways: (a) to test the predictive capacity of the Gatekeeper, which was described in Chapter 2 as the device to screen brands that should receive further investment, separating them from those that should not; (b) to look at the three inputs, STAS, Advertising Intensity, and Promotional Intensity, separately and in combination; and (c) to examine the 39 brands that increased their shares over the course of the first year of the research, and by doing this, attempt to tease out the relative importance of the causes of that growth. A separate section on sales promotions is inserted between points (b) and (c).

Testing the Gatekeeper

Readers will remember from Chapter 2 that a STAS Differential of 120 or more should permit a brand to pass through the gate and qualify for further investment. Also allowed through should be those brands with a STAS Differential in the marginal 105–119 range that also command a significantly above-average consumer price. With the latter brands, it can be realistically assumed that the advertising is justifying to consumers a higher-than-average price, in addition to boosting volume to a modest degree. These two groups provided, respectively, 31 and 7 different brands, or a total of 38.

We can plot the progress of these brands. We can also review the progress of the 40 brands that did not pass through the gate and whose campaigns would normally have been stopped while fresh advertising was being developed. The Gatekeeper was a hypothetical concept as it related to my original 78 brands. But the analysis of the sales progress of these brands enables the hypothetical Gatekeeper to be transformed into an operational tool for the management of advertising. This analysis was made in the following way.

For all the brands, I made four separate calculations—all based on the brand's competitive position—and averaged each for the brands in each group:

- *Growth.* This is based on market share, to measure the brand in relation to its competitors. It specifically shows the brand's average share during the last 9 months of the year in comparison with its share during the first 3 months. It thus demonstrates progress through the year itself: an ongoing measure of the brand's success or failure in the medium term.
- *STAS Differential.* This measures the endemic strength of the campaign.[3]
- *Advertising Intensity.* This examines the media budget put behind the campaign and expresses the advertising investment *relative to the size of the brand.* Two brands of the same size can have greatly different advertising budgets (measured as two different advertising intensities), but even a large budget for a small brand will generally be smaller than the budget for a large brand.[4] It is however important to compare like with like: small with small and large with large.
- *Promotional Intensity.* This measures the brand's expenditure on consumer promotions relative to the competition.[5]

The results of this analysis are shown in Table 4.1.

The meaning of Table 4.1 is clear. The 38 brands that passed through the gate grew by 13%. This is a very substantial increase for brands in highly competi-

TABLE 4.1 Brands That Pass/Do Not Pass Through the Gate

Pass Status	No. Brands	Average Growth Index	Average STAS Differential Index	Average Advertising Intensity Index	Average Promotional Intensity Index
Brands that pass through the gate	38	113	153	2.3	109
Brands that do not pass through the gate	40	100	96	2.3	110

tive product categories that show no aggregate growth, as was the case with the 78 brands analyzed. The 40 brands that did not pass through the gate showed no growth.

The average STAS Differential shows a large gap between the brands that pass through the gate and those that do not; however, there is no difference between the two groups in Advertising Intensity and in Promotional Intensity.

The difference between the two groups can therefore be robustly explained by the STAS Differential, a measure of the innate strength of the advertising campaign. The Gatekeeper was formulated to be a measure of this campaign strength, and it is predictive. The Gatekeeper effectively guards the gate.

This conclusion is unambiguous. But it conceals certain internal relationships between the inputs. These are examined by the method described in the next section.

Three Inputs and How They Operate Together

I started by ranking all 78 advertised brands according to their growth over the year and divided them into deciles from high growth to low. For each decile, I averaged the STAS Differential, Advertising Intensity, and Promotional Intensity. These data appear in Table 4.2.

Note that the figures describing the medium-term growth of the brands are much smaller than the STAS Differentials in Table 2.1. Table 4.2 shows weaker effects from the most strongly growing brands, and there are more brands that are declining. The obvious explanation is that, over the course of a year, the

TABLE 4.2 Medium-Term Growth Deciles Analyzed by Three Separate Marketing
Inputs

Decile	Average Growth Index	Average STAS Differential Index	Average Advertising Intensity Index	Average Promotional Intensity Index
Top	182	163	3.9	121
9th	121	125	4.3	91
8th	113	110	2.7	105
7th	109	120	2.0	122
6th	104	117	1.4	105
5th	98	126	1.4	107
4th	95	110	2.2	117
3rd	90	132	1.5	108
2nd	84	112	2.1	115
Bottom	69	129	1.8	106
Average	106	124	2.3	110

increases shown in the STAS figures have been tamed by consumers' responses
to competitive advertising. The STAS effect has been repeated over a year's
time, but there has been a countervailing force. With inevitable gaps in the advertising schedules, consumers have responded to competitive advertising during these gaps.

All the brands taken together show a net growth of 6%. Because this measure
is based on market shares, this increase demonstrates that the advertising of
brands is not a totally zero-sum game (i.e., with pluses balanced by minuses).
What has happened is that the advertised brands have managed to grow in the
aggregate at the expense of store brands and price brands, which receive no advertising support. This conclusion provides an interesting general endorsement
of the value of consumer advertising.

The data in Table 4.2 do not otherwise produce clear lessons. The top decile
shows the highest STAS and also a very high level of both Advertising Intensity
and Promotional Intensity. But below the top decile, there is no obvious and un-
interrupted progression of the other marketing inputs. It therefore seemed appropriate to look at combining the inputs and seeing what came out of this.

Table 4.3 examines brand growth. It is a matrix relating two influences on
this growth: STAS Differential and Advertising Intensity. With both of these I
split the data into two groups: (a) average and above and (b) below average. The

TABLE 4.3 Matrix Relating STAS Differential to Advertising Intensity

	Advertising Intensity Below Average	*Advertising Intensity Average and Above*	*Total*
STAS Differential Average and Above	13 brands Average Growth Index 112	11 brands Average Growth Index 135	24 brands Average Growth Index 122
STAS Differential Below Average	36 brands Average Growth Index 96	18 brands Average Growth Index 104	54 brands Average Growth Index 99

average STAS Differential was 124, with 24 brands being average or above and 54 below average. The average Advertising Intensity was 2.3.

Table 4.3 demonstrates a number of interesting points:

- The 24 brands with the top STAS measures (average and above) grew by 22%.
- The 54 brands with the below-average STAS measures showed no growth.
- Of the 24 brands with the top STAS measures, only 11 combined their high STAS with high Advertising Intensity, and these achieved an average growth of 35%, which is spectacular in the field of repeat-purchase packaged goods.
- With the brands that generated a below-average STAS Differential, high Advertising Intensity made little difference in their performance. In sales terms, the brands with heavy advertising were 4% in the black; those without it were 4% in the red. Extra repetition had very little influence on a basically ineffective campaign.

The two important points revealed so far—the key importance of STAS as Gatekeeper and the role of the media budget in prolonging sales growth by engineering a repeated short-term effect—support the proposition that *the short-term effect of an advertisement determines whether or not that advertisement will have a medium-term effect. A repetition of short-term effects over a period (normally 12 months)—effects felt exclusively during the periods when the brand is advertised—adds up to a medium-term effect.*

The STAS Differential and Advertising Intensity are, of course, natural partners. They work together for the simple reason that Advertising Intensity determines (in conjunction with the brand's media strategy, discussed in Chapter 5)

TABLE 4.4 Matrix Relating Advertising Effort to Promotional Intensity

	Promotional Intensity Below Average	Promotional Intensity Average and Above	Total
Advertising Effort Average and Above	12 brands Average Growth Index 111	13 brands Average Growth Index 132	25 brands Average Growth Index 122
Advertising Effort Below Average	32 brands Average Growth Index 96	21 brands Average Growth Index 101	53 brands Average Growth Index 98

whether or not the advertising will be exposed often enough to prolong the short-term effect of the campaign over a longer period.

The two measures should therefore be knitted together, quantity being added to quality. This can be done quite simply, by multiplying the STAS Differential Index for each brand by its Advertising Intensity. The resulting calculation is called the Index of Advertising Effort.[6] (Figures for individual quintiles are shown in Table 4.6 later in this chapter.)

The analysis in Table 4.4 is in the form of another matrix, this time relating Advertising Effort to Promotional Intensity. The average figure for Advertising Effort is 283; 25 brands exceeded this average, and 53 were below it. The average Promotional Intensity was 110.

The conclusions from Table 4.4 are striking:

- Medium-term growth is exclusively associated with above-average Advertising Effort (22% growth for the 25 high Advertising Effort brands, compared with no growth for the 53 brands whose Advertising Effort was low).
- Among the brands with above-average Advertising Effort, *Promotional Intensity provides a significant extra stimulus to sales.*
- With low Advertising Effort, Promotional Intensity, whether high or low, makes little difference to a brand's progress.

This analysis generates an important concept. At the higher levels of Advertising Effort, sales promotions work synergistically to boost the already high influence of the advertising, or in the words of the Gatekeeper Model, *Sales promotions can add to the effect of advertising; such synergy is strongest when promotions coincide with the most powerful advertising campaigns.* This is a topic important enough to be examined separately and in detail.

Sales Promotions—Their Upside and Downside

Sales promotions directed at the consumer account for about 25% of large consumer goods companies' combined advertising plus promotional (A&P) budgets. Trade promotions account for another 50% and consumer advertising for the remaining 25%.[7] As hinted earlier in this chapter, trade promotions do not have an influence on the consumer commensurate to their cost to manufacturers and so are not discussed here. However, consumer promotions—as the name implies—are aimed at the consumer, although not totally because they also have an indirect effect on the retail trade by encouraging in-store display.

Consumer promotions, which, like trade promotions, are really discounts—a euphemism for a reduction in revenue—have five important characteristics. The first and fifth are positive, the others are very negative. Consumer promotions are mostly variants on the theme of offering lower prices to the consumer—for example, coupons, reduced price packs, and banded packs (4 for the price of 3). We can generalize about the effect of price reduction on consumer purchases. Based on published averages of typical cases, the effect on purchasing of a given percentage reduction in consumer price is almost nine times as large as the effect of the same percentage increase in advertising expenditure.[8] The immediate and powerful effect of consumer promotions makes them dangerously attractive to manufacturers. This is the first point about promotions.

The word "dangerously" is used deliberately. This is because of the second characteristic of promotions, both those directed at the consumer and those directed at the trade. The extra sales volume increases direct costs (raw material, packaging, etc.), which generally represent a high proportion of a manufacturer's total expenses. This increase in costs, allied to the reduction in revenue from the promotion (which could be 10% or more) will generally pinch out the brand's profitability. This means that a typical brand will earn less from the larger volume sold on deal than from the smaller volume sold at normal prices.

The third characteristic of promotions is that they have a mostly finite effect. The boost to sales generally stops when the promotion stops. This is something that has been known for decades.[9] Sometimes, promotions are followed by an

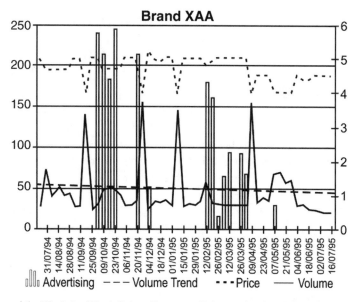

Figure 4.1. Week-by-Week Sales, Consumer Price, and Advertising: Brand XAA

actual reduction in sales because they will have brought forward future sales that would have been made at full prices. Nielsen calls this the "mortgaging" effect of promotions.

The extremely short-term nature of promotional sales increases is illustrated in Figure 4.1, which shows the weekly sales pattern of a typical brand, code-named XAA. The large but temporary response of sales to price cuts can be seen in all four instances in which the price has been reduced. Note that the volume sales trend for this brand is downward, which means that the price-cutting has had the opposite of a positive long-term effect.

The fourth point explains why manufacturers continue to pursue a sales strategy so apparently self-destructive as sales promotions. Manufacturers are forced into it by double pressure from both the retail trade and their competitors in the marketplace. Promotions are a cost of doing business with the retail store chains, whose executives know perfectly well that one manufacturer can be played off against another to bid up promotional discounting. Promotions are therefore inevitable, and the best that manufacturers can do is to maximize any benefits that promotions can provide.

For a start, additional sales volume makes an increased contribution to the general overhead, despite the loss of profit from the individual brand. But there

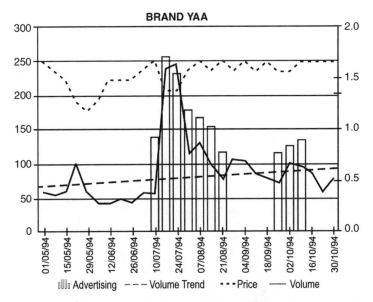

Figure 4.2. Week-by-Week Sales, Consumer Price, and Advertising: Brand YAA

can be an additional compensation, which is the fifth point about consumer promotions. They can quite often work hand in glove with consumer advertising to
nudge a brand's sales trend upward. There is fairly recent aggregated evidence
that this type of synergy can take place in about half of all cases.[10] It should be
emphasized that such synergy does not call for advertising that features the promotion; the normal "theme" advertising serves. But it is important that both activities should take place coincidentally so that the consumer is stimulated from
two different directions at the same time.

This point is illustrated in Figure 4.2, which shows how, for Brand YAA,
advertising and promotion were planned to coincide, with the result that we see
a rising sales trend across the months illustrated in the diagram.

The joint planning of advertising and promotions is still relatively rare,
despite all the debate surrounding the doctrine of Integrated Marketing Communications. Much more commonly, advertising and promotions are planned
separately and sometimes kept deliberately apart to prolong the number of
weeks when there is at least some marketing support behind a brand. As can be
seen in Figure 4.1, such separation cut off all possibility of synergy for Brand
XAA.

TABLE 4.5 Growing Brands' Medium-Term Growth Compared With Individual Marketing Stimuli

Growing Quintile	Growth Index	STAS Differential Re-indexed	Advertising Intensity Re-indexed	Promotional Intensity Re-indexed
Top	209	134	217	109
4th	139	102	238	82
3rd	130	90	150	95
2nd	125	98	111	110
Bottom	120	96	78	95
Baseline: Average of declining brands	100	100	100	100

The cooperation that can take place between advertising and consumer promotions is especially fruitful with those advertising campaigns that are qualitatively and quantitatively the strongest. This point is discussed in the concluding section of this chapter.

Growing Brands—and Why They Grow

I now concentrate on the 39 brands that show medium-term growth. These form the top five deciles of the whole range of 78 brands shown in Table 4.2. I took the average growth of the five bottom deciles—the declining brands—and indexed this average as 100; this provides the base from which the increases in the growing brands can be measured. The data relating to each of the deciles of growing brands—those describing the growth and also the three main marketing inputs—are indexed on this base. Since there are five growing deciles, these are now more correctly labeled as the five growing quintiles.

Table 4.5 compares the growth in each quintile with the equivalent figure for each stimulus separately—STAS Differential, Advertising Intensity, and Promotional Intensity. With this analysis (as with the parallel examination in Table 4.2), none of the three separate stimuli is an accurate predictor of growth. The least efficient of them is Promotional Intensity, which confirms the point made in this chapter that promotions have no effect beyond the short term.

TABLE 4.6   Growing Brands' Medium-Term Growth Compared With Combined
Marketing Stimuli

Growing Quintile	Growth Index	Advertising Effort Index	Advertising Effort Plus Promotional Intensity Index
Top	209	260	306
4th	139	199	167
3rd	130	139	123
2nd	125	105	109
Bottom	120	79	72
Baseline: Average of all declining brands	100	100	100

We get much more promising results when we combine the stimuli, by looking at the relationships between growth and Advertising Effort and between
growth and Advertising Effort plus Promotional Intensity. These relationships
are shown in Table 4.6 and plotted in Figure 4.3. The effects can be seen most
dramatically in the diagram.

The direction of the figures is unmistakable. The two combinations of marketing inputs succeed in predicting marketplace performance.

The trajectory of the input figures—the steepness of the curves—is more
pronounced than the final outturn in brand growth. The input figures start lower
and end higher. But there is no break in the series, and it can be seen that the fit
of the curves is good. There is actually some advantage in producing input
curves that are steeper than the outturn because the operational lessons from the
analysis become clearer.

This analysis is made with the aim of helping advertisers boost their brands
in large competitive and often stagnant markets. Here are four guidelines.

1. The competitive functional performance of their brands must be good enough to
   support advertising investment. In the eyes of consumers, the brand must justify
   repurchase.

2. Manufacturers should make sure that their brand's advertising generates a high
   STAS Differential. If not, they must persist until they produce a campaign that
   does, otherwise the campaign should not be allowed through the gate.

3. A brand's budget will inevitably be governed by its present and/or anticipated
   profitability. Within these limits, above-average investment is strongly recom-

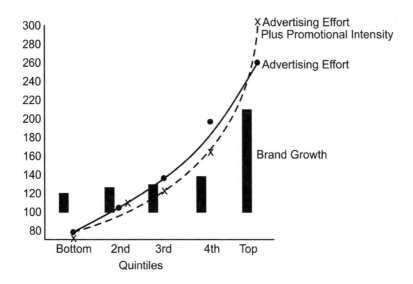

Figure 4.3. Quintile Analysis of 39 Brands Showing Medium-Term Growth
NOTE: Index on 39 declining brands = 100.

mended for those campaigns that generate a high STAS Differential. This will certainly be the case for new brands, which must invest at a high level in order to get established.

4. It is less desirable to boost consumer promotions in view of their uneconomic cost. However, pressures in the marketplace will force manufacturers to promote, and when this happens there is merit in concentrating the promotional support on those brands with a high STAS Differential plus high Advertising Intensity. In all events, advertising and promotions should coincide in time so as to maximize synergy.

Consider the four examples of real brands in Table 4.7, which appear in ascending order of sales effect (reading left to right). Note in particular the fundamental importance of the STAS Differential and how Advertising Intensity reinforces its effect.

In summary, this chapter has described four phenomena from which it is possible to draw operational lessons.

First, the STAS Differential guards the gate. It should control whether or not an advertising campaign justifies further investment.

Second, the range of medium-term effects is much less pronounced than the range of STAS Differentials. This demonstrates that, over time, the STAS effect erodes as a result of competitive activity in the marketplace.

TABLE 4.7   Medium-Term Growth Compared With Combined Marketing Inputs
for Four Successful Brands

Category	Breakfast Cereal	Liquid Detergent	Bar Soap	Packaged Detergent
STAS Differential	121	133	193	253
Advertising Intensity	2.2	5.0	2.0	3.5
Promotional Intensity	70	108	122	163
Advertising Effort	266	665	386	886
Advertising Effort plus Promotional Intensity	186	718	471	1,444
Medium-term growth (%)	+22	+25	+78	+119

Third, to minimize this erosion, an advertiser should support a campaign that achieves a high STAS Differential with the highest affordable Advertising Intensity. Consumer promotions should be timed to support the advertising, and within a general policy of using promotions sparingly, should be used for brands that have effective advertising rather than to compensate for ineffective advertising.

Fourth, the indexes of Advertising Effort and of Advertising Effort plus Promotional Intensity can be used to predict the sales growth of successful brands.

Are the lessons in this chapter a shadow of the Holy Grail of advertising? We cannot make any such claim until we have built into our model an evaluation of advertising's long-term effect. This is the concern of Chapter 6 and the rest of the book. Before getting to this dense, complex, and fascinating topic, we must first consider the tactical application of above-average Advertising Intensity and discuss how this can be used to build advertising continuity, which (as explained at the beginning of this chapter) is one of the eight determinants of the growth of a brand.

Notes

1. This information comes from research among a sample of large advertisers contacted regularly by Cox Communications. John Philip Jones, "Trends in Promotions," in *The Advertising Business: Operations, Creativity, Media Planning, Integrated Communications,* ed. John Philip Jones (Thousand Oaks, CA: Sage, 1999), 321-324.

2. John Philip Jones, *When Ads Work: New Proof that Advertising Triggers Sales* (New York: Simon & Schuster-Lexington Books, 1995).

3. As explained in Chapter 2, the STAS Differential measures the difference in a brand's market share between its ad households and adless households. The former had received advertising for the brand during the 7 days before the brand was bought; the latter had not.

4. Advertising Intensity is a measure of the size of the brand's advertising media budget in relation to that of its competitors in the same product category. It is based on the brand's share of voice (all advertising in the category). Advertising Intensity is the ratio of a brand's share of voice to its share of market. For example, if Advertising Intensity is 2.0, then the brand's advertising share is twice as high as its market share—say, 6% compared with 3%. For most brands, share of voice is larger than share of market because there are always some unadvertised brands in all categories. Therefore, the average share of voice will be larger than share of market because the latter is based on *all* brands whereas share of voice is derived from the advertised brands alone; for the unadvertised brands it will be zero.

5. Promotional Intensity is also based on competitive activity within a brand's product category. It is measured by the percentage of the brand's volume sold on deal (i.e., at a special, reduced price) compared with the category average (indexed at 100).

6. I have chosen the simplest way of making the calculation. It does not matter precisely how the calculations are carried out so long as the same method is used consistently in all cases. The purpose of this piece of arithmetic is simply to make *comparisons between brands* on the basis of their relative Advertising Effort. An alternative system of calculating the Advertising Effort would put different brands in the same relationship to each other, although the numbers might be different.

7. See Note 1.

8. These averages are based on a substantial number of cases. See Gert Assmus, John U. Farlet, and Donald R. Lehmann, "How Advertising Affects Sales: A Meta-Analysis of Econometric Results," *Journal of Marketing Research,* February 1984, 65-74; Gerard J. Tellis, "The Price Elasticity of Selective Demand: A Meta-Analysis of Econometric Models of Sales," *Journal of Marketing Research,* November 1988, 331-341; and John Philip Jones, "The Double Jeopardy of Sales Promotions," *Harvard Business Review,* September-October 1990, 145-152.

9. James O. Peckham, Sr., *The Wheel of Marketing* (Privately published, 1981; available from A. C. Nielsen), 52-70.

10. Abbas Bendali, "Do Promotions Need Media Support?" *Commercial Communications: The Journal of Advertising and Marketing Policy and Practice in the European Community,* January 1997, 13-16.

5

Keeping the
Brand in the Window

Erwin Ephron, a New York media consultant who combines a researcher's understanding of principles and underlying causes with pragmatic knowledge derived from a lifetime of practical experience of media planning and buying for major brands, once used this striking metaphor: "Visualize a window of advertising opportunity in front of each purchase. Advertising's job is to influence that purchase. Recency planning's job is to place the message in that window."[1]

This chapter is devoted to the concept of recency, which embraces two factors: continuity and propinquity. Continuity means planning the advertising to appear "in the window" for as many weeks over the course of a year as the budget will permit. Propinquity means ensuring that the advertising message appears near the time when the consumer experiences an impulse to buy one or another brand in the category. The decision to buy a *product* (irrespective of the particular brand chosen) is generally uninfluenced by advertising. It is governed, in the case of packaged goods, by whether the last box in the home has been used up; in other fields, it happens when the need arises. However, there is no doubt at all that advertising can influence the choice of *brand* for the replacement purchase, and it does this generally by reminding, which means evoking prior brand experience. This is a more realistic description of the process than the rational phrase "influencing a decision."

The Buying Process

The buying process for all consumer goods is more turbulent than nonspecialist observers imagine. The purchasing of brands by individual consumers is complicated (as we will shortly see). And the aggregate purchasing in a market, made up as it is of millions of consumers buying a multiplicity of brands with great regularity, introduces an exponential degree of further complication, which means we need a research technique as data-intensive as Pure Single-Source to dig out the effects of advertising.

Advertising is quite capable of influencing sales, as was seen in Chapters 2 and 4. But to explain more fully how an immediate short-term effect can be prolonged into the medium term, I must start by making three general points about consumer purchasing.

First, in the majority of categories, consumers buy repeatedly. With day-to-day purchases, such as extremely inexpensive ones like individual telephone calls or e-mails, the repetition takes place with great regularity within an extremely short period. At the other end of the range are durables like cars, which we buy regularly but where the repurchase period is extended over years. Goods sold in supermarkets and drugstores fall between the two extremes, with the repetition interval usually 1 to 4 weeks. The latter products account for the majority of household expenditure and are the main concern of this chapter.

The second characteristic of purchasing is that in the majority of categories most buyers are women, for the simple reason that homemakers tend to be female. Social evolution—in particular, change in the roles of the sexes—has brought about a diminishing proportion of female buyers, but women homemakers are still prevalent enough for me to adopt the widespread convention of calling buyers "she" and not "he." Housewives have a good relationship with their brands, but the sheer number of different brand purchases they make in all the product fields they buy reaches in most cases more than 1,000 in a year. It follows that the individual decision to choose one brand over another is not too serious a matter. It is rarely planned beforehand and equally rarely subject to post hoc examination. The process has been described as "low involvement."

The third point, and the one that is most relevant to the role of advertising, is that consumers buy a number of different brands; it is fairly rare for more than 20% of purchasing over the course of a year in any category to be made by buyers of one brand only (a group known technically as solus buyers).[2] The group of brands bought by a consumer is described as her brand repertoire.

Here is a typical example of one homemaker's purchases in one heavily bought category over a two-year period. The brand names are coded by letters of the alphabet:[3]

BOODGBOCOBGBGABBGBBDBGBCBBGGBBB

This consumer "shows a trend toward brand B and a cycle in buying brand G which recurs on average 4.4 times."[4] Over the period, this housewife made 31 separate product purchases, and she had a repertoire of 6 different brands. She bought brand B, 15 times; G, 7 times; O, 4 times; C twice; D twice; and A once. This pattern is typical. Most buyers have a favorite brand (B), a second favorite (G), and a rotating third brand (either O, C, D, or A in our example).

The importance of this analysis to an advertiser is that his buyers will be using and comparing both his own and his competitors' brands. These buyers will therefore be appropriate targets for his and his competitors' advertising. And since the buyers use all these brands either regularly or intermittently, they will be modestly inclined to pay attention to the advertising of these because of Selective Perception. We tend to look, or at least half-look, at the advertising for the brands we use.

With repeat-purchase packaged goods, household purchasing tends to take place weekly, generally on Thursday, Friday, or Saturday. But much buying takes place on other days as well. If we add together the buying of all the consumers in any product category—many millions of people in most cases—it is easy to visualize the massive amount of buying that takes place every day, with an even larger amount toward the end of the week. People buy when their household stocks are low or depleted. Each household has a purchase interval for its brands: the period between purchases (e.g., about three weeks for toothpaste or one week for breakfast cereals). But repurchase takes place on different days in different weeks for different households. And people who buy one brand today will possibly or even probably buy a different brand next time.

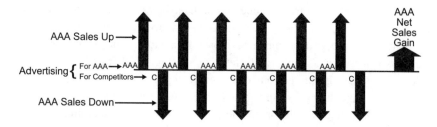

Figure 5.1. Schematic Diagram of Sales Gains and Losses for Brand AAA Over the Course of a Year

There are huge numbers of potential buyers at all times for all established brands in every category. And in every category, the pattern of buying shows a constant interchange of brand shares, the "ups" for a specific brand reflecting its advertising at the time—provided, of course, that the campaign has a positive STAS. If only one brand is advertised, this will directly attract customers from all others. If more than one is advertised at the same time, the brand whose campaign generates the highest STAS Differential will do best. The gaps in a brand's schedule will therefore cause losses of business because millions of potential buyers have been missed. This process is illustrated in Figure 5.1, a hypothetical picture, although the lesson it contains is real enough. Each short-term sales increase represents the size of the STAS Differential. The net gain at the end of the year represents the sum of short-term gains minus the sum of short-term losses.

The end result is as we see in Figure 5.2, which describes a real German brand, ZAA, whose STAS Differential index (B minus A) showed a rise of 50% but whose medium-term sales improvement (D minus C) was only 14%. The difference between the two numbers was the result of the gaps in ZAA's schedule when consumers were responding to the advertising for competitive brands.

The performance of brand ZAA, despite the drop from 50% to 14%, is actually good. The losses of business below the STAS Differential are greater for most other brands. In many cases the effect of a positive STAS completely disappears as a result of the stronger campaigns for competitive brands, which means that the brands which lose their STAS end the year in negative territory.

In view of the vigorous forces of competition, it is obvious that if advertising for a brand is to be placed "in the window" in order to be seen by the countless numbers of people who are in the market, then it must have a permanent

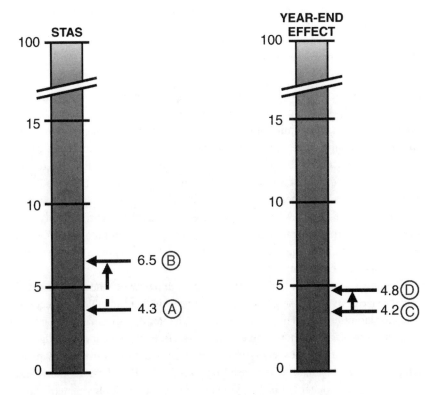

Figure 5.2. STAS Differential and Medium-Term Sales Effect for Brand ZAA

advertising presence or at least as permanent a presence as the budget will allow. Advertising presence naturally means *effective* presence, reaching a large
enough number of consumers every week to influence the total volume of
sales. Also, advertising should appear immediately before the buying takes
place, when it has the greatest effect (as we shall see). This is the meaning of
propinquity.

This then is the basic rationale for the strategy of recency:

• Large amounts of buying take place weekly; media should therefore be planned
weekly. Since the advertising is required to influence the buying, the weekly
reach must be sufficiently large for an effect in the marketplace. We should aim
for a minimal effective coverage of targeted homes but without extravagance.

- Buying tends to take place toward the end of the week; media should therefore be planned similarly.
- Buying never stops; media exposure should therefore never stop—or only stop when it is constricted by the budget.

When this doctrine was first propagated, it upset many deeply rooted beliefs. Indeed, the importance of continuity, in particular, is still not universally accepted, although the skeptics now represent a diminishing minority. But in addition to the doubts of these most conservative practitioners, there are two factors that inhibit our ability to achieve continuity. The first is the size of the budget. In most cases, we simply cannot afford to advertise all year round, and this represents a permanent problem. In the real world, the budget for an ongoing (as opposed to a new) brand is governed inevitably by its profitability. It is unrealistic to expect manufacturers to accept advice to spend more money and thereby sacrifice immediate profit, no matter what benefits greater media continuity can offer in the longer term.

Despite a rather subtle but important relationship between the size of a brand and the size of its advertising budget—a relationship that can yield scale economies for larger brands (a matter reviewed in Chapter 7)—the size of the media budget is not discussed in this present context. Here I take the media budget as given and just say that a successful marketplace outcome from recency planning will probably lead to increased budgets in the long term as the brand grows. We must concern ourselves with the most effective deployment of existing media dollars. This brings me to the second problem with the application of continuity: namely, the extent to which traditional patterns of media buying unconsciously build waste into media plans, thus misusing resources that could be used to provide continuity. To evaluate this second point, we must examine a technical matter: the shape of the advertising response function.

The Advertising Response Function

The response function is an example of a theory with a directly practical application. It describes the amount of advertising needed to trigger buying. In particular, it illustrates the sales effect of additional amounts of advertising and whether they generate increments of sales at an increasing or diminishing rate. These points become clearer by comparing Figure 5.3 with Figure 5.4.

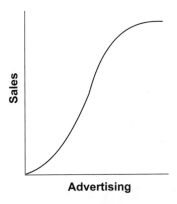

Figure 5.3. Advertising Response Function With Threshold (S-shaped curve)

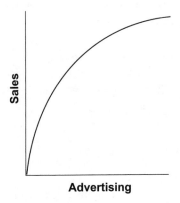

Figure 5.4. Advertising Response Function Without Threshold (concave-downward curve)

In Figures 5.3 and 5.4, the horizontal axis plots equal "doses" of advertising. These can be measured in a number of ways: in dollars, television gross rating points (GRPs), or consumer impressions ("opportunities to see"). The vertical axis plots the *incremental* sales that are generated by the progressive doses of advertising. We see therefore *varying* amounts of sales output that have resulted from *equal* amounts of advertising input.

In Figure 5.3, extra advertising causes sales to increase at a growing rate, building up to a threshold shown by the bend in the curve (known as the inflexion point), where the increasing sales increments change to diminishing ones. The amount of advertising that produces the greatest sales effect for the advertising dollar is measured at the inflexion point: where the marginal—or additional—dose of advertising produces the greatest return.

In Figure 5.4, all doses of advertising produce sales results, but the increments decline from the beginning. For example, the first advertising generates the most sales, the second produces extra volume but less than the first, and the third produces more still but less than the second—hence, diminishing returns.

Two Response Functions: Two Strategies

These alternative theories are used to support two different ways of deploying advertising money. Figure 5.3 underpins a once-popular belief that a fixed number of advertisement exposures (generally considered to be 3) have to be received by the consumer before the advertising will seriously influence her purchasing behavior. This number of exposures was considered to be the threshold representing maximum effect. The result was the popular policy of compressing the advertising into confined periods to obtain an "effective frequency" of 3.

With the alternative theory of diminishing returns shown in Figure 5.4, the first dose of advertising is seen to be the most productive one, and extra doses produce increases that become progressively smaller. These are less economic because each diminishing sales increment costs the same advertising budget as the one before. The way to exploit diminishing returns is to create during each week a strong effect by covering a large audience *once* and no more. We can then move on to the next week, when the advertising can be used to stimulate fresh sales, again with 1 strong exposure. This is a broad description of continuity planning.

As I have suggested, the theory embodied in Figure 5.3 once received wide support. This meant that the advertising schedules of the majority of brands in most countries around the world were for many decades made up of 2- or 3- or 4-week periods of advertising, each concentrated to achieve "effective frequency." These periods were separated by intervals during which there was no advertising. The gaps were, of course, unavoidable because advertising budgets could not run to year-round exposure at a heavy rate. The pockets of concentration in such schedules are known as flights in the United States and as bursts in Europe.[5]

Until the 1990s, the shape of the advertising response function was not a subject of great interest to the advertising business.[6] As I have said, the majority of media plans employed flights, a policy that was, of course, tacitly based on the S-shaped response function shown in Figure 5.3. It was unlikely that media planners, who are practical people, were much concerned with the theoretical basis of the strategy of media concentration that was automatically—and perhaps unthinkingly—applied in virtually all circumstances.

The influential research study *Effective Frequency: The Relationship Between Frequency and Advertising Effectiveness,* sponsored by the Advertising Research Foundation and published by the Association of National Advertisers in 1979, gave academic support to a flighting strategy.[7] The main piece of evidence in this book came from Colin McDonald's pilot study carried out in Great Britain in 1966 (described in Chapter 2). This showed an S-shaped curve of a very extreme type. Unfortunately, this was a result of the way in which McDonald analyzed the data. He used an incomplete method because he measured the response of purchasing to increments of advertising solely by the amount of switching from brand to brand. This tells us only half the story since it ignores repeated purchase of the same brand, which can be influenced by advertising just as much as brand switching can.

I used a more straightforward method of analyzing all the data from the first large-scale piece of Pure Single-Source research in the United States. I measured the change in purchasing caused by advertising—both in absolute and in incremental terms—by a simple change in market share. This struck me at the time as the commonsense approach, and my method has not been disputed since my work was first published in 1995. When McDonald recomputed his 1966 figures using my simpler method, his findings echoed mine—a straightforward pattern of diminishing returns. McDonald's results are shown in Figure 5.5;[8] mine are in Figure 5.6.

My research was planned to measure the sales response to any amount of advertising for a brand during the 7 days before it was bought. It was, however, reasonably simple to isolate the sales response in the homes that had received a single advertisement. As can be seen in Figure 5.6, the average share of market for all 78 brands was 7.8% in the adless households: the level of the baseline. The share in the ad households that had received only one advertisement was 8.4%; in the ad households that had received any number of advertisements, the share was 8.7%.[9]

My research demonstrated a sharp pattern of diminishing returns, with households receiving a single advertisement buying 73% as much as households

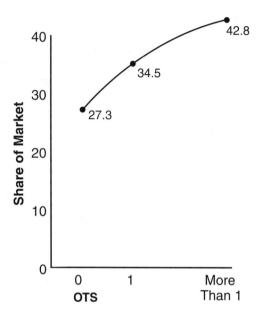

Figure 5.5. Response Function: McDonald's 1966 British Pure Single-Source Data Recomputed Using the Jones Method

receiving any number of advertisements. Additional advertisements beyond one generated only about a third more business. My finding, namely a 73:27 ratio between the effect of 1 exposure and subsequent exposures, had some remarkable effects on American advertising practice. The research was also replicated and the subsequent studies have confirmed broadly what I found.

The first repeat of my American research was in Germany.[10] This showed quite clearly that a single advertisement can be effective—often highly effective. This conclusion has also been confirmed by other American data, from among others Lawrence Gibson,[11] and by British data both from Andrew Roberts[12] and from Colin McDonald's large-scale *Adlab* study.[13] McDonald makes an important point by emphasizing propinquity. The greatest sales effect comes from advertising one day before purchase. Fewer sales come from advertising two days before, and fewer still from three days before.[14] McDonald found the same thing in his 1966 investigation.[15]

My count of published response functions shows more than 200 brands whose campaigns show diminishing returns and slightly more than 10—mainly

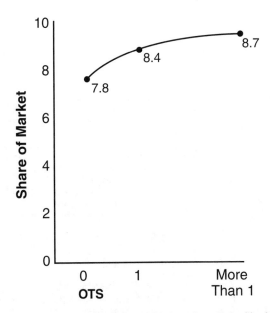

Figure 5.6. Response Function: Nielsen 1991 American Pure Single-Source Data From 78 Brands

new brands—whose campaigns show S-shaped thresholds. The logic of (at least temporary) media concentration for new brands is that new product concepts and new advertising campaigns need a degree of repetition before consumers can understand them. However, even in this exceptional circumstance, it can be shown that the most efficient plan is a single weekly exposure. The research to support this contention is discussed in the Coda at the end of this chapter.

Diminishing Returns in Europe

There is a special point worth making about the difference between my findings from the United States and Germany. This illustrates dramatically the waste involved in concentrating advertising money in ignorance of the vicious effect of diminishing returns. The normal reduction in advertising efficiency caused by

TABLE 5.1 STAS Minus Year-End Sales Change (in percentage points)

Decile	United States (High Falloff)	Germany (Low Falloff)
1st	−54	−16
2nd	−43	−7
3rd	−26	−1
4th	−12	No difference
5th	−13	No difference
6th	−10	No difference
7th	−9	−4
8th	−7	−5
9th	−5	−3
10th	−4	−1

diminishing returns will effectively cause a large difference between an immediate sales lift from STAS and a year-end sales increase. As I have mentioned, it is common to find a positive immediate effect ending up in a year-end *sales reduction.*

In the United States, I found a very sharp pattern of diminishing returns in the advertising response function: as explained, an average 73:27 ratio of effects from, respectively, 1 exposure and multiple exposures. Media concentration—which swallows large amounts of money—causes the average advertising budget to run down very fast, and the loss of potential sales caused by the diminishing returns means that any short-term sales gain simply cannot be maintained across a year. Table 5.1 examines the falloff of short-term effects by the end of the year. All the brands from my American study are ranked in deciles from the campaigns with the strongest STAS (first decile) to the weakest (10th decile). The inefficiency of concentrated scheduling is amply illustrated by the consistent dissipation of the short-term effects.

The situation in Germany is different. Here the rate of diminishing returns is much less sharp than in the United States, with a sales effect from the first exposure compared with additional exposures in the ratio of 46:54. Additional exposures beyond one are still generating a good deal of business. In Germany therefore, concentrated pressure leads to *less falloff in sales and less decay of the short-term effect* than in the United States.

The difference in the rate of falloff between the two countries is startling, and it emphasizes the terrible loss of potential sales in the United States that concentrated advertising schedules will bring about. The data reported in my book *When Ads Work* point up this loss in very simple terms:[16] 70% of campaigns generate short-term sales increases; of these, 46% maintain higher sales at the end of the year, although the effect was always less than the original STAS, and 24% (i.e., 70 minus 46) totally lost their positive effect on sales, for reasons connected with media weight and scheduling.

An additional discovery of McDonald's is worth mentioning. Although most sales come from the homes that receive a single advertisement, additional exposures *do* generate some extra business—a very small amount in the United States but more in Europe where the onset of diminishing returns is less steep. In Europe, it is likely that the buyers who watch an above-average amount of television will receive extra advertisements for a brand. And heavy television viewers in Europe tend to buy more of a brand than do light viewers (because of the number of children in the household). Similarly, light viewers buy less.

McDonald called this effect Purchasing/Viewing (P/V) bias.[17] It goes both ways, causing European STAS figures to go up or down. We must, however, bear in mind the band of inaccuracy I am using to interpret the data in this book and only consider STAS variations outside this range.

How we use the data depends on the distribution of heavy and light viewers in the target audience for our brand's media schedule. As a general rule, covering all television viewing in most countries, about 40% of homes are heavy viewers (in varying degrees), 20% of homes are average viewers, and 40% of homes are light viewers (again in varying degrees).

The 60% of average and heavy viewers are obviously unaffected by this analysis. Their STAS will be either average or above average. The light viewers are more problematical, although more in theory than in practice. This is because advertisers commonly spend at least 10% of their total advertising budgets on general and specialist magazines to reach light television viewers, who are often the better educated and more affluent families. There is therefore a built-in compensation for the likelihood of these consumers generating a below-average STAS from television on its own. They receive additional stimuli from print media.

As mentioned, the P/V bias is a European problem rather than an American one. In the United States, purchasing levels are relatively uniform across the different viewing groups. But to be on the safe side, remember that in Chapter 2, I advised that the brands with a STAS Differential of under 120 should only be allowed through the gate if there is additional evidence (e.g., premium price) that the advertising is effective.

Recency in the Marketplace

The Gatekeeper model says *the size of the medium-term effect is determined not only by the creative content of the campaign but also by the brand's budget and its media strategy. Budget and media are devices to engineer the advertising continuity needed to protect the brand from competitive assaults.*

The most effective media strategy for a brand can be described simply. However, it is not easy to implement such a strategy because of the complexities of the media marketplace:

1. Aim to cover a substantial proportion of the brand's target group once every week with as little duplication as possible. "Substantial proportion" is a judgment call based on the size of the brand, its target group, and knowledge of the effectiveness of defined levels of reach achieved in the past.

2. To attain this minimum reach, determine the optimum number of weekly GRPs and establish the best types of day parts and television programs to use in order to minimize audience duplication. These procedures are again judgmental, and they require expert knowledge of the television audience and of the fast-changing field of programming. During recent years, Erwin Ehpron has done more than any other analyst to put flesh on these theoretical bones.

3. Run the weekly advertising pattern for as many weeks as the budget will allow. Any inevitable gaps in the schedule should occur during the low season.

My recommendations call for redeploying advertising budgets to achieve a greater continuity than many schedules achieve at present, and of course this means less short-term concentration—an economically favorable outcome because of the way it manages to reduce the effect of diminishing returns. Regional test programs are also a good idea so long as these can be carried out efficiently and economically.

These thoughts, which would at one time have been considered highly unorthodox, are not falling on deaf ears in either the United States or Europe.

In the late 1970s, when I was working at J. Walter Thompson in London, the client and agency commissioned an econometric study of the advertising response function for Andrex, a very powerful brand and market leader in the bathroom tissue category. This response function—although it came in the form of a rather weak regression—seemed to show a pattern of diminishing returns. This was nevertheless good enough to persuade the client and agency to plan and run a pattern of continuous advertising in a number of typical television areas. A careful analysis of sales at the end of one year showed significantly stronger sales in the test areas than in the rest of Great Britain, which acted as the statistical control.

As a result of this test, the national advertising was changed to a pattern of continuous advertising. This was a very unusual undertaking for an important national brand. However, it has been acknowledged by both the client and the agency to have benefited the brand enormously over the years. It did this by maintaining the brand's already high penetration and purchase frequency and by preserving Andrex's comfortable market leadership:

> [J. Walter Thompson] believe[s] that this high level of carry-over and behavior maintenance is in some measure attributable to the disposition of advertising weight within and between sales periods. Andrex has, for many years, disposed advertising weight continuously. It is not clustered in bursts.[18]

Such an unprejudiced, experimental mind-set has also been adopted by many American advertisers—an attitude that must be welcomed by the research community. During the course of 1996, I gradually learned about eight major advertisers, with an aggregate national billing of more than $4 billion, who were seriously experimenting with continuity scheduling on an area basis and in some cases were producing demonstrably positive results.

I possess full details of the media experiments carried out by one of these organizations—an extremely prominent advertiser and a company with nine major marketing divisions whose brands are all household names. In 1995, the average number of weeks of advertising across all these divisions was 16, at an average weekly advertising weight of 97 GRPs. As a result of successful experimentation during the course of 1996, eight of the nine divisions adjusted the distribution of their advertising funds. In 1997, the average number of advertised weeks in all nine operating divisions had increased to 22, and the average weekly GRP level had been decreased to 84.[19] The company has taken—after good research and careful deliberation—a measurable step toward recency scheduling. The plans also accommodated a good deal of detailed media innovation aimed at stretching the net reach of the schedules and reducing wasteful duplication.

During 1996, the pace of interest in continuity scheduling increased. By December, 53% of major clients and 70% of senior media executives in agencies were aware of the research into single-exposure effectiveness and the value of continuous advertising. Similar numbers also claimed to be either implement-

TABLE 5.2 Relative Effectiveness of TV Schedules Based on Different Combinations of Continuity and Weekly Weight

Continuity	Weeks on Air	Maximum GRPs* per Week	Index of Sales Effectiveness
Low	9	240	61
Medium	22	163	106
High	38	193	132

* GRPs = gross rating points.

ing or considering implementing plans to advertise more continuously than before. Interest was particularly strong among packaged goods and automotive advertisers.[20]

In 1999, the celebrated *AdWorks2* study was released to subscribers, and selected extracts were published. This was a cooperative enterprise between Media Marketing Assessment, Inc. (MMA) and Information Resources, Inc. (IRI). It was an econometric study of more than 800 brands in 200 separate categories, using sales data from 4,000 grocery, drug, and mass merchandiser stores over the two years 1995-1996. This research compared the effectiveness of Continuity and Flighted media plans and reached an unambiguous conclusion:

> Continuity plans are more effective than Flighted plans. This supports findings from other studies that point to the importance of Recency. Brands that are planning to increase weight should first consider adding weeks instead of adding weight to existing flights. Brands with high levels of GRPs delivered per week should consider shifting some weight across additional weeks.[21]

This conclusion was derived from a special calculation of the relative effectiveness of different schedules, based on the average (indexed at 100) for all television schedules covered by the *AdWorks2* research. The relative effectiveness of three mixes of Continuity and weekly weight are shown in Table 5.2.

The greater effectiveness of high Continuity scheduling over low Continuity is a manifestation of diminishing returns. The Continuity schedule benefits from operating every week on a lower—more productive—part of the advertising response curve. In contrast to this, the low Continuity (concentrated) schedule soon hits diminishing returns.

Another way of expressing this same point is that if two brands with the same budget, size, media costs, and advertising elasticity choose to raise their

GRP support by, say, 20% we would see very different volume returns as a result of different patterns of Continuity. With additional weeks but no change in the weekly concentration of GRPs, the extra budget would generate extra sales. But if weekly GRP levels are lifted drastically and weeks on-air not increased, we would consistently and quickly see saturation, and overall television effectiveness would not be improved in line with the budget increase. The extra money would be essentially wasted.

As if to write *finis* to this debate, the Advertising Research Foundation (ARF), which had sponsored the 1979 *Effective Frequency* study, formally announced at the end of 1997 the termination of its support for the doctrine of effective frequency. Using a slightly macabre metaphor, the ARF declared that "we agreed to amputate the rule of thumb. And like any amputation, it was painful."[22]

Coda: Recent Research Demonstrating the Universal Efficiency of Single Weekly Exposure

Earlier in this chapter, I discussed the probability that an S-shaped response function operates in exceptional circumstances, in particular for a brief period during the introduction of new brands.

Shortly before this book went to press, important new research revealed that, even with an S-shaped response function, the most efficient media strategy is a single weekly exposure. This research was carried out jointly by Erwin Ephron (whose work has been discussed in this chapter) and Melissa Heath of Kantar Media Research, Inc.[23] The analysis was derived from Kantar's Optimizer system, a widely used media model based on substantial data inputs. The media coverage information came from the Nielsen Television Index, and a leading media planning organization, MindShare, provided the respondent data. (Both Kantar and MindShare are parts of WPP, the largest advertising and communications group in the world.)

The analysis was based on media planning for a typical national brand, with a television budget of $13.5 million. The demographic target was the typical but relatively unselective group of women aged 25-54. The research covered a range of weekly net reach levels, but they all disclosed the same patterns. The following conclusions concentrate for simplicity's sake on a single reach target of 35%.

TABLE 5.3 Two Alternative Minimum Weekly Exposure Levels

Exposure Group	Minimum of 1 Exposure	Minimum of 2 Exposures
1	21.3	(19.0)
2	7.9	11.5
3	3.1	6.7
4+	2.7	16.8
Total	35.0	35.0

Two related findings emerge from this research. The first is that if we establish a minimum target of 1 weekly exposure of the audience this can be accomplished with 62 GRPs. Targeting a minimum of 2 exposures calls for 181 GRPs. This large increase in the number of GRPs is a reflection of viewing patterns. To reach viewers a minimum of twice a week forces us to use a range of spots viewed by many permutations of the same audience. A large number of our viewers will see three, four, or more spots, and there is no way of avoiding this because it is dictated by the fact that many television programs are seen to a large degree by the same people.

A single exposure, accomplished by 62 GRPs, can be bought for $366,000. The annual budget of $13.5 million therefore provides 37 weeks of advertising. On the other hand, a minimum of 2 exposures, accomplished by 181 GRPs, will cost $1,127,000. The annual budget will therefore only provide 12 weeks of advertising. *There is therefore a large loss of continuity as a result of an increase in a minimum weekly exposure from 1 to 2.*

The second part of this analysis is more subtle. It involves estimating the actual selling power of alternative schedules. This is done by multiplying the number of viewers covered by a schedule by these people's volume of purchases. The detailed procedure is to multiply the two figures described as follows:

1. The incremental net reach for each level of exposure. The figures for each incremental exposure are shown in Table 5.3.
2. The weekly sales generated by each increment of exposure. With a typical S-shaped response function, the increments will be approximately as follows:
   35% from first exposure
   80% from first and second exposures
   95% from first, second, and third exposures
   100% from all exposures

TABLE 5.4 Comparison of Selling Power of Two Alternative Weekly Exposure
Levels

Exposure Level	Weeks on Air	Index of Selling Power
Schedule for minimum of 1 exposure	37	100
Schedule for minimum of 2 exposures		
S-shaped response function:		
Weak	12	76
Moderate	12	65
Strong	12	64

For each scheduling pattern, the multiplication of the two numbers produces
a figure described technically as a Frequency-Value Weighted Reach. This is, in
effect, a surrogate for the selling power of each schedule. Using this technique,
Ephron and Heath calculated the relative selling abilities of 1-exposure and 2-
exposure schedules as these would apply to S-shaped response functions of
varying degrees of steepness (i.e., responsiveness to incremental pressure).
Indexing as 100 the selling potential of a 1-exposure schedule, the authors demonstrated that the selling ability of the various schedules providing 2 exposures
is in every case less efficient. This point is illustrated in Table 5.4.

The data in Table 5.4 are dramatic. In every case, irrespective of the actual
steepness of the S-shaped function, *a media plan based on a minimum of a
single exposure will generate more sales than a media plan based on 2 exposures.* This is substantially the result of the very few weeks that the concentrated schedule can afford to be on air.

Conclusion

This chapter has demonstrated how a single weekly exposure is the most efficient pattern for response functions which show the general although not universal pattern of diminishing returns. The new data from Ephron and Heath
show that this conclusion also applies to all S-shaped response functions. The
strategy that works best—namely, minimum concentration and maximum continuity—is therefore the most efficient one in all circumstances. It is a genuine
example of "one size fits all."

Notes

1. Erwin Ephron, "A Car Is Like a Box of Frosted Flakes" (Advertising Research Foundation and European Society for Marketing and Opinion Research: *Worldwide Electronic and Broadcast Research Symposium,* San Francisco, April 1996).

2. John Philip Jones, *When Ads Work: New Proof That Advertising Triggers Sales* (New York: Simon & Schuster-Lexington Books, 1995), 145.

3. John Philip Jones, *What's in a Name? Advertising and the Concept of Brands* (New York: Simon & Schuster-Lexington Books, 1986), 105. This particular analysis is based on the work of Michael Baines, whose original paper is described on page 128 in *What's in a Name?*

4. Ibid.

5. A purely instinctive drive to concentrate media weight was commonplace during the period 1953-1980 when I worked as an advertising practitioner.

6. This field is reviewed in Jones, *What's in a Name?,* 183-224.

7. *Effective Frequency: The Relationship Between Frequency and Advertising Effectiveness,* ed. Michael J. Naples (New York: Association of National Advertisers, 1979).

8. Colin McDonald, "The Effective Frequency Debate," *Admap,* February 1995, 27.

9. Jones, *When Ads Work,* 42-47.

10. John Philip Jones, *When Ads Work: The German Version* (Frankfurt am Main: Gesamtverband Werbeagenturen, 1995), 21-24.

11. Lawrence D. Gibson, "When Can One TV Exposure Do?" *Conference Proceedings of Copy Research Workshop* (New York: Advertising Research Foundation, 1994), 16.

12. Andrew Roberts, "What Do We Know About Advertising's Short-Term Effects?" *Admap,* February 1996, 42-45.

13. Colin McDonald, "How Frequently Should You Advertise?" *Admap,* July/August 1996, 22-25.

14. However, Walter Reichel and Leslie Wood's analyses of the American Nielsen database suggest that the short-term effect of advertising can be felt up to *4 weeks* before the date of purchase. The importance of this conclusion—if it is generally valid—is that continuous weeks of advertising may be able to generate an effect that increases slightly as a result of tiny additional effects from past periods. (This matter is discussed in Chapter 6.) See Walter Reichel and Leslie Wood, "Recency in Media Planning Redefined," *Journal of Advertising Research,* July/August 1997, 66-74.

15. Jones, *When Ads Work,* 184.

16. Ibid., 27, 30.

17. Colin McDonald, "Short-Term Advertising Effects: How Confident Can We Be?" *Admap,* June 1997, 36-39.

18. Evelyn Jenkins and Christopher Timms, "The Andrex Story: A Soft, Strong and Very Long-Term Success," in *Advertising Works: Volume 4. Papers From the Institute of Practitioners in Advertising (IPA) Advertising Effectiveness Awards,* (Charles Channon, Ed.) (London: Cassell, 1987), 185. This case study is one of two devoted to Andrex published by the IPA. The second came out in 1993.

19. Private information.

20. *Myers Report* (New York: Myers Report Industry Research, December 16, 1996). The data came from surveys of 711 and 300 executives respectively in advertiser companies and advertising agencies.

21. Media Marketing Assessment, Inc. and Information Resources, Inc., *AdWorks2: Report of Presentation,* 1999.

22. *Myers Report* (New York: Myers Report Industry Research, November 1997).

23. Erwin Ephron and Melissa Heath, "Less Is More: New Thinking About Reach/Frequency. Adding the Dimensions of Time and Frequency Value Shows the Shape of the Response Function Is Unimportant for Scheduling" (paper written March 2001; publication forthcoming).

6

The Bridge to the Long Term

The first five chapters of this book concentrated on advertising's short- and medium-term effects. Because a medium-term effect represents a mere repetition of short-term effects, the two can be discussed together. They are essentially the same thing except for the time dimension. Both are discrete and closed-ended. There is little delayed effect from the short term to the medium term, and as a general rule, a second short-term effect is no greater than a first one because there is no hangover from what has gone before. (There is a small exception to this, which is discussed at the end of this chapter.)

When we move beyond the medium term and try and evaluate the effects of advertising over a period of years, an important new concept must be introduced. The long-term effects of advertising (in the plural) accumulate over time. They may occasionally do this by making the advertising more deeply etched in the psyche of the consumer, although measuring this is more difficult than it might appear. Some analysts, including me, believe that the traces of advertising from previous years that may linger with the consumer do not normally have much influence on the sales of a brand. In most circumstances, advertising's long-term effects are manifested therefore through *an enrichment of the brand itself,* and in particular by advertising's ability to build added values in the minds of consumers. These added values come partly from favorable impressions caused by experience of the brand in use and partly from advertising working to reinforce these.

If the long-term effects of advertising are (as I believe) mainly brought about through reinforcing the psychological associations of the brand, it is a difficult job to isolate them. This is nevertheless the task I begin in this chapter. Much of what I say is devoted to a bird's-eye view of the sales of a number of brands measured over a year, quantifying the specific contributions to these sales made by the consumer advertising (in different media) and by trade and consumer promotions. In other words I first look at medium-term effects at an aggregated level.

However, at the end of this chapter, these data are examined longitudinally, and this makes it possible to begin our examination of long-term effects. As the chapter title suggests, I begin to build a bridge between the medium term and the long term.

Different measures of long-term effects are described in Chapters 7 through 10. The information in this chapter, and most of that in the rest of the book, comes from a leading American econometric organization, Media Marketing Assessment (MMA).[1]

Econometrics is a statistical discipline that MMA applies to marketing problems by using the mathematical techniques developed in the academic world for the analysis of microeconomic and macroeconomic phenomena. The most important technique used is multivariate regression, which examines the relationship between a number of independent variables examined in turn, and a single dependent variable. This statistical device makes it possible to estimate the relative importance of each of the independent variables. And by adding them all together, the dependent variable can often be explained in its entirety in terms of the varying importance of its causes, the independent variables. This process is described as model building.

The most common dependent variable that MMA examines is the sales of a brand (measured in volume and share of market), and the independent variables are the causes of these sales. One of these causes is invariably the consumer advertising. MMA therefore attempts to quantify the specific contribution of advertising (and also the other marketing stimuli) to a brand's sales, with the object of increasing the efficiency of marketing practice, in particular by comparing the financial return from each of the various inputs with its dollar cost. This process makes it possible to manipulate these stimuli so as to maximize the value of the total marketing investment.

The following six inputs are described in this chapter:

1. The brand's equity or base volume (i.e., the sales that would have been achieved in the year in question without other marketing support); equity can rise or fall year by year
2. Television advertising
3. Print advertising (mainly magazines)
4. Radio advertising
5. Trade promotional allowances
6. Coupons (the most important type of consumer sales promotion)

These independent variables need some comment.

- Brand equity is normally discussed in marketing circles in qualitative rather than quantitative terms because equity expresses in a general way the innate strength of a brand, something often considered unquantifiable. However, equity is measured in the MMA model as a residual (i.e., nonincremental) influence on sales after deducting the contributions of the other marketing inputs. It can (as mentioned) rise or fall year by year in response to the success of the marketing inputs in the previous year. For mathematical reasons, a high equity percentage means a relatively low contribution from the other independent variables. Generally speaking, high equity means a low promotional contribution, which implies a high average consumer price. High equity = high price is a commonsense and generally applicable concept.
- Price effects are captured virtually entirely by trade promotions and coupons. In the United States, list prices of brands are of only nominal importance, and price competition in most categories is manifested through changes in the amount of promotional activity.
- Because the MMA database comprises established brands, independent variables important to new brand introductions, notably the development of retail distribution, are omitted as not very relevant.
- Likewise, variables such as seasonality, which are relevant to categories rather than to brands, are also omitted.

The six-part MMA model has been used for six years to deconstruct and forecast the sales of the brands described in this book, and it has been found to be predictive.

As a matter of definition, consumer advertising in the main media is commonly referred to as above-the-line investment; the various types of sales promotion are called below-the-line expenditures.[2] These are simple descriptions, although they have implications for sales and profit. As a broad generalization, above-the-line advertising normally achieves modest (although sometimes profitable) sales increases. Below-the-line expenditures on promotions can achieve large (but generally unprofitable and temporary) boosts in sales. This topic is discussed in detail in Chapter 9.

An Initial Review of the MMA Data

The facts described in this chapter are derived mainly from 35 brands of repeat-purchase packaged goods. These are all well-established, large in market share, and familiar to the public, but because the data are proprietary I am not allowed to publish the actual names. (These are coded, using numbers 1 through 35.) A number of years' data are available for each of the brands, and I shall call each year's figure for a brand a Brand/Year (B/Y) observation.

This chapter describes a number of different measures relating to these brands, each providing a B/Y observation. For these different measures, the numbers of observations differ quite a lot. For example, the majority of brands receive television support, which provides many B/Y observations, but few use radio, hence fewer observations. The measure that applies most extensively to most brands is, in fact, television advertising, and this provides a total of 147 observations.

At first glance, 147 seems a small number to support a quantitative investigation. But this conclusion is wrong. The main information described in this chapter relates to the individual contributions of the main marketing stimuli to the sales of individual brands. To make this calculation possible, *each separate figure is the result of a complete research study.*

Each regression calculation is based normally on 2 to 3 years of data, comprising thousands of individual statistical readings. Once an estimate has been made of the contribution of a single marketing input to a brand's sales, statistical tests are applied to ensure that the estimate is reliable. These analyses are then repeated over time.

Each B/Y observation, although it is a single number, is the distillation of a substantial *tranche* of statistical information that embraces both a large number of raw facts and multiple analyses of these. A B/Y observation resembles the visible part of an iceberg, the largest amount of which lies below the surface of the sea.

TABLE 6.1 Sales Deconstruction: 10 Brand Study (in percentages)

Brand Code	Year	Equity	TV^3	Print	Radio	Trade Promotions	Coupons	Total
3	1996	91.3	3.2	1.6	0.1	0.9	2.9	100.0
16	1995	80.7	6.3	1.6	0.7	10.4	0.3	100.0
16	1997	78.3	6.2	0.9	0.3	13.6	0.7	100.0
17	1994	78.0	5.3	1.2	0.2	14.3	1.0	100.0
2	1994	76.6	4.7	1.1	0.1	16.8	0.7	100.0
17	1995	75.9	6.4	0.5	1.3	15.1	1.8	100.0
2	1997	73.3	4.0	1.4	0.2	20.6	0.5	100.0
24	1998	72.1	4.7	3.1	1.3	16.9	1.9	100.0
14	1996	72.2	4.9	2.9	1.1	17.4	1.5	100.0
14	1994	71.2	4.9	4.6	1.6	16.9	0.8	100.0
24	1994	69.3	4.2	4.8	0.4	18.6	2.7	100.0
8	1998	66.9	4.3	0.9	0.1	26.6	1.2	100.0
8	1995	67.3	1.9	3.8	0.7	24.8	1.5	100.0
5	1997	65.4	6.7	1.4	0.4	22.8	3.3	100.0
24	1997	66.3	6.3	5.6	2.0	17.9	1.9	100.0
8	1996	65.7	4.7	2.3	0.7	25.3	1.3	100.0
8	1997	66.0	5.3	2.8	0.3	24.5	1.1	100.0
24	1996	63.4	7.2	3.9	2.2	20.8	2.5	100.0
24	1995	63.2	5.1	4.9	3.3	21.6	1.9	100.0
8	1994	61.6	3.5	2.0	1.5	29.6	1.8	100.0
15	1996	59.2	9.3	0.1	3.2	27.5	0.7	100.0
29	1997	55.3	14.5	0.9	0.7	21.0	7.6	100.0
Average		69.9	5.6	2.4	1.0	19.3	1.8	100.0

Of the 35 brands, 10 received all 6 marketing stimuli in certain years. These brands yielded 22 B/Y observations, which are shown in Table 6.1. This first analysis I call the 10 Brand Study.

Although, as explained, all the individual figures in Table 6.1 are robust, we must also consider whether the range of brands is typical of consumer goods categories as a whole in the United States. In particular, the average market share of the brands in Table 6.1 is 32.0%, which is very much above-average for repeat-purchase packaged goods. To examine this problem, I looked again at a pilot study I had earlier conducted using a much broader range of MMA data, scrutinizing information from an extensive range of brands which I am not allowed to publish for reasons of confidentiality. There is considerable similarity between the two data sets. I therefore believe that what we see in Table 6.1 and

TABLE 6.2 Summary of Average Sales Attributable to 6 Marketing Inputs: 10 Brand Study (in percentages)

Total	100.0	
Equity/base	69.9	
Advertising	9.0	
Television		5.6
Print		2.4
Radio		1.0
Promotions	21.1	
Trade		19.3
Coupons		1.8

the other tables in Chapters 6 through 10 represents broad general patterns as they relate to the sales generated by the six main marketing inputs. The individual figures and also the ranges of data are reasonably typical of the consumer goods field as a whole. There are no problems so long as we exercise the usual care in interpreting the information.

Table 6.1 shows both the individual B/Y observations and the averages for the sales generated by the main marketing inputs. The latter are presented separately in Table 6.2.

The equity of the brand itself is shown by all the MMA analyses to be substantially the most important contributor to a brand's sales. This is an important subject that I examine in later chapters. In this chapter, I devote most attention to the other influences on sales, which are the above-the-line and below-the-line expenditures. Totaling the relevant figures from Tables 6.1 and 6.2 as 100%, the contributions of the individual types of advertising and promotional activity are shown in Table 6.3.

Two things are worth noting about Table 6.3. First, the ratio of 30:70 in the relative contributions of advertising and promotions should be no surprise to people with direct knowledge of the marketing practices of sophisticated consumer goods organizations. Data published by an objective monitoring organization called Cox Direct demonstrate that the average expenditures of leading manufacturers of repeat-purchase packaged goods are distributed in a not dissimilar way. The above-the-line/below-the-line ratios they published for 1994, 1995, and 1996 were, respectively, 25:75, 24:76, and 24:76.[4] But note that advertising's sales productivity (30%) is actually greater than its share of total

TABLE 6.3 Summary of Average Sales Attributable to Advertising and
Promotions: 10 Brand Study (in percentages)

Total advertising and promotions	100.0	
Advertising	29.9	
Television		18.6
Print		8.0
Radio		3.3
Sales promotions	70.1	
Trade		64.1
Coupons		6.0

cost (24%–25%). In other words, advertising is more productive than sales promotions.

This happens specifically because advertising focuses on repetition of purchase, and it is the depth of such repetition that boosts brands. It should also be remembered that advertising focuses on both the short and long term, whereas the effects of promotions are felt virtually exclusively in the short term. Therefore, the massive (and slowly increasing) amount of money spent on sales promotions is indirect but powerful evidence of the gradual shift of emphasis in business planning away from long-term objectives. This is a matter that has serious implications for marketing practice in the present and the future.

The second point—and a very important one—is that the contributions to sales made by the various above-the-line and below-the-line activities are the end product of the total combination of factors influencing each activity. With advertising, these influences are the campaign itself, the budget, and the media. With promotions, they are the type of promotion used and its financial cost. With the promotions that take the form of price reductions, the cost is represented by the fall in receipts below normal net sales value (NSV).[5] In accounting terms, advertising is considered a positive investment. On the other hand, price reductions both at the retail level and at the consumer level are considered reductions in manufacturers' receipts.

There is a way to separate the qualitative influences (i.e., the advertising campaign and the type of promotion) from the financial factors (budget and media), and the data in Tables 6.4 and 6.5 show how this is done.

TABLE 6.4 Summary of Average Sales Attributable to 6 Marketing Inputs: 35 Brand Study

Stimulus	Percentage of Sales		Number of Brand/ Year Observations
Equity/base	75.4		122
Advertising	7.5		
Television		4.6	147
Print		1.7	72
Radio		1.2	30
Sales promotions	18.3		
Trade		16.4	123
Coupons		1.9	119

Different Marketing Stimuli and How They Vary in Their Productivity

Tables 6.4 and 6.5 examine the total database (35 brands, not just 10). There is a slight problem in doing this. The measures relating to the different marketing stimuli are based on different numbers of B/Y observations, which means that the battery of B/Y observations from which each average is calculated is slightly different from every other one. This accounts for rounding discrepancies and other small differences within and between the tables.

Table 6.4 summarizes the average contribution of each marketing stimulus to the sales of all 35 brands in the sample. Table 6.5 (which examines mostly the same brands) disregards the equity component and averages the dollar expenditures on each above-the-line and below-the-line stimulus. There are differences between contribution and cost in every case.

Tables 6.4 and 6.5 raise two points:

1. The advertising achieves a marginally better total return against total advertising dollars than sales promotions' return against total promotional dollars. The tables examine the average of medium-term effects, and it is also important not to neglect the additional long-term effects. Advertising is capable of strong long-term effects, although it does not achieve these with every campaign. On the other hand, promotions, with rare exceptions, have a zero or negative long-term

TABLE 6.5 Summary of Average Marketing Dollars Spent on Advertising and Promotions: 35 Brand Study

Stimulus	Percentage of Marketing $	Number of Brand/ Year Observations	Percentage of Attributable Sales*
Advertising	27.7		29.1
Television	19.9	144	17.8
Print	5.2	74	6.6
Radio	2.6	31	4.7
Sales Promotions	72.3		70.9
Trade	63.8	108	63.9
Coupons	8.5	104	7.4
Advertising plus promotions	100.0		

* Ads and promotions only (from Table 6.4).

effect. They produce sales and not customers, and sales today are often at the expense of sales tomorrow because promotions tend to mortgage future sales by bringing forward purchases that might have taken place (at full price) in later periods. In addition, by cheapening the image of the brand, extensive promotions can permanently devalue future business (i.e., encourage people to buy only at reduced prices).[6] Because of the importance of long-term effects, the balance between the relative productivity of advertising and promotions is weighted—perhaps strongly—in favor of advertising. This is a matter discussed in later chapters.

2. The second point is that there is a remarkable difference in the cost-productivity relationship between the three advertising media analyzed. This is given special attention later in this chapter.

The relationship between the productivity and cost of the different marketing stimuli was sufficiently important to encourage MMA to look for a way of analyzing the *qualitative* value of the different inputs (i.e., factoring out the relative sizes of their budgets). This measure is called Payback. It quantifies *the percentage return from a dollar spent* on each of the above-the-line and below-the-line activities. In other words, it estimates the number of cents returned by a dollar invested in each activity. Payback, as defined here, represents what has until now been regarded as the Holy Grail of advertising—an accurate method of measuring Return on Investment (ROI).

TABLE 6.6   Average Percentage Payback From Above-the-Line and Below-the-Line Activities: 35 Brand Study

Stimulus	Percentage Payback (cents per dollar)		Number of Brand/ Year Observations
Advertising	68.4		
Television		49.0	140
Print		90.6	67
Radio		114.1	27
Sales promotions	54.8		
Trade		61.3	101
Coupons		47.3	95

The data for the total sample of 35 brands are shown in Table 6.6.

Table 6.6, like the others presented thus far in this chapter, describes average medium-term effects. What comes across clearly is that in the medium term *above-the-line and below-the-line activities do not pay their way.* There are three important points to be made about this:

1. First, advertising must be seen as a cost of doing business, in a similar way to how raw materials and other direct costs are regarded. For new brands, marketing activities are carried out aggressively with the aim of sowing seeds for the future. For existing brands, the advertising and promotional money is, to a large degree, spent defensively so as to protect the brand against competitive brands that also spend substantial sums.

2. Second, existing brands will generally generate a large enough sales volume to yield scale economies in raw material purchasing, in production, and in marketing. One of the objectives of marketing activity is therefore to maintain volumes at least at their existing levels and facilitate low costs. Competitive forces drive manufacturers to pass these low costs on to consumers in the form of low prices. These in turn maintain the high level of demand that keeps costs down. The process works in a benevolent spiral.

3. The third point is the one already mentioned. Advertising is capable of long-term effects that can be added to those produced in the medium term. This book attempts to quantify these long-term effects and consequently help us determine how close advertising gets to breaking even when the full range of its influence on sales is taken into account. Promotions, on the other hand, have little or no long-term effect.

TABLE 6.7 Productivity Compared With Investment, by Medium

Medium	% Sales Productivity per $	% Share of Marketing $
Radio	114.1	2.6
Print	90.6	5.2
Television	49.0	19.9

Table 6.6 also demonstrates that, between the three media examined, print is more productive, dollar for dollar, than television, and radio is more productive, dollar for dollar, than both television and print. There is a degree of synergy between the three media. Two of the media examined offer synergy; one medium obviously does not. And all three offer more than two media.

The *average* figure for radio productivity is, surprisingly, in positive territory, showing that radio advertising appears to generate more sales value than the cost of the media time. However, we may here be on shaky statistical ground. The radio average was calculated from 27 B/Y observations: 12 positive (i.e., showing sales value as greater than media cost) and 15 negative. Of the positive readings, 9 came from only 2 brands, and this is a very small sample.

Nevertheless, I believe that the general lesson is valid: Radio is more productive, dollar for dollar, than print, and in turn, print is more productive than television. These relationships point to an important general conclusion about how media work.

Table 6.7 shows that each medium's rank in its sales productivity is the reverse of its rank in the number of dollars spent on it.

Chapter 5 demonstrated the virtually universal prevalence of diminishing returns at the level of the individual advertised brand. This new evidence of the relative productivity of different media conveys a similar lesson: that there are diminishing returns at the aggregate level of the advertising medium. Infrequently used media pay off best while they remain infrequently used.[7]

The lesson for advertisers is the importance of looking searchingly but sensitively at new media opportunities. The more heavily employed any medium becomes, the more it is laden with the clutter of advertising messages from everybody in the market. With increasing concentration on television alone, more and more advertisers will encounter progressively lower productivity from their advertising dollars. Magazines and radio offer ways of stretching cost-efficient reach. However, there are limits to the value of these supplemen-

TABLE 6.8 Ranges of Sales Attributable to Each Marketing Input: 35 Brands
(in percentages)

Stimulus	Top of Range	Bottom of Range (excluding outliers)	Average
Equity/base	90.8	56.0	75.4
Television	14.5	1.2	4.6
Print	4.5	0.3	1.7
Radio	2.5	0.3	1.2
Trade	36.5	1.5	16.4
Coupons	4.6	0.3	1.9

tary media. They can never offer the mass audience of television, and heavy use of magazines and radio can, in turn, lead to diminishing returns similar to those encountered on television. The planning of multiple media is an increasingly valuable process, but it requires finely tuned judgment.

The percentage contribution to sales made by each marketing activity differs a good deal according to brand. The ranges of effects are shown in Table 6.8.

The variability from the averages contains clues that should help us explain the varying performance of the different marketing inputs, and some of these variations are referred to in later chapters.

Payback Varies According to Level of Investment

A brand's payback to advertising investment is not totally uniform for all levels of advertising. As the budget moves up or down, so does the payback. This is illustrated in Table 6.9, which describes 14 MMA brands not analyzed thus far in this book. In this table, the effect on payback for each brand is described for a 50% reduction and a 50% increase in the advertising budget.

These brands are all responsive to changes in advertising pressure. This is shown in Table 6.10, which also looks at a 50% reduction and a 50% increase in advertising investment and estimates the resultant effect on sales.

Comparing Table 6.9 and 6.10, we can draw the following conclusions:

TABLE 6.9 Change in Payback in Response to Changes in Advertising Investment: 14 Typical MMA* Brands

	Payback (in cents per TV advertising)		
Brand	50% Reduction in TV Advertising	Current TV Investment	50% Increase in TV Advertising
A	0.20	0.16	0.14
B	0.46	0.37	0.33
C	0.13	0.12	0.11
D	0.18	0.15	0.13
E	0.55	0.30	0.25
F	0.85	0.71	0.61
G	0.37	0.27	0.22
H	0.21	0.19	0.17
I	0.32	0.25	0.20
J	0.97	0.72	0.57
K	1.56	1.30	1.12
L	0.52	0.41	0.33
M	0.76	0.62	0.51
N	0.81	0.73	0.67
Unweighted average	0.56	0.45	.038

* MMA = Media Marketing Assessment.

- As advertising pressure is reduced, payback improves. As pressure is increased, payback worsens.
- As advertising pressure is reduced, sales fall (as expected). As pressure is increased, sales rise (as expected).
- For both advertising payback and sales volume change, there is a greater response from budget *reductions* than from budget increases. This is a clear signal of diminishing returns; that is, with each upward step in advertising expenditure, there is a progressive reduction in the actual sales generated and in the financial productivity of the advertising.
- There is a trade-off between payback and sales, and manufacturers must carry out a balancing act between the two to optimize their profit return. Budget reductions mean more efficient use of advertising dollars but also substantial volume decreases. On the other hand, budget increases mean more volume sales, but a less efficient use of the advertising budget.

This trade-off is illustrated in Figure 6.1, which shows a full range of data on budget decreases and increases for Brand B, a relatively typical example of the range of brands shown in Tables 6.9 and 6.10.

TABLE 6.10 Sales Volume Change in Response to Changes in Advertising
Investment: 14 Typical MMA* Brands

Brand	50% Reduction in TV Advertising (% volume change)	50% Increase in TV Advertising (% volume change)
A	−38	+27
B	−37	+33
C	−45	+38
D	−39	+28
E	−38	+26
F	−41	+29
G	−31	+26
H	−45	+37
I	−36	+23
J	−33	+19
K	−40	+30
L	−36	+23
M	−38	+25
N	−45	+38
Unweighted average	−39	+29

* MMA = Media Marketing Assessment.

Large and Small Brands; Growing and Declining Brands

The average share of market for all the brands in this research is 32% (coincidentally the same as those in the 10 Brand Study). This is a very high average share, certainly in American product categories, although it does not seem to distort the figures describing the effects of the different marketing stimuli discussed in this and subsequent chapters.

Table 6.11 breaks the brands down into two groups. There are 30 brands for which we have reasonably complete information; 13 brands have a share above the average, and the other 17 have a share below it. There are instructive differences between the two groups in the productivity of the most important advertising stimulus, television advertising. The average proportion of the total

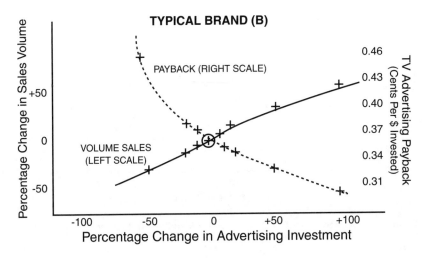

Figure 6.1. Incremental Change in TV Advertising Investment: Resultant Change in Volume Sales and TV Advertising Payback

TABLE 6.11 Large and Small Brands: Payback Differences (30 Brands)

Share of Market	Number of Brands	% Average Share of Market	Average Television Productivity (cents per $)
Total	30	32.0	50.6
Larger than average	13	61.6	56.0
Smaller than average	17	9.4	46.5

marketing expenditure accounted for by television is 23% for all these brands, although the figure for the quintile of largest brands is only 19%. (Larger brands normally underspend in advertising.)

But looking at the average television productivity—that is, the sales attributable *to each dollar of television advertising investment*—the productivity of the larger brands is 21% greater than that of the smaller ones (56.0 percentage points compared with 46.5 percentage points).

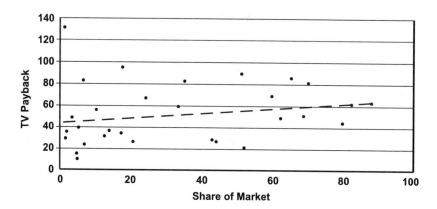

Figure 6.2. Scatterplot of Television Payback and Share of Market

The data are shown as a scatterplot in Figure 6.2. The overall fit between the two statistical variables is by no means precise, but it is strong enough to support my general conclusions.

Share increases are normally easier for small brands than for big ones. This is because large brands have a large mass, and an increase as small as 1 percentage point in share of market means that a very large volume of extra merchandise is being sold. This is not true for small brands, which show a considerable responsiveness to advertising and promotional activity—these being increases from a low base.

But in the long term, advertising for large brands can cause their profits to rise slightly. Remember that large brands benefit from scale economies in all aspects of their production and marketing, especially in raw material purchasing, manufacture, sales force employment, and (as discussed later) advertising. These scale economies continue, solidify, and, if anything, increase over time. And the long-term role of advertising, to the extent that it enables a large brand to maintain its high volume, is an important influence on the extra profitability that stems from this high volume.

Advertising also helps justify the generally above-average prices of large brands. This is a reflection of the above-average valuation that consumers put personally on brands they have used for a long time and which have benefited from the long-term effects of successful advertising.

The scale economies that are directly derived from advertising are important enough for us to quantify and add them as a supplementary long-term benefit,

TABLE 6.12 Growing and Declining Brands: Payback Differences (30 Brands)

Growth/Decline	Number of Brands	Average Growth/ Decline Index	Average Television Productivity (cents per $)
Total	30	97	47.7
Growing	15	108	53.6
Declining	15	87	41.8

using the method described in Chapter 7. These economies are ultimately derived from the breadth—the above-average penetration—of large brands.

This means that a large brand has a broader body of users than a small brand has. It is known that viewers and readers tend to pay at least some attention to the advertising for the brands they use themselves, as a result of selective perception. A large brand therefore has a higher proportion of its audience engaged mentally with its advertising than is the case with a small brand, hence the greater productivity, dollar for dollar, of the advertising for large brands compared with small ones.

Table 6.12 makes a comparable analysis of growing versus declining brands. The full data are set out in a scatterplot in Figure 6.3. As in Figure 6.2, the fit between the two variables is not particularly tidy, but the direction of the relationship is clear.

Table 6.12 describes the growth of all brands in the total sample. With most brands, the period covered is 5 years. As in Table 6.11, there are 30 brands for which reasonably full figures are available. The measure of growth and decline is the comparison of *market share*. Each growth/decline figure on which Table 6.12 is based takes the last year for which information is available and indexes this on the first year (which has a value of 100).

In the aggregate, the brands show very little change over the period. The average of all the brands together is an index figure of 97 (i.e., 3% decline). Since, as explained, this calculation is made from market shares, it is probable that many categories will have grown to some extent in total volume so that an overall 3% decline in share means a small increase in sales measured in absolute terms. In competitive categories, it is almost impossible for big brands to increase their sales to a significant degree. To make modest improvements is a general sign of success.

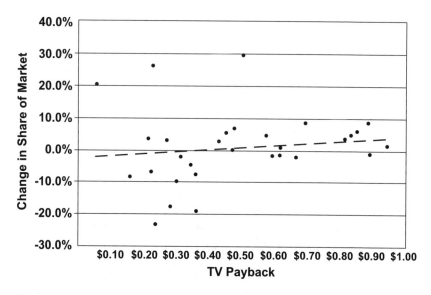

Figure 6.3. Scatterplot of Television Payback for Growing and Declining Brands

The 15 growing brands showed an average index of 108; the 15 declining brands, an index of 87. These are small changes considering that we are measuring mainly a 5-year period. It should however be remembered that these stable figures may not be totally typical. They relate to repeat-purchase packaged goods, and there is more general growth in some categories outside this field.

In a similar pattern to Table 6.11, the growing brands show a different pattern of television productivity than the declining brands show. That for the growing brands is 28% greater (53.6 percentage points percentaged on 41.8 percentage points).

I believe that brand growth is driven by increasing advertising productivity—or at least by the increasing productivity of effective campaigns. But how is this effect manifested in specific sales-related terms? It can best be described diagrammatically as in Figure 6.4, which shows sales stemming from advertising as occurring in three phases. This is a schematic picture.

STAS (Short-Term Advertising Strength), as discussed in Chapter 2, is the change in a brand's market share that follows household reception of advertising for that identified brand within 7 days of the advertisement's appearance. It is measured by Pure Single-Source research.

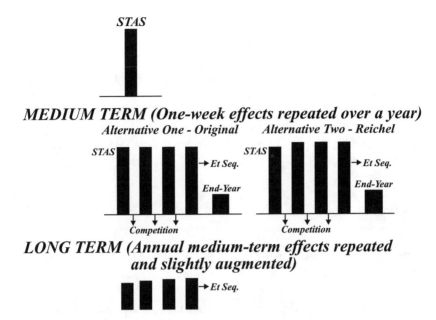

Figure 6.4. Schematic of Sales Effects of Advertising in 3 Phases

In the short term, the STAS effect is immediate and temporary.

In the medium term, the weekly STAS effects, minus the countervailing effects of advertising for competitive brands, produce a (year-end) medium-term effect that will invariably be smaller than any individual STAS.

Alternative Two in the description of the medium term refers to the work of Walter Reichel (described in Chapter 5).[8] Reichel's analysis of data from the A. C. Nielsen household panel suggests that, although most of the effect of advertising comes within seven days of its exposure, advertising *can* have a very small effect over a longer period—up to 28 days.

The implications of Reichel's analysis are shown in Figure 6.4 as Alternative Two. Here the first STAS in a year—that generated by a new campaign—will have no longer-range effect from earlier advertising. But the second and subsequent STAS sales increases will receive a small extra boost from the advertising that has gone before. In the second period, this will have come from the prolonged effect of the first period of advertising; in the third, it will come from the second period; and the effect continues, which means that the second and subsequent STAS effects will be at a slightly higher level than the first.

I believe that Reichel's modification provides a modest but plausible supplement to the analysis of medium-term effects.

In the first paragraph of this chapter I mentioned that there was a small exception to the general rule that advertising in the short term produces no hangover effect. It is Reichel's work that I had in mind.

Finally, *in the long term,* as advertising gradually increases in productivity, the (annual) medium-term effect of advertising on sales will be seen as gradually rising year by year. This hypothesis underlies the analyses in the remaining chapters of this book.

Five Conclusions

I draw five conclusions from the data in this chapter. Although these all have reasonable validity, some of the conclusions are firmer than others.

1. It is clear that the greatest contribution to a brand's sales is made by the equity of the brand. The proportion of sales attributable to the equity averages somewhere between 70% and 75%, but there is a variability of 20 percentage points on either side. However, even at the lower end of the range, the equity still accounts for over half of a brand's sales volume.

   New brands are in the process of building equity, and at the beginning they have very little—with the exception of a small "halo" effect in the cases of brands that are introduced with a brand name already used by another product (generally in a different market segment). This points to the need for a new brand to build a consumer franchise and advertising-related added values with maximum speed so that the new brand will be able to rely at the end of a year on an established and growing equity/base volume. This is one of the strongest reasons for high advertising investment in a new brand.

   Of the remaining influences on sales, the relative contributions of above-the-line and below-the-line inputs are in an average ratio of 1:2. Again, there are substantial variations on a brand-by-brand basis. As a broad generalization, advertising on its own accounts for a little less than 10% of a brand's sales.

2. It is also clear that all paid-for sales stimuli—both above-the-line and below-the-line—are uneconomic in the medium term. They represent a cost of doing business and are engines to maintain the levels of sales necessary for scale economies in raw material purchasing, production, and marketing; in other words they enable prices to be kept down. The overall ROI of advertising is slightly better (i.e., less negative) than that of promotions. Advertising is also capable of long-term effects, which can be added to its medium-term effect. This enables advertising expenditures in some circumstances to reach a break-even level of productivity.

The same is not generally true of promotions, which can sometimes depress sales in the long term.

3. The relative ROI, dollar for dollar, of the main advertising media differs significantly one from another. The most productive individual medium is radio, followed by magazines and then television. This ranking suggests the existence of diminishing returns at an aggregate media level. The sales response to radio advertising is at a lower point on the medium's response curve than is the case with print advertising. This in turn is at a lower point on its response curve than television's place on its own curve. The lesson to be drawn from this is the need to avoid the excessive use of any single medium. *It points to the benefit of planning campaigns using multiple media.*

4. Measured in terms of contribution, large brands produce a greater response to advertising than do small brands. This confirms the presence of advertising-related scale economies. The bigger the brand, the more efficiently advertising appears to work.

5. The sales response to advertising for growing brands is stronger than that for declining brands. This underscores the importance of effective advertising as a contributor to brand growth.

The first 2 of the 5 conclusions are not, I believe, seriously disputable. Conclusions 3, 4, and 5 form to a substantial degree the agenda for the rest of this book.

Notes

1. Media Marketing Assessment (MMA) is part of the Aegis group, a diversified public company based in London. The largest single component of the group is Carat, the most prominent media-buying organization in Europe and which also operates in the United States. MMA was founded in 1989 and is based in Wilton, Connecticut. It is one of the most important companies specializing in the commercial application of econometrics, and it operates in the United States and 20 foreign countries. Its list of over 40 clients includes many of the most sophisticated marketing organizations in the world. MMA's staff of 70 includes 50 hands-on specialists in the field of econometrics. The company's work has been extensively validated by its clients, many of whom have employed MMA for a number of years, which is presumptive evidence that the company's estimates have been found accurate and useful.

2. The word *expenditure* is used to describe below-the-line activity because the money is, in effect, an income reduction to achieve a short-term effect; it is not a positive investment aimed at long-term growth.

3. There are two ways in which television advertising generates sales. The greater effect comes directly from advertising for the brand. For a minority of brands, a smaller additional amount comes from the "halo" effect from advertising for other products that carry the same brand name. In the estimates in this chapter, I have added together the two effects.

4. John Philip Jones, "Trends in Promotions," in *The Advertising Business: Operations, Creativity, Media Planning, Integrated Communications,* ed. John Philip Jones (Thousand Oaks, CA: Sage, 1999), 321-324.

5. See Note 2.

6. John Philip Jones, "The Double Jeopardy of Sales Promotions," *Harvard Business Review,* September-October 1990, 145-152.

7. This plausible hypothesis was first suggested by Erwin Ephron (whose views are also referred to in Chapter 5). The point was raised in personal discussion.

8. Walter Reichel and Leslie Wood, "Recency in Media Planning Redefined," *Journal of Advertising Research,* July/August 1997, 66-74. Reichel's hypothesis of advertising having a relatively prolonged effect is not a new idea. The notion is often referred to as the Adstock model, also discussed in Appendix A. It is measured by the number of weeks taken for an advertising effect (however this is measured) to fall to half the level of what it was in the first week of advertising. This "half-life" period normally varies between 3 and 6 weeks. Insofar as the hypothesis is valid—and Adstock is based on modeling not observation—it would have the result of boosting each individual STAS to a level slightly higher than it would otherwise be, since we are now adding the decayed effect of previous advertising. This whole matter is of more theoretical than practical importance. A recent piece of research based on British data has demonstrated that a model derived from Adstock produces sales estimates that are almost identical with STAS. STAS is of course the simpler measure. This research is to be found in Lotte Yssing Hansen, *Advertising and Promotions Effectiveness—Learning from a Five-Year Study* (Copenhagen, Denmark: *asi* European Advertising Effectiveness Symposium, 2001). asi@dial.pipex.com

7

A First Measure
of Long-Term Effects

*Advertising can also have long-term effects which operate beyond a year and
into the future. This process is cumulative (unlike the short-term and medium-
term effects). A brand initially grows as a result of expanding penetration—an increase in the number of users—a process that gives the brand breadth and which
is influenced by advertising in its short-term role. The long-term effects of advertising work by adding to this a depth of repeat-purchase, an increased perception
of value, and a boosted salience.*

*The long-term effects of advertising take the form of an enrichment of the
brand and a strengthening of its relationship with the consumer. There are at
least six ways in which this enrichment can be evaluated. The most important of
them can be measured in terms specific to the advertising itself.*

This extract from the Gatekeeper model provides the agenda for the rest of
this book. This chapter is devoted to the last point mentioned: how the long-
term effect can be measured in terms related specifically to the advertising itself. Brands are a part of our everyday life, and writers about brands are often
tempted to discuss them in qualitative or somewhat inexact terms. In contrast,

my approach is very specific and quantitative. The measure described here is derived from share of voice, which is a precise expression of advertising weight and is defined as a brand's share of measured media advertising in its product category during a particular period.

Estimating the dollar value of measured media advertising is a relatively simple matter. In most developed countries, there are efficient commercial media-auditing services that provide estimates of the advertising budgets of individual brands and the category totals. The data are presented in much detail and on a continuous basis. A brand's *share* of the category total is easy enough to calculate. Nevertheless, it is less easy to see how this share influences sales.

We can understand how a brand's advertising measured in absolute dollars can affect the sales of a brand: other things being equal, more dollars will produce more sales. But 20% and 10% shares of voice seem to be concepts far remote from a consumer buying a brand in a retail store. It is inconceivable that consumers should be so conscious of the overall volume of advertising in a category that they would respond to the varying proportions of such advertising that are contributed by different brands by buying those brands in the same proportions.[1]

The way to understand how share of voice influences a brand's sales is to forget about calculating the share in the normal way, that is, as a percentage. Instead, we should measure a brand's advertising in terms of the *number of consumer impressions* it achieves. This is represented by the number of consumers *(x)* who receive an average number *(y)* of advertisements for a brand in a given period. We multiply x by y to estimate the number of consumer impressions.

If 1% of a year's media advertising in a category achieves about 50 million consumer impressions (a relatively realistic figure), then the advertising for Brand A with a 10% share of voice will generate 500 million consumer impressions, and Brand B with a 20% share of voice will generate 1 billion. These represent vast numbers of opportunities for the advertising to influence consumer purchasing, although the actual number of occasions on which the advertising "bites" is only a small proportion of these large numbers. Nevertheless, the huge differences between the consumer impressions generated by the two brands' campaigns enable us to see how—other things being equal, and in particular if both brands have similarly effective campaigns—Brand B will probably outsell Brand A in the ratio of 2:1.

This analysis is totally harmonious with everything I have said in this book. The decision to buy a product in a category (irrespective of brand) is not influenced by advertising but, rather, by the fact that the household supplies of the product are running low. In developed markets where there is little category growth, advertising is planned almost invariably to engineer the choice of one brand in preference to another. Advertising works in a relatively simple way, with no build-up from repeated advertisements. Although campaigns often reflect rather subtly the psychographics of the potential user, there is no ambiguity in the message she receives and to which she (perhaps unconsciously) responds. People will buy Brand A or Brand B and will be influenced to a greater or lesser degree by the campaigns for the two of them.

Since (as I am assuming) A and B have similarly effective campaigns, the short-term effect of both campaigns is virtually the same. However, since B outspends A by a ratio of 2 to 1, then B's campaign has twice the repetition of A's, with the result that B is likely to sell twice as much as A over the course of a year.

The definition of share of voice is based on a year's advertising, which means that it is concerned with medium-term effect. However, the most important analysis in this chapter will show how this medium-term measure has an additional—and highly robust—long-term dimension.

How Share of Voice Influences a Brand's Growth (or Decline)

The cost structure of any brand in a category is similar to that of others in the same category. Major brands are mostly the products of large manufacturers, and such brands can only compete effectively if they have similar prices and comparable product quality as the prices and quality of their competitors. This means that the sales volumes and the manufacturing processes for all brands must generate equivalent levels of scale economy.

Brands of a similar size will have approximately similar levels of direct and indirect cost, and they will enjoy comparable margins and deploy advertising budgets of about the same size. If one brand has twice the market share of another, it will have approximately twice the absolute level of direct and indirect cost and deploy an advertising budget twice as large.

A brand's advertising budget expressed as its share of voice (SOV) therefore drives, or is at least closely associated with, its share of market (SOM). The normal relationship—the relationship with which all exceptions should be compared—is that the two are equal. In other words SOV = SOM, which can be described as the category-average rate. If SOV exceeds SOM, the brand is investment-spending; it is putting more money into its advertising than the norm for the category. If SOV is smaller than SOM, then it is profit-taking; it is underspending in its advertising investment.[2]

A common strategy for manufacturers in most categories is occasionally to make an above-normal advertising investment in order to boost sales. With the important proviso that the manufacturer has developed an effective campaign, such a strategy has a reasonable chance of succeeding. This policy is indeed followed in all launches of important new brands and in the vast majority of restages (known in Europe as relaunches) of existing brands.

Table 7.1 returns to the 35 MMA brands discussed in Chapter 6. The focus of Table 7.1 is on share of market and share of voice. Thirteen of the brands analyzed in Chapter 6 have been dropped from Table 7.1 for two reasons. The first is that a number of the brands discussed in Chapter 6 have untypical advertising characteristics, in that they are either dominating advertisers in their category or else have such small budgets that they hardly advertise at all. The second reason is that a few brands described in Chapter 6 have incomplete data. The SOV data in Table 7.1 are based on dollar expenditures on television advertising. (Television is by a large margin the most important advertising medium for all the brands in the table.)

Table 7.1 contains relatively full information for 22 brands. These are all well-established in the marketplace; they are all significant advertisers; and they all have strong direct competitors within their categories. (The figures in parentheses are based on a limited number of years.) I have divided these 22 brands into two equal groups, based on share of market—large and small brands. Table 7.2 averages the figure for each group separately.

The difference between SOV and SOM is the measure of *advertising intensiveness*. It enables us to compare the advertising investments of competitive brands of a similar size. When advertising is measured in absolute dollars, the expenditure behind a large brand is virtually always greater than that behind a small brand. But it is perfectly possible—in fact, it is generally the case—that large brands are *less* advertising-intensive than small brands.

Table 7.2 demonstrates a number of points to be picked up later in this chapter and illustrated with additional data.

- Note the decline in average share of voice and how this has almost certainly caused a reduction in share of market. The 11 top brands are in positive territory for both measures; the bottom 11 are negative.

TABLE 7.1 Share of Market (SOM) and Share of Voice (SOV)

Brand	% Average SOM	% Average TV SOV	TV SOV Minus SOM, % Points	SOM Growth Index	TV SOV Growth Index, 1999 (compared with each brand's average = 100)
Top 11 brands					
2	87.7	27.0	−60.7	101	127
22	63.2	10.2	−53.0	106	74
25	59.7	20.1	−39.6	129	81
33	51.5	5.6	−45.9	(103)	9
34	43.7	21.4	−22.3	(103)	217
11	36.0	10.2	−25.8	(105)	(216)
7	33.4	13.8	−19.6	98	118
5	24.5	32.4	+7.9	98	106
1	21.0	9.7	−11.3	93	65
26	18.5	25.2	+6.7	96	38
21	18.1	17.3	−0.8	101	106
Bottom 11 Brands					
18	17.8	6.6	−11.2	80	168
10	12.9	10.2	−2.7	(98)	75
14	10.5	25.4	+14.9	104	80
6	7.0	30.6	+23.6	63	80
15	6.5	6.6	+0.1	105	121
19	6.1	2.1	−4.0	45	33
35	4.7	16.6	+11.9	(92)	(46)
20	4.5	1.7	−2.8	120	(29)
27	2.1	2.1	0	(96)	19
30	1.7	2.8	+1.1	(94)	125
29	0.8	0.8	0	(96)	88

- There is a very large difference between the advertising investments of the brands in these two groups. In the top group, an average 17.5% SOV supports an average 41.6% SOM. This means that each percentage point of market share is supported by only about 0.4% SOV. In the bottom group, an average SOV of 9.6% does not quite maintain an average SOM of 6.8%. This means that each percentage point of market share is weakly supported by about 1.4% SOV.

- If each percentage point of advertising investment ("voice") in a category represents $1 million, then each point of market share in the top group needs only approximately $400,000 support, whereas each point in the bottom group needs about $1.4 million support. *This says something about the strength of the brands*

TABLE 7.2 Share of Market (SOM) and Share of Voice (SOV) Averages of Two Groups of Brands

Brand	% Average SOM	% Average TV SOV	TV SOV Minus SOM, % Points	SOM Growth Index	TV SOV Growth Index, 1999 (compared with each brand's average)
Top 11 brands	41.6	17.5	−24.0	103	105
Bottom 11 brands	6.8	9.6	+2.8	90	79
All brands	24.2	13.6	−10.6	97	92

in the top group. The legacy of their previous advertising is so strong—the long-term effect of earlier advertising is so great—that they only need a modest "prod," whereas the smaller brands in the bottom group need an all-out advertising assault.

- The top group of the largest brands shows the greatest average SOM growth, and this group shows the highest *increase* in share of voice. It is a reasonable hypothesis that increasing advertising investment is encouraged by the fact that since sales are obviously buoyant the advertising is productive. Specifically, the SOV in the top group is *significantly below the share of market.*

- In the two groups, the relationship between SOV growth and SOM growth is exactly as might be expected, with SOV driving SOM. In the bottom group describing the smallest brands—which also show below-average growth—the relative unprofitability of the advertising (with SOV higher than SOM) does not encourage advertisers to increase their investment.

- Examining the individual brands in Table 7.1, we see that in the top group, 9 of the 11 brands are underinvestors (and the 2 overinvestors are low in the ranking). In the bottom group, there are only 4 underinvestors. This is general confirmation that large brands are almost invariably strong, although there are a few powerful small brands, like the underinvestors among the smaller brands in the table.

- The overall conclusion from Table 7.2 is the high productivity of advertising for large brands (with SOV below SOM); and the low productivity of advertising for small brands (with SOV higher than SOM). This is a uniform pattern that has been confirmed by much research in a number of different countries. As a general rule, the extent to which share of market exceeds share of voice *becomes progressively greater as we examine brands of increasing size.* This in effect demonstrates a progressive increase in the economic productivity of advertising dollars for progressively bigger brands.

TABLE 7.3 Share of Market (SOM) and Share of Voice (SOV) for Leading
Automobile Marques in Country M

	Marque MAA		*Marque MAB*		*Marque MAC*	
Year	*SOM %*	*SOV %*	*SOM %*	*SOV %*	*SOM %*	*SOV %*
1991	20.8	13.4	19.6	12.8	16.4	12.8
1992	19.2	15.6	19.8	13.7	17.2	13.3
1993	20.8	17.4	19.5	15.8	17.0	14.7
1994	19.3	17.9	19.0	13.6	18.7	13.4
1995	17.3	10.8	20.1	13.6	18.5	10.8
1996	17.6	11.3	19.4	12.7	17.8	11.1

- This analysis raises the important point that there is likely to be a level in each product category at which SOV can comfortably be set below SOM without endangering the stability or even the growth of sales. Data from other sources help us determine this level in specific cases. I offer three examples.

Table 7.3 describes the automotive category in an overseas country. In the market in question, there are three leading brands (which in the car field are called marques), that are approximately equal in shares of market.[3]

As mentioned, MAA, MAB, and MAC are the three largest marques in their category. Note the consistency of their SOM-SOV relationship, with SOV in every case below SOM. However, the manufacturers of MAB and MAC succeeded in maintaining their sales level more efficiently than did the manufacturer of MAA, and the dip in MAA's share of market in 1995 is clearly related to the sharp fall in its share of voice. This was reduced to a level that cut into the muscle and caused an important loss of sales for MAA, leading to a traumatic loss of market leadership. Note also the reduction in MAC's share of voice in 1995 and 1996, which had an influence on MAC's loss of share in 1996.

The experience of this product category suggests that (a) SOM will suffer if there is a sharp drop in SOV and (b) marques can underinvest in advertising to the extent that SOV can be below SOM by about 5 percentage points. But an underinvestment of 6 percentage points represents a level that will endanger sales, causing a likely stagnation or decline.

The second example (Table 7.4) is an unusual one because it describes the multinational experience of a global brand: Lux Toilet Soap, manufactured by

TABLE 7.4 Share of Market (SOM) and Share of Voice (SOV) for Lux Toilet Soap in 30 Countries (mid-1980s)

Aggregate SOM (%)	17
Aggregate SOV (%)	14
SOV in countries where sales were under pressure (%)	12

TABLE 7.5 Share of Market (SOM) and Share of Voice (SOV) for 200 Typical Brands With SOM of 13% or More

Brand Group	Number of Brands	Average Underinvestment (SOV below SOM), % Points
Brands with growing trend	83	− 1
Brands with static trend	53	− 3
Brands with declining trend	64	− 4

Unilever, and by a large margin the biggest-selling bar soap in the world. The brand is positioned in a similar way everywhere and is advertised with the same advertising campaign in every country.

In the mid-1980s, Lux's aggregate SOM in its 30 leading markets was 17%. This was supported by an overall SOV in these same markets of 14%: a level quite high enough to enable Lux to hold its market position, despite active competition from many other strong brands. But there was a limit to the degree of acceptable underinvestment. Experience in a number of countries demonstrated that a reduction in Lux's SOV to 12% would lead to a loss of market share. The critical level of underinvestment for this well-established brand was therefore a share of voice 3 percentage points below Lux's SOM.[4]

The third example describes the experience of 200 typical large brands of repeat-purchase packaged goods, again in a number of countries. Table 7.5 divides these brands into three groups, depending on their sales trends.[5]

With this group of large brands, the cutoff for "safe" underinvestment is a share of voice 3 percentage points below share of market, a similar figure to Lux (Table 7.4). The broad empirical base of this particular inquiry provides a final and firm support for the notion of "safe" underinvestment.

These three variegated examples demonstrate consistently that large brands can be undersupported in advertising and still maintain their market position.

TABLE 7.6 "Safe" Underinvestment: Share of Voice (SOV) Below Share of Market (SOM)

Case	Share of Market		"Safe" Underinvestment	
	% Points	*Index*	*% Points*	*Index*
Table 7.2 top group	42 (rounded)	100	−24	−57
Table 7.3	20	100	−5	−25
Table 7.4	17	100	−3	−18
Table 7.5	13	100	−3	−23

The degree of "safe" underinvestment varies from case to case, and this is especially true if we compare the last 3 cases with the 22 MMA examples described in Tables 7.1 and 7.2.

With such large variations in the "safe" underinvestment levels, the most useful way to compare them is to factor out the brand's SOM. This is because the large differences in SOM exaggerate the raw variations in the "safe" underinvestments. The arithmetical procedure is in each case to index the "safe" underinvestment on the average SOM of the brand(s) to which it relates. This is done in Table 7.6.

The last two columns (labeled "Safe" Underinvestment) should be interpreted as the amounts by which advertising expenditure is actually reduced. Basing the calculation on the SOV-SOM comparison, the investment in the top group of brands in Table 7.2 is 57% below SOM. (This is a percentage, not percentage points, and is calculated by comparing the reduction below SOM, which has been given the value of 100.)

This calculation means that this group of large brands can maintain its market position with an advertising budget *only 43% of the norm.* There is enough marketing impetus driving these brands that their advertising, which is at such a low rate, operates as efficiently as if it were at the normal category-average (SOV = SOM) level. *This estimate of the actual advertising budget as a percentage of the normal (SOV = SOM) budget is given the name Size-Weighted Budget Index (SWBI).* It plays a role in calculating the value of the long-term effect of advertising. The arithmetic is carried out by taking a brand's actual SOV and indexing this on the brand's SOM (which would equal SOV under normal circumstances).

The levels of "safe" underinvestment in Table 7.6 are all large, but they vary a lot from case to case. Most of the variations can be explained by the facts that the examples involve different categories and different countries. However, much the largest individual example of "safe" underinvestment relates to the 11 largest brands in the MMA sample (Tables 7.1 and 7.2). This very substantial "safe" underinvestment is clearly connected with the average SOM of these brands, which is more than twice that of the brands in Tables 7.3 through 7.5. As explained already, other analyses of this type all demonstrate that the larger the brand, the greater the progressive degree of "safe" underinvestment that can support it without loss of sales.

If we are to turn this analysis into a device of operational value, we must base our figures on the specific category and brand we are examining. With the large degree of variation in the "safe" underinvestment that we see in Table 7.6, it is absolutely necessary to use brand-specific data and not estimates derived from miscellaneous collections of examples, no matter how typical these might be.

Large Strong Brands and Small Weak Brands

The preceding section examined the relation between advertising underinvestment and a brand's marketplace performance. The general conclusion was that within limits—determined brand by brand—such underinvestment does not inhibit a brand's ability to maintain and sometimes increase sales. This is the underlying reason why large brands virtually always underinvest in media advertising, with the beneficial result that they manage to boost their profit.

Advertising underinvestment is a topic that has been widely explored, and the basic facts are not seriously in dispute. Figure 7.1 plots the SOV-SOM relationship for 666 brands from 23 different countries.[6] Three-quarters of the data come from the various fields of repeat-purchase packaged goods and the rest come from other types of advertising. The regression in Figure 7.1 was first published in 1989 and has been replicated in many additional investigations, with substantially similar results. The link between share of market and overinvestment/underinvestment is called the Advertising-Intensiveness Curve (AIC).

The AIC is valuable to marketing practice in helping us determine the advertising budget for any brand. This is because the SOM-SOV relationship tells us the average level of expenditure for a brand of any particular size. But as indi-

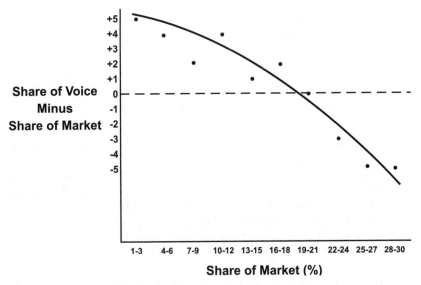

Figure 7.1. Share of Market and Share of Voice Advertising-Intensiveness Curve

cated already, an AIC should be constructed from specific brands in the category in which we are interested.

The AIC also helps us evaluate the sales-generating ability of the advertising for a brand of any size. Consider a selection of the brands in Figure 7.1.

- A small brand, with a share of market of 9%, will overspend in advertising by 3 percentage points above SOM; it will thus account for a total of 12% SOV. This means that each percentage point of SOM must be supported by 1.3% of SOV. Another way of looking at the same relationship is that *1% SOV will support 0.8% SOM.*

- A medium-size brand, with a share of market of 20%, will spend at the category-average on advertising, or 20% SOV. Each SOM will be supported by 1% SOV. And *1% SOV will support 1% SOM.*

- A large brand, with a share of market of 26%, will underspend on advertising by 5 percentage points below SOM; it will therefore account for 21% of SOV. This means that each percentage point of SOV can be supported by 0.8% SOV, and *1% SOV will support 1.2% SOM.*

What this arithmetic shows is that the advertising investment behind large brands is more productive, dollar for dollar, than the investment behind small brands. This difference is robustly quantifiable, and if we are able to understand the reasons for this phenomenon, we will receive valuable clues to measuring the long-term effects of advertising.

Making the customary assumption that we are comparing equally effective campaigns, a dollar spent behind a large brand will provide higher sales than a dollar spent behind a small brand. There are at least five reasons for this:

1. The large brand has a bigger consumer franchise, or user base, than a small brand. Since people tend to pay at least some attention to the advertising for the brands they use themselves, this means that the attentive (or semi-attentive) audience produced by a given amount of advertising for a large brand is greater than that for the same amount of advertising for a small brand.

2. The average user of a large brand will buy that brand slightly more often in a defined period than the average user of a small brand. This extremely important point is demonstrated in detail in Chapter 8.

3. A large brand, because of its above-average user base, will occupy a high "share of the mind" of more consumers than is the case with a small brand. The ubiquity of a large brand can be a valuable asset. For instance, if any particular brand is out-of-stock at the store where the consumer is shopping, there is almost a 60% chance that she will buy another brand in the product field.[7] This is more likely to be a large than a small brand because of the high display level for the major brands in any category.

4. A large brand is valued more than a small brand by the consumer, and this justifies the generally higher-than-average prices that large brands can command. This point is also examined in Chapter 8.

5. As explained in Chapter 3, I believe that most advertising acts as a reminder, or an evocation of previous brand experience. However, some advertising goes beyond this, and the advertising message itself and how it is communicated leave traces in the memory of the consumer. Such high-profile advertising has a greater overall effect for large than for small brands for the simple reason that the large brands have the bigger budgets measured in absolute terms. It must not, however, be thought that high-profile campaigns are always better at generating sales than low-profile campaigns. It all depends on the endemic characteristics of the brand and its position in the market. But in the cases in which high-profile advertising is particularly effective, the memorability of the campaign favors large brands.

These five factors add up to what I have earlier described as the *marketing impetus driving large brands.* And there is no doubt at all that previous advertising for the brand—by its ability both to encourage repeat purchase and to build psychological added values in the minds of consumers—contributes to a very large degree to this. The marketing impetus is therefore substantially a description of the contribution made by previous advertising.

The Sales-Weighted Budget Index is a measure of this marketing impetus. This device can therefore be used as a measure of the long-term effect of advertising, or more precisely a measure of how much the long-term build-up of advertising has contributed to a strengthening and enrichment of the brand itself. The feature of the measure that makes it so relevant to this analysis is that it is calibrated in terms of the advertising itself. It summarizes the advertising-related effects of a number of factors that are themselves only indirectly related to the advertising.

In this discussion, the phrase *large brand* has been assumed to mean *strong brand,* and the phrase *small brand* has been assumed to mean *weak brand.* This is substantially although not totally correct. As mentioned in the discussion of Table 7.1, small strong brands are not uncommon. They are, however, more prevalent than large weak brands. Strong minor brands can have a diminutive consumer base but high purchase frequency, which means that they tend to appeal to specialist market niches and have a loyal consumer franchise (e.g., certain high-fiber breakfast cereals and specialist laundry detergents). Major brands invariably have a high consumer penetration and an above-average purchase frequency, which means that they have endemic strength unless they are on a downward sales path because of underinvestment (as in the case of some of the examples in Tables 7.3, 7.4, and 7.5).

Calculating the Long-Term Effects of Advertising

The method described here is based on the medium-term payback to advertising, described in Chapter 6. This is expressed by the results in sales (measured in cents) for each dollar of advertising investment. If the advertising budget is reduced and sales remain unchanged, then the payback goes up. If the budget is increased and sales remain unchanged, then the payback goes down. What we see from this calculation is changes in the brand's *profitability*. A lower budget to maintain the same sales as at a higher budget means a more effective use of advertising funds. This means an increase in the sales generated by each dollar of investment and therefore greater profit.

The concept introduced in this chapter is that some brands—the large ones—are effectively and economically underadvertised by not spending at the category-average rate (SOV = SOM); thus their medium-term payback can be inflated to the extent of this underinvestment to reflect the brand's greater profitability. On the other hand, small brands must overadvertise by spending above their category-average rate (SOV = SOM); thus their overinvestment must be used to deflate their medium-term payback to reflect the brand's lower profitability. The arithmetic used follows three simple steps:

1. Compute the SWBI. This is done by indexing the brand's share of voice on its share of market (which in turn represents its SOV in normal circumstances).

2. Apply the SWBI to the medium-term advertising payback represented by cents of sales resulting from each dollar of advertising investment. We do this by multiplying the medium-term payback by the fraction 100/SWBI. (If we wish to isolate the long-term effect, we deduct the medium-term contribution from the new total.) This weighting applied by the SWBI will provide a new total estimate of the *medium-term plus long-term advertising payback.*

3. Using the financial return from the medium-term plus long-term payback, calculate by subtraction the number of cents of advertising investment that are still uncovered by the business generated by the advertising itself. By applying this to the actual advertising budget, we can also compute the dollar sum of net uncovered investment.

This procedure is illustrated in Table 7.7, which describes two notional (but typical) brands. Brand ZAA has a large SOM and can safely underinvest in advertising. ZAB is a small brand that must advertise at an above-average rate to maintain its market position.

Table 7.7 shows the following:

- The value of ZAA's advertising has been increased because the brand can afford to underinvest to a significant degree. The brand spent $17 million, but this represents a campaign that in normal circumstances would be valued at $21 million ($17 million is 81% of $21 million). ZAA benefits from the accumulated long-term value of previous advertising, and its medium-term payback is effectively increased from 50 cents to 62 cents.

- ZAB must overinvest in advertising, which means that the value of its medium-term productivity is reduced in proportion. The brand does not benefit yet from any long-term effects of previous advertising. This will only happen when the brand grows enough to generate advertising-related scale economies. ZAB's necessary over-investment in advertising effectively reduces the brand's medium-term payback from 50 cents to 38 cents.

TABLE 7.7 Medium-Term Plus Long-Term Effects of Television Advertising for Two Notional but Typical Brands

		Part 1		
Brand	*% Share of Voice (SOV)*	*% Share of Market (SOM)*	*SOV Minus SOM % Points*	*Sales-Weighted Budget Index*
ZAA	21	26	−5	81
ZAB	12	9	+3	133

		Part 2		
Brand	*(Medium-Term) Percentage Payback (cents per advertising $)*	*(Medium-Term Plus Long-Term) Weighted Percentage Payback (cents per advertising $)*	*Advertising Deficit (cents per $)*	*Absolute Advertising Deficit ($ million)*
ZAA	50	62	38	6.5
ZAB	50	38	62	5.6

The discussion of the valuation of advertising's long-term effects does not end here. In Chapter 10, I examine how this method of calculating long-term effects applies to actual brands and then look at some cases in which advertising produces sales value that exceeds its cost when the long-term effects are taken into account.

Notes

1. The ways in which share of voice are able to influence a brand's market share are discussed in John Philip Jones, *What's in a Name? Advertising and the Concept of Brands* (New York: Simon & Schuster-Lexington Books, 1986), 235-236.

2. There is a small complication to this calculation. All brands in a category will share the sales between them; they will all have their own measurable shares of market. However, a few brands are usually unadvertised, which means that the advertising expenditure is divided between a more limited number of brands. This means that a typical *advertised* brand's share of voice (divided among the fewer brands) will be slightly higher than its share of market (divided among the total

number of brands in the category). However, unadvertised brands tend to be relatively unimportant, and this mathematical complication is ignored in the discussion in this book, where the normal relationship is described as SOV = SOM.

3. Based on private information.

4. John Philip Jones, *Does It Pay to Advertise? Cases Illustrating Successful Brand Advertising* (New York: Simon & Schuster-Lexington Books, 1989), 97.

5. Ibid., 300.

6. Ibid., 293-300. Also John Philip Jones, "Ad Spending: Maintaining Market Share," *Harvard Business Review,* January/February 1990, 38-42.

7. James O. Peckham, Sr., *The Wheel of Marketing,* 2nd Edition (Privately published, 1981, but available from A. C. Nielsen), 27.

8

The Depth of Advertising's Long-Term Effects

The long-term effects of advertising take the form of an enrichment of the brand and a strengthening of its relationship with the consumer.

Chapter 7 described a direct, advertising-related measure of the long-term effects of advertising. We are now going to immerse ourselves in the brand itself with the aim of understanding *and also in turn measuring* the underlying causes of this advertising-related measure. What is there within a brand that enables it to maintain and sometimes increase its sales despite consistent under-investment in advertising?

To find out more, we need to concentrate on a brand's sales, or more precisely on its consumer purchases. We can do this—examining sales from the consumer's point of view—by using a formula which specifically focuses on consumers and their buying, the end result being the sales of a brand. We must analyze the buyers of brands in this way in order to plan efficiently an advertising strategy, since media advertising is concerned exclusively with consumers' influence on sales. The packs do not disappear from the store shelves in

TABLE 8.1 Sales in Consumer Terms

Sales Formula	Brand JBL in Volume	Brand JBL in Consumer $
Household population (in millions)	120	120
× household penetration	12% (6 months)	12% (6 months)
× purchase frequency	2 (6 months)	2 (6 months)
× packs bought per purchase occasion	1	1
× average size of pack	2.6 KG (42 loads)	$7.50
= sales	(Approx.) 146,000 metric tons per annum	(Approx.) $430 million per annum

response to advertising's serenade. It is the consumer who is serenaded, and it is the consumer who, it is hoped, will put the packs in her shopping cart.

The formula is simple, as set forth in Table 8.1 where it is applied to a specific major brand of laundry detergent coded JBL.

JBL is a very large brand, indeed a household name. The manufacturer can compare the calculations in Table 8.1 with his own ex-factory shipments, which are of course delivered to the retail trade. And he can see the extent to which his sales are passing through to the consumer and how much are being used to build retail inventories. Most important, Table 8.1 helps the manufacturer plan his advertising with the consumer in mind—whether he should be concerned with building penetration by finding new users or boosting purchase frequency by getting his existing users to buy more.

If we compare different brands in any category, three parts of the formula in Table 8.1 provide similar figures for every brand we examine. The household population is the same for all. In any category, the number of packs bought per purchase occasion tends to be the same for every brand; and the average size of pack is also approximately uniform brand by brand.[1]

The parts of the formula that discriminate between brands are *penetration* (the proportion of households that buy a brand at least once in a defined period) and *purchase frequency* (how often they buy the brand, on average, during that same period).

These are the two key components of sales, and this chapter is devoted to analyzing them. Penetration directly drives a brand's sales and gives the brand *breadth.* Purchase frequency—an especially important sales-driver for a large brand—makes the major contribution to giving it *depth.* The most common measure of depth is purchase frequency, but it is not the only one. There is a parallel measure, share of requirements, described in the next paragraph. Advertising, in cooperation with consumers' satisfaction with the functional efficiency of the brand, is the engine to increase depth of purchase.

Penetration

Table 8.2 returns to the MMA brands discussed in Chapters 6 and 7. Table 8.2 shows figures for one year, 1997 (chosen because this is the year for which the richest battery of data is available). The table provides data for 31 brands on their shares of market and 12-monthly penetration. MMA also provides a very good measure of consumer loyalty, which (like purchase frequency) indicates depth of purchase of a brand. This measure is *Share of Requirements.* It concentrates on the households that buy the brand and percentages their purchases of the brand on their total category volume purchases. It shows how important the brand is within the average household's brand repertoire.[2]

As in Chapters 6 and 7, the brands are divided into groups. In Table 8.3 (and also in all the other tables in this chapter), I break the brands into quintiles, each representing one-fifth of the total number. The brands are ranked from largest to smallest before being divided into these five separate groups. The table gives average figures for share of market and penetration for each quintile of a defined average SOM. The figures are also indexed (i.e., for share of market), the average for all 31 brands is given the base index number of 100, and the separate figures for each quintile are calculated from this base. The same thing is also done for penetration. The index figures in Table 8.3 are set out diagrammatically in Figure 8.1.

A brand grows mainly by gaining new users; and penetration—the measure of the size of the user base—drives market share. But there is an obvious top limit to penetration. In Table 8.3, the threshold penetration is 31.2%, which drives an average SOM of 23.4%. The brands in the MMA sample are, as discussed in Chapter 6, larger than the norm for repeat-packaged goods, with an average SOM in Table 8.3 of 32.2%. This large average size has caused penetration to peak at a relatively low level in the ranking of the brands. To examine a

TABLE 8.2 Penetration and Depth of Purchase for MMA* Brands, 1997

Brand	% Share of Market	% 12-Monthly Penetration	% Share of Requirements
2	88.0	43.4	100.0
8	81.3	33.6	75.1
31	79.9	6.5	84.3
24	68.9	26.7	55.9
25	68.4	21.3	76.7
22	65.2	21.4	84.2
17	62.3	43.2	52.0
16	60.0	24.4	44.8
33	52.3	28.6	73.7
32	51.3	8.9	48.3
34	44.4	5.2	30.8
3	43.0	19.4	65.9
11	37.0	26.2	50.9
7	33.2	42.1	33.6
5	24.2	35.0	41.6
1	20.7	22.0	50.6
21	17.6	38.4	46.3
26	17.2	20.6	34.5
18	13.9	34.5	34.5
10	12.8	11.6	29.2
14	10.6	7.9	52.5
4	7.0	8.0	58.0
6	6.8	18.8	77.9
23	6.8	10.8	86.1
15	6.7	12.9	46.1
20	4.8	6.6	52.4
35	4.5	3.5	38.9
19	3.3	10.1	56.3
27	2.0	5.6	7.9
30	1.6	10.7	7.2
29	0.8	10.6	4.4

* MMA = Media Marketing Assessment.
NOTE: Brands are grouped in quintiles.

(more common) situation where the average share of market is smaller, we should examine also a range of brands distributed in size in a more typical way.

We now look at four further SOM/penetration relationships. Three of these examine complete packaged goods categories: cold breakfast cereals, regular domestic beer, and laundry detergents.[3] The fourth example covers 78 brands in

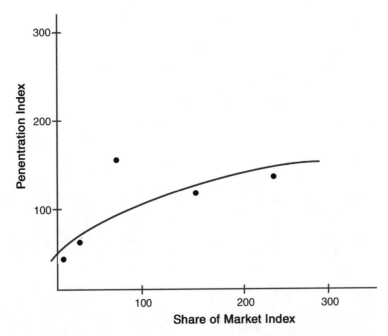

Figure 8.1. Average Share of Market and Penetration of MMA* Brands, 1997
* MMA = Media Marketing Assessment.

TABLE 8.3 Average Share of Market and Penetration for MMA* Brands, 1997

Brand	Number of Brands	% Average Share of Market	Share of Market Index	% Average 12-Month Penetration	Penetration Index
All brands	31	32.2	100	20.0	100
Top quintile	6	75.3	234	25.5	128
4th quintile	6	52.2	162	21.6	108
3rd quintile	7	23.4	73	31.2	156
2nd quintile	6	8.5	26	11.7	59
Bottom quintile	6	2.8	9	7.9	40

* MMA = Media Marketing Assessment.

12 different categories, which were researched in 1991 by the Pure Single-Source technique.[4]

TABLE 8.4 Average Share of Market and Penetration for Cold Breakfast Cereals, 1991

Brand	Number of Brands	% Average Share of Market	Share of Market Index	% Average 6-Month Penetration	Penetration Index
All brands	95	1.1	100	4.6	100
Top quintile	19	3.1	282	11.3	246
4th quintile	19	1.0	91	5.6	122
3rd quintile	19	0.6	55	2.9	63
2nd quintile	19	0.3	27	2.0	43
Bottom quintile	19	0.2	18	1.4	30

TABLE 8.5 Average Share of Market and Penetration for Regular Domestic Beer, 1997

Brand	Number of Brands	% Average Share of Market	Share of Market Index	% Average 6-Month Penetration	Penetration Index
All brands	36	2.8	100	1.6	100
Top quintile	7	9.5	339	4.3	269
4th quintile	7	2.5	89	1.7	106
3rd quintile	8	1.2	43	1.1	69
2nd quintile	7	0.7	25	0.8	50
Bottom quintile	7	0.3	11	0.4	25

The data, tabulated in a similar way to Table 8.3, are presented in Tables 8.4 through 8.7. The share of market/penetration relationships are plotted diagrammatically in Figures 8.2 through 8.5.

We can draw four inferences from these five groups of brands just described:

1. There is a direct relationship between penetration and market share. As penetration builds, so does SOM—more users, more sales. This is basic common sense and can be taken as a formal rule describing all brands except the largest ones, mostly the top 20%. For these there is a more subtle conclusion discussed in point 3.

2. With four of the five collections of brands, there is a large gap separating the top quintile from the remaining four quintiles; the top-quintile brands are *very much*

TABLE 8.6 Average Share of Market and Penetration for Laundry Detergents, 1998

Brand	Number of Brands	% Average Share of Market	Share of Market Index	% Average 6-Month Penetration	Penetration Index
All brands	39	2.6	100	4.1	100
Top quintile	8	6.6	254	9.5	232
4th quintile	8	2.9	112	4.8	117
3rd quintile	7	1.8	69	2.9	71
2nd quintile	8	1.0	38	2.3	56
Bottom quintile	8	0.4	15	1.1	27

TABLE 8.7 Average Share of Market and Penetration for Brands in 12 Categories, 1991

Brands	Number of Brands	% Average Share of Market	Share of Market Index	% Average 6-Month Penetration	Penetration Index
All brands	78	6.8	100	11.9	100
Top quintile	16	18.7	275	26.9	226
4th quintile	15	6.8	100	18.6	156
3rd quintile	16	3.9	57	11.0	92
2nd quintile	15	2.8	41	7.7	65
Bottom quintile	16	1.8	26	6.3	53

larger. The exception is the MMA brands (Table 8.3 and Figure 8.1), but with them the average SOM for the top three quintiles is exceptionally high—75.3%, 52.2%, and 23.4%, respectively—and sets them all well apart from the rest of the pack. The size factor separates the top three quintiles of the MMA data from the bottom two quintiles, but with the other four groups of brands, it is only the top quintile that is separated.

3. Where the top quintiles have a particularly high market share (Tables 8.3 and 8.7), this is accompanied by a flattening of the penetration curve (Figures 8.1 and 8.5). There is also a commonsense reason for this. The larger a brand grows, the more it runs out of potential users. The original-formula Listerine finds it difficult to attract new users who will accept the brand's strong medicinal taste, despite the brand's widely understood efficiency at killing bacteria—a functional benefit, which to some users is actually signaled by the taste. Tide finds it diffi-

(text continues on p. 140)

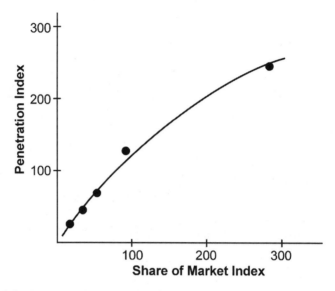

Figure 8.2. Share of Market/Penetration Relationship: Cold Breakfast Cereals, 1991

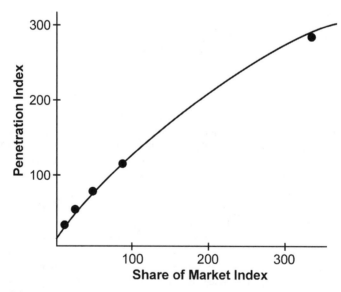

Figure 8.3. Share of Market/Penetration Relationship: Regular Domestic Beer, 1997

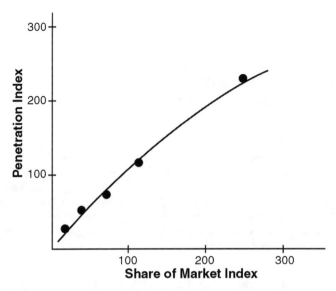

Figure 8.4. Share of Market/Penetration Relationship: Laundry Detergents, 1998

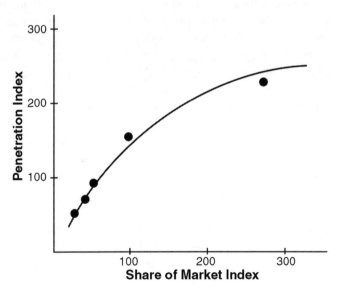

Figure 8.5. Share of Market/Penetration Relationship: Brands in 12 Categories, 1991

cult to find new users who will accept the brand because some people regard Tide as hard on fabrics, despite its ability to wash clothes with maximum efficiency. And Budweiser, despite the fact that its American sales volume alone makes it the widest-selling beer in the world, finds that some potential users regard the brand as too downmarket for their (perhaps snobbish) taste.

4. The relatively small number of big brands tend, of course, to be the oldest established ones: those that have had years to build and reinforce a loyal franchise. It is rare for a new brand to join this group of large players because the latter have the strength to block serious competition. The big brands are generally made by very large manufacturers to whom they offer two benefits: (a) the market strength of the big brand itself and (b) the resultant scale economies that provide funds for new brands in the same or different categories. However, these scale economies occasionally produce a negative effect. A manufacturer is often so enthusiastic about new brand ideas (most of which fail) that he neglects his own large brands. In the bar soap category, Dial lost SOM for a few years in the 1970s, and Ivory suffered more permanent damage in the 1990s.

When a brand becomes a very large competitor in a category, penetration reaches a plateau, with very little potential to grow and increase sales *pari passu*. Nevertheless, some brands have a larger SOM than others despite similar penetration levels. And some large brands grow larger over time, and they do this despite a relatively stable penetration. The dynamic force driving large brands upward is clearly the loyalty of their users: their depth of purchase.

Summarizing what has been said so far, it is clear that there is something especially important about the largest 20% of brands that sets them apart from the majority of brands in their category. What makes them so special is not so much their large penetration but their depth of purchase. The large brands not only have greater breadth than the small brands, but—more important—they also have greater loyalty. This quality, which is at the heart of strong brands, is now described in detail.

Depth of Purchase

Table 8.8 sets out in compressed form a large amount of information on depth of purchase. The five groups of brands described in this chapter are compared with one another in this one table. The actual figures are indexes based in each case on the category average, and the quintiles are ranked according to the average size of the brand in each quintile (as in Tables 8.3 through 8.7). With the MMA

TABLE 8.8 Depth of Purchase, by Quintiles

Quintiles Ranked by Share of Market	MMA* Brands 1997	Breakfast Cereals 1991	Regular Domestic Beer 1997	Laundry Detergents 1998	12 Categories 1991
All brands	100	100	100	100	100
Top quintile	154	133	137	127	125
4th quintile	102	91	124	109	97
3rd quintile	81	100	110	112	92
2nd quintile	113	91	63	80	94
Bottom quintile	54	86	63	71	84

* MMA = Media Marketing Assessment.

brands, the measure used is share of requirements (explained earlier in this chapter). For the others, the measure is of the average number of purchase occasions in the research period (6 months in the cases of the 3 all-category analyses, and 12 months in the 1991 study of 12 categories). Despite the differences in methodology, the index figures for the five groups of brands are comparable.

The data for the five groups of brands are plotted diagramatically in Figures 8.6 through 8.10.

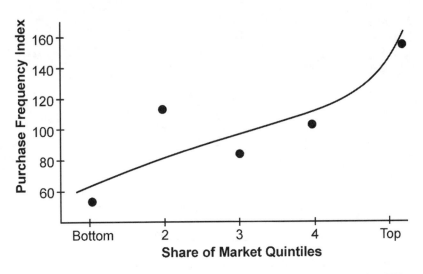

Figure 8.6. Purchase Frequency, by Share of Market Quintiles: MMA Brands, 1997

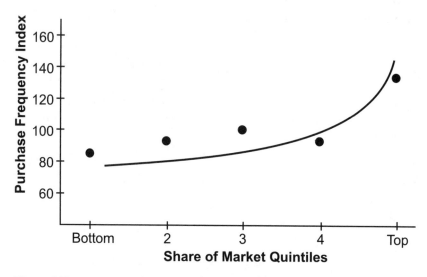

Figure 8.7. Purchase Frequency, by Share of Market Quintiles: Breakfast Cereals, 1991

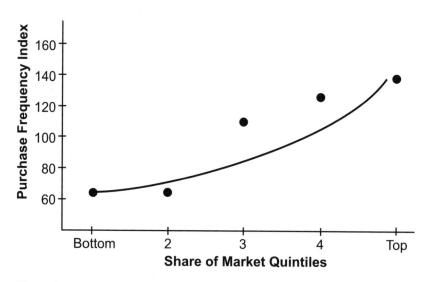

Figure 8.8. Purchase Frequency, by Share of Market Quintiles: Regular Domestic Beer, 1997

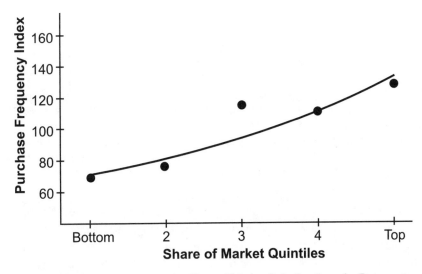

Figure 8.9. Purchase Frequency, by Share of Market Quintiles: Laundry Detergents, 1998

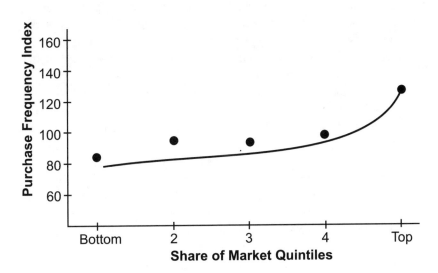

Figure 8.10. Purchase Frequency, by Share of Market Quintiles: Brands in 12 Categories, 1991

The meaning of these five cases is clear, and their findings are consistent:

- The share of market of large brands is the end product of significantly enhanced loyalty/purchase frequency.

- Looking at brands on a continuum ranging from smallest to largest, greater loyalty/larger purchase frequencies are related to larger shares of market, with very few discontinuities in the ranking.

- Finally, and most important, loyalty/purchase frequency kicks up sharply in the top quintile of brands, opening up the generally large distance that separates this quintile from the remaining four-fifths of brands on the continuum.

These conclusions may surprise some readers, but they are not new. The connection between above-average purchase frequency and high share of market was first noted by Andrew Ehrenberg many years ago, although he uses the curiously negative phrase "Double Jeopardy" to describe it. By this, he means that small brands suffer from the double disadvantage of *low* penetration and *low* purchase frequency.[5] Also many years ago, I first used the more positive phrase "Penetration Supercharge" to explain the same phenomenon.[6]

If we compare Table 8.8 with Table 7.6 (in Chapter 7), the obvious question raised is whether it is possible to connect the greater loyalty/higher-than-average purchase frequency of large brands with their lower-than-average advertising-intensiveness (i.e., their share of voice being significantly below their share of market).

Table 8.9 and Figure 8.11 examine this connection for the 21 brands in the MMA sample for which full data are available.

Of the 21 brands in Table 8.9, 13 underinvest in advertising. These are mostly the larger brands, with an average SOM of 34.7%. Eight of the brands overinvest, and these are mostly the smaller brands, with an average SOM of 11.2%.

The underinvestors are, I am convinced, the brands that benefit from the long-term effects of their advertising campaigns, effects that can be measured (as explained in Chapter 7) by dollar estimates of the specific extent of their advertising underinvestments. The advertising of the overinvestors is obviously less productive. They have (as explained) a lower average share of market, and overinvestment is normal for small brands; also, the few large overinvestors have weak campaigns, hence the need for higher expenditure.

Figure 8.11 concentrates on the 13 brands that benefit from campaigns with positive measurable long-term effects. In this diagram, the extent of the under-

TABLE 8.9 Consumer Loyalty and Advertising Under-/Overinvestment for MMA*
Brands, 1997

Brand	% Share of Market	% Share of Requirements	TV Share of Voice Minus Share of Market, % Points
2	88.0	100.0	−64.8
25	68.4	76.7	−43.5
22	65.2	84.2	−50.2
33	52.3	73.7	−45.1
34	44.4	30.8	−13.8
11	37.0	50.9	−28.3
7	33.2	33.6	−22.2
5	24.2	41.6	+3.2
1	20.7	50.6	−13.0
21	17.6	46.3	−0.5
26	17.2	35.4	+1.9
18	13.9	34.5	−11.6
10	12.8	29.2	+0.1
14	10.6	52.5	+13.0
4	7.0	58.0	+24.0
6	6.8	77.9	+24.5
15	6.7	46.1	+1.9
20	4.8	52.4	−3.2
35	4.5	38.9	+13.4
19	3.3	56.3	−4.5
27	2.0	7.9	−0.5

* MMA = Media Marketing Assessment.

investment for each brand is related to its share of requirements: a measure of consumers' brand loyalty. As can be seen, the fit between the two variables, while not perfect, is both in the right direction and also reasonably close. *The stronger the brand, signaled by high consumer loyalty, the greater the degree of advertising underinvestment the brand can support.*

In this chapter, I reviewed penetration and loyalty/depth of purchase as contributors to the long-term effects of advertising and examined how depth of purchase—the most striking cause of these long-term effects—is related to advertising underinvestment, which in turn provides a simple dollar estimate of their value.

But the underlying causes and signals of advertising's long-term effects do not end here. An important factor is the price that a brand can command in the marketplace.

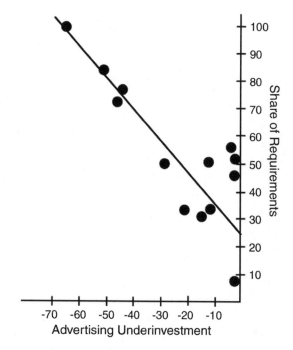

Figure 8.11. Scatterplot of Brands That Underinvest in Advertising: MMA Brands, 1997

Pricing

Pricing data should be simple to collect, and many analysts might expect extensive pricing data to be available for all product categories. But the supply of good information is unfortunately not very generous. There are two reasons for this.

First, pricing information must be calculated within each product category. Listerine must be compared with Scope and not with Kellogg's Corn Flakes. The best method is to average the consumer price in any category, giving this an index number of 100, and to calculate the price of each brand in comparison with this. Unfortunately, most investigators do not follow this procedure.

The second problem is that it is only relevant to show current ruling prices. This means we must use the actual prices paid by consumers, taking account of the direct effect of consumer promotions and the indirect effect of trade promo-

TABLE 8.10   Marketplace Prices of Brands in 12 Product Categories, 1991:
Indexes Compared With Category Averages

All brands	100
Largest 10 brands	114
Second-largest 10 brands	110
Remaining 58 advertised brands	99
64 unadvertised brands	97

tions. A brand's list price on its own is quite misleading, since it is rare to see a brand sold at its nominal list price.

Robust price information is available for the 78 brands in 12 different categories whose penetration and purchase frequency have already been examined (in Tables 8.7 and 8.8). With these brands, the actual price of each brand was calculated in the recommended way, by indexing it on the category average. The 78 brands were all advertised, and there were in addition 64 small unadvertised products, making a total of 142 different brands covered by the investigation. Their prices are summarized in Table 8.10.

The picture from Table 8.10 is clear. The largest brands in any category not only have an above-average penetration and greatly above-average loyalty, but they are also able to *command above-average prices.*

This conclusion is harmonious with a finding described in Chapter 9 (Table 9.11) concerning the price-elasticity of different brands. Brands that spend heavily on advertising—those mostly large in size—have a *lower* price-elasticity than brands that spend less. This means that the degree of advertising investment to some extent determines whether or not brands can profit from price increases. Low elasticity means a small loss of volume from a price increase and therefore a likely increase in profit.

Knitting the Threads

The evidence in this chapter shows that large brands, which in most cases are measured as the top quintile by SOM, have more users than small brands and are valued by their consumers more than small brands are. This valuation is expressed both by these brands' greatly above-average loyalty/purchase frequency and by the above-average prices they can command in the marketplace.

These beneficial outcomes, which are behavioral and quite robust, are partly the result of users' continuous satisfaction with the brands' functional properties. But this satisfaction has been underscored and reinforced by the consumer advertising. It is virtually certain that a brand having these characteristics has been influenced—in many cases for years and sometimes for decades—by effective advertising. It is difficult to find exceptions when this has not happened.

The relationship between share of voice and share of market, which enables us to give a dollar value to the long-term effects of advertising, is a long-term phenomenon. If SOV is below SOM by a large gap, this means that the brand in question possesses values to the consumer that drive her to use it more often and pay more money for it. It is because of these values, which generally cause a brand to be a major participant in the brand repertoire of large numbers of buyers, that *advertising does not have to work very hard to generate sales,* and a single advertisement has greater-than-average effect. The advertising will be seen by large numbers of people because a large brand has a big user base, and many of these people will pay some attention to the advertising because of selective perception. In addition, the brand itself will mean more to these users both in money terms and in overall salience because the brand is likely to be their first preference.

Dollar for dollar, the advertising for larger brands is more productive than that for smaller brands because the larger brands have a stronger place both in the buyer's pattern of buying and on her scale of brand values. Because of this high valuation—a valuation that has been positively influenced to a greater or lesser degree by the large amounts of previous advertising—the brand can afford to advertise relatively less than would be the case if the brand were smaller and weaker. With large brands, advertising reinforces. Advertising works on more fertile ground. Advertising generates more sales per dollar invested. The causes lie below the surface in the relationship between the brand and the consumer, but the effect of these causes can be quantified surprisingly simply by comparing a brand's share of voice and its share of market: two pieces of uncomplicated and readily available marketplace data.

Notes

1. The analyses in this chapter are substantially based on the work of the British academic and business consultant Andrew Ehrenberg, who is the first person to have examined empirically the patterns of consumer buying and drawn some conclusions of seminal importance. His work is reg-

ularly brought up-to-date and extensively published, but his basic ground rules are found in A. S. C. Ehrenberg, *Repeat Buying: Facts, Theory and Applications,* 2nd edition (New York: Oxford University Press, 1988). The 1st edition was published in 1972.

2. *Share of requirements:* the average percentage of category purchases (normally in a year) accounted for by the brand being measured.

Purchase frequency: the average number of purchases (normally in a year) by buyers of a brand.

Share of requirements and purchase frequency are both expressions of depth of purchase. However, as can be seen from the definitions, they are not the same thing. Both cover users of a brand, but they differ in their treatment of light and heavy category users. It is possible for light category users to have a high share of requirements for a brand but low purchase frequency, and it is possible for heavy category users to have high purchase frequency of a brand but low share of requirements (because such consumers are also buying quantities of other brands). The two leading sales measurement organizations, A. C. Nielsen and Information Resources, Inc. (IRI), report both measures. Both can be used, with judgment, to indicate consumers' depth of purchase, which signals loyalty to a brand.

3. The data on the three packaged goods categories are calculated from the annual reports published by Mediamark Research, Inc. (MRI). The information from cold breakfast cereals dates from 1991, regular domestic beer from 1997, and laundry detergents from 1998.

4. John Philip Jones, *When Ads Work: New Proof That Advertising Triggers Sales* (New York: Simon & Schuster-Lexington Books, 1995). The data relate to 1991.

5. Ehrenberg, *Repeat Buying,* 200, 265.

6. John Philip Jones, *What's in a Name? Advertising and the Concept of Brands* (New York: Simon & Schuster-Lexington Books, 1986), 114, 116, 126.

9

Can Doses of Advertising Produce Doses of Profit?

We saw in Chapter 6 that advertising, when its cost is compared with the value of the sales it produces over a year, only very rarely pays for itself. This does not mean that advertising is a profligate and self-indulgent activity, although ineffective campaigns *are* totally wasteful and this is why the advertising industry does its best to detect and eliminate them.

When we conclude that, in the medium term, advertising can produce strong sales but the sales increases are almost always unprofitable, we must look at this in a broader context:

- Advertising should be seen as a part of the expense of doing business, in the same way as a manufacturer's direct and indirect costs.
- Advertising is an engine to generate demand, which in turn makes large-volume manufacture an economic proposition, and this in turn lowers costs and prices, and low prices also stimulate demand.

- Although there may be losses in the medium term, it should be possible to offset some of these by the positive value—particularly the extra profit—generated by advertising in its long-term role.

There is another important aspect to this matter of advertising profitability. Although the medium-term effect of advertising is usually uneconomic, we have seen in Chapter 5 that the short-term effect is invariably much stronger than the medium-term effect. We should therefore examine whether an advertising exposure which produces a sometimes substantial immediate sales increase is also always fated to achieve an uneconomic return. Can a strong advertisement generate enough immediate sales to cover its cost, at the very least, before its effect is eroded over a year by the countervailing influence of the advertising and other marketing activities of competitors? To test this point, we must measure this short-term effect, and we do this by examining the effect of fresh exposures of advertising.

When we do this, we find many cases in which the short-term effect of advertising *can* be economic. The measure that we use not only compares immediate advertising against immediate return, but there is also an extension of the measure that has unmistakable long-term overtones. This will be described later in this chapter.

How Doses of Advertising Generate Doses of Sales and (Sometimes) Extra Profit

The way in which we measure the short-term effect of increases or decreases in advertising is with a statistical device called an advertising elasticity. Elasticity means responsiveness (in this case, of sales) to a given stimulus (in this case, advertising). The calculation is carried out by regression analysis of multiple changes in advertising expenditure (and other marketing stimuli) related to their effect on sales of an individual brand. The end product of the calculation is *an estimate of the percentage rise in sales that results from a 1% increase in advertising expenditure,* the extra sales having come from advertising alone since the effect of the other influences on sales has been allowed for.

Any estimate on these lines is of course predicated on the basic assumption that the campaign is creatively strong enough to produce some degree of short-term effect. As we saw in Chapter 2 (Table 2.2), a third of campaigns do not fulfill this condition.

The complicated calculations of advertising elasticity have been made with hundreds of brands. In 1984, three American analysts, Gert Assmus, John U. Farlet, and Donald R. Lehmann, published a summary of the advertising elasticities of 128 separate advertising campaigns.[1] The elasticity varies according to the product category, the brand, and most of all the campaign itself. The average published figure was +0.22. If we round this to +0.2, we see an approximate 5 to 1 relationship. A 1% increase in advertising produces a 0.2% boost in sales; a 5% lift in advertising will generate 1% extra sales; a 10% advertising increase boosts sales by 2%; a 20% advertising lift will increase them by 4%. Increments in advertising are normally in minimum amounts of 10%; 20% is common for brand restages. A 5 to 1 relationship is a fairly low response rate, but I shall show that the sales return can sometimes be economic (i.e., the value of extra sales *can* exceed the outlay).

In my own experience, some elasticity calculations are made with a year's data, which means that the results are likely to be diluted because the period will be long enough for the effect of the advertising to be contaminated by the influence of competitive activity. This analysis will however be confined to short-term effect, and all the figures in the following tables refer to notional quantities during the relatively short period when the brand is advertised. This period is not necessarily uniform but in many cases it would be a month.

I have also found that +0.2 is rather a high figure. This is confirmed by data from MMA with typical elasticities in the range of 0.06 to 0.09, varying according to the level of advertising investment behind a brand. This general experience, together with my usual caution about interpreting statistics, has led me to concentrate on the lower range of elasticities, with +0.2 at the top of the range and not the average. I have examined the following levels: +0.05, +0.1, +0.15, and +0.2. In Table 9.1, these elasticities are applied to four hypothetical brands whose net sales value (NSV) is a uniform $100 million.[2] The table examines the immediate sales results of a 20% increase in advertising expenditure.

Each of the brands shows a sales increase in accordance with its advertising elasticity. However, this table tells us nothing about whether or not the sales increases are economic. We must now see how costs have been affected. There are three separate expenses that must be factored into the calculation:

1. The dollar cost of the extra advertising. The amount depends on the Advertising: Sales (A:S) ratio for the brand.

TABLE 9.1 Effect of Extra Advertising on Sales of 4 Brands With Net Sales Value of $100 Million During Advertised Period

Effect	Brand EAA	Brand EAB	Brand EAC	Brand EAD
Advertising elasticity	+0.05	+0.1	+0.15	+0.2
Additional advertising (%)	+20	+20	+20	+20
Additional sales (in millions)	+$1	+$2	+$3	+$4

2. The increase in direct costs (raw material, packaging, etc.) for the extra volume of output sold. This depends not only on the amount of extra sales but also on the share of a brand's total cost that is accounted for by direct costs.

3. The increase—if any—in indirect costs.

Tables 9.2 through 9.5 respectively use a grid for each of the four brands. Each table looks at two variables: the brand's A:S ratio and its ratio of direct costs out of total NSV. With such relatively small sales increases, 1%, 2%, 3%, and 4%, respectively, for the four brands, I am making the realistic assumption that these will not cause indirect costs to go up. The assumption is made that the firm's general overhead has enough slack in it to cover these modest sales increases. I am therefore estimating only the extra advertising cost and the additional direct costs.

In Tables 9.2 through 9.5, the additional advertising cost is signified by A, the extra direct costs by D, and the total of the two by T.

In the cases in which the extra advertising is profitable (i.e., the value of the incremental sales exceeds the extra costs), I have put an asterisk (*) in the appropriate box.

These four tables contain a total of 36 statistical cells representing varying advertising elasticities, A:S ratios, and proportions of total cost accounted for by directs. In 16 cases, the extra advertising is profitable; in 4 cases, the extra advertising breaks even; and in 16 cases—generally those with low elasticities—the advertising does not pay for itself.

With 20 positive and 16 negative examples, the odds are better than even that, in the short term, advertising expenditure will lift sales and also keep the brand in the black. With advertising run as a more-or-less continuous series of exposure periods (as recommended in Chapter 5), there is a better chance of it running profitably than if it runs intermittently over a 12-month period. This is

TABLE 9.2　Incremental Costs for Brand EAA ($ million) (advertising elasticity +0.05; incremental sales $1 million)

Direct Cost Ratio	A:S Ratio		
	4%	6%	8%
40%	A 0.8	A 1.2	A 1.6
	D 0.4	D 0.4	D 0.4
	T 1.2	T 1.6	T 2.0
50%	A 0.8	A 1.2	A 1.6
	D 0.5	D 0.5	D 0.5
	T 1.3	T 1.7	T 2.1
60%	A 0.8	A 1.2	A 1.6
	D 0.6	D 0.6	D 0.6
	T 1.4	T 1.8	T 2.2

TABLE 9.3　Incremental Costs for Brand EAB ($ million) (advertising elasticity +0.1; incremental sales $2 million)

Direct Cost Ratio	A:S Ratio		
	4%	6%	8%
40%	A 0.8	A 1.2	A 1.6
	D 0.8	D 0.8	D 0.8
	T 1.6*	T 2.0	T 2.4
50%	A 0.8	A 1.2	A 1.6
	D 1.0	D 1.0	D 1.0
	T 1.8*	T 2.2	T 2.6
60%	A 0.8	A 1.2	A 1.6
	D 1.2	D 1.2	D 1.2
	T 2.0	T 2.4	T 2.8

because, with the latter alternative, the advertised brand will suffer from the marketing activities of competitors. Continuity planning will therefore not only maintain sales at a higher level than a schedule with interruptions but is also *likely to be an economic rather than a loss-making activity.*

TABLE 9.4　Incremental Costs for Brand EAC ($ million) (advertising elasticity +0.15; incremental sales $3 million)

Direct Cost Ratio	A:S Ratio		
	4%	6%	8%
40%	A 0.8	A 1.2	A 1.6
	D 1.2	D 1.2	D 1.2
	T 2.0*	T 2.4*	T 2.8*
50%	A 0.8	A 1.2	A 1.6
	D 1.5	D 1.5	D 1.5
	T 2.3*	T 2.7*	T 3.1
60%	A 0.8	A 1.2	A 1.6
	D 1.8	D 1.8	D 1.8
	T 2.6*	T 3.0	T 3.4

TABLE 9.5　Incremental Costs for Brand EAD ($ million) (advertising elasticity +0.2; incremental sales $4 million)

Direct Cost Ratio	A:S Ratio		
	4%	6%	8%
40%	A 0.8	A 1.2	A 1.6
	D 1.6	D 1.6	D 1.6
	T 2.4*	T 2.8*	T 3.2*
50%	A 0.8	A 1.2	A 1.6
	D 2.0	D 2.0	D 2.0
	T 2.8*	T 3.2*	T 3.6*
60%	A 0.8	A 1.2	A 1.6
	D 2.4	D 2.4	D 2.4
	T 3.2*	T 3.6*	T 4.0

In the words of the Gatekeeper model, *although econometric estimates show that the medium-term effect of advertising is generally uneconomic (with costs greater than receipts), elasticity calculations often demonstrate that advertising can pay for itself in the very short term. This confirms the value of planning media to achieve a repetition of short-term effects, with maximum continuity.*

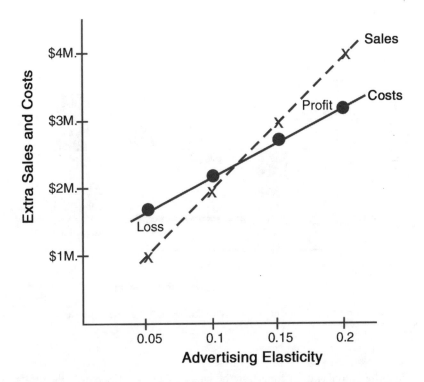

Figure 9.1. Extra Sales and Extra Costs for Brands With Different Advertising Elasticities
NOTE: A:S ratio 6%; direct cost proportion 50%.

Figure 9.1 concentrates on the average brand, with the middle A:S ratio (6%) and the middle proportion of direct costs (50%). It plots the incremental income/incremental cost relationship for the four different levels of advertising elasticity.

As an extension of Figure 9.1, the profit or loss for each level of advertising for our average brand is plotted in Figure 9.2. This diagram also suggests that advertising produces an incremental, long-term effect, and that one way of evaluating this is by measuring increases over time in the brand's advertising elasticity.

A progressive increase in advertising elasticity in subsequent years is a signal of advertising's ability to generate measurable long-term effects. The increase may be partly due to the extra, lagged effect on buying behavior that

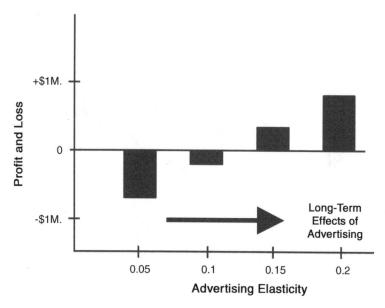

Figure 9.2. Profit and Loss for Brands With Different Advertising Elasticities
NOTE: A:S ratio 6%; direct cost proportion 50%.

follows the initial sales increase. In the language used in Chapter 8, the effect may be coming to some extent from increased purchase frequency from the new consumers triggered by the initial advertising stimulus. There is a well-known published example of this process. This describes the leading British brand of toilet tissue, Andrex, which had a short-term advertising elasticity of +0.06, and a boosted elasticity of +0.15 when the added effect of repeat purchase was included in the calculation.[3]

But although the idea of measuring the long-term effects of advertising by monitoring increasing advertising elasticity is a persuasive concept, how *practicable* is it to measure not only the elasticity for a single period but also to repeat the difficult calculations year after year?

Changes in Advertising Elasticity Over Time

Evidence exists from a small number of brands that an individual brand's advertising elasticity—measured repeatedly and accurately with state-of-the-art econometric techniques—can go up and down year by year. The problem is that the data cannot be published for reasons of confidentiality.

These annual variations rise and fall in response to changes in campaign, and thus they provide a valuable measure of each campaign's medium-term effect. The changes in the actual numbers are not very large, and small variations above and below the average do not necessarily indicate any long-term effects from advertising. However, in the examples that illustrate consistent (albeit small) annual improvements, long-term effects are making themselves felt. Most important, progressively rising figures can be extrapolated to provide year-by-year estimates of increases in profit (or reductions in loss) from measured doses of advertising, as shown in Figure 9.2. The value of an increasing advertising elasticity is its ability to provide another advertising-related measure of a gradual strengthening of the brand.

We need not feel totally frustrated by the lack of statistical material on the elasticities of specific brands that we are free to publish. Cases are available to demonstrate how advertising's productivity can be shown to increase over time, although these cases fall short of providing specific profit-and-loss estimates of this long-term effect. I describe two of them in the following sections.

Orkin Exterminating Company

Orkin is an organization in the business of protecting homes from termites and roaches: an activity concentrated in the warmer parts of the United States, where infestation is the greatest problem. The information that follows dates from the 1980s,[4] during which Orkin was the market leader (as it is today), providing a premium service in terms of both quality and price. At the time, the company treated about 17% of the 16 million American homes that used the services of professional exterminators every year.

The total market was declining. The most important reason for this was that, although the total housing stock increased slightly every year, the houses that had been treated for insect infestation removed themselves from the market because the protection lasts for a number of years. Out of the total housing stock, the proportion of protected homes therefore rose year by year, and the proportion of unprotected ones fell.

Orkin's advertising followed an unchanging strategy, and there was also much continuity in the creative expression. The campaign had always worked relatively directly to generate a stream of inquiries. The advertising was, in fact, an important driving force for the whole business. During the 1980s, the num-

bers of inquiries every year showed no signs of decline—in fact, just the opposite, with a general buoyancy and frequent increases in the number of leads that
came in.

Even with no significantly increased media investment behind the Orkin
campaign, the maintenance of, and even improvement in, response to the advertising among a shrinking total target audience provided clear evidence every
year of *progressive improvement in the medium-term response of advertising to
uniform media pressure.* Another way of saying this is that there was at the time
a gradually increasing advertising elasticity.

United States Marine Corps (USMC)

The facts from this case also date from the 1980s.[5] As with Orkin, the United
States Marine Corps recruitment advertising was addressing a declining target
population. This was partly because of a shrinkage in the number of young men,
aged 16 to 21, to whom the campaign was directed, as a result of population
trends and also because of reductions in some years in the propensity to join any
branch of the armed services, as a result of the competition of civilian job opportunities. The "propensity to join" is measured by regularly repeated research among a large sample of potential recruits. The data predict accurately
the actual number of recruits that join shortly afterward.

The USMC advertising plays an important role in stimulating recruitment. It
does two jobs:

1. It works directly to generate leads that eventually encourage a potential candi-
   date to visit a recruiting office, a task carried out by a large volume of direct mail
   literature.
2. It works indirectly to stimulate and nurture awareness of the ethos and spirit of
   the Corps, a job carried out by skillfully crafted television advertisements.

The strategy of the USMC campaign has not changed for decades, and there is
also strong continuity in the creative execution of this strategy.

The way to evaluate the productivity of the Marine Corps advertising is to
compare its yield with that of the advertising for the other branches of the armed
services, the army, navy, and air force. The proportion of young men indicating
a propensity to join the USMC increased steadily from 30% to 35% over the
period 1976 through 1986. This was almost certainly proof of the long-term effectiveness of the television campaign. The marines' improvement was specifi-

cally at the expense of the navy and the air force and was accomplished with an average advertising budget significantly lower than that for any other branch of the services. The USMC signed on 14% of all military recruits in the United States, with the support of an advertising budget for recruitment that was on a continuous basis only 12% of the total for all the armed services.

We can conclude from these facts that not only was the USMC advertising more productive, dollar for dollar, than that of the other services, but its advertising had done a *progressively more efficient job.* The advertising campaign was generating more responses per dollar, year by year, which is another way of saying that it was producing an increasing elasticity of response from a constant advertising investment.

Other Cases

It would be very surprising if there were not many more cases showing similar effects to those produced by Orkin and the United States Marine Corps. However, it is not sufficient merely to demonstrate increasing sales year after year. The cases must (as with these two examples) have the following characteristics:

1. There must be no change in the campaign during the period being examined: It must use the same creative concept, with approximately the same media expenditure.
2. There must be clear evidence of a direct influence of the campaign on sales in the short and medium term.
3. There must be a trend, year by year, showing *either* very strong share growth in a rising total category, *or* increasing sales in a stable category (hence an increasing share of market), *or* stable sales in a declining category (which also means increasing SOM).

A Further Look at Consumer Prices

Chapter 8 demonstrated that the largest brands—those that are generally strong because they have benefited from a positive long-term advertising heritage—can command significantly higher consumer prices that the average brands in their categories. The rather obvious reason is that the largest brands represent greater subjective value to the consumer, who will therefore pay the premium price.

A measurement exists to quantify this subjective value, a device well-established in the field of microeconomics. It is a parallel concept to advertising elasticity, discussed earlier in this chapter. The measure is price elasticity, a quantification of the responsiveness of a brand's sales to changes in consumer price, specifically *the measured response of sales to a 1% price reduction.* Because the relationship between price and sales is reciprocal (the first down, the second up), a price elasticity in almost all circumstances is preceded by a minus symbol.

If Brand A has a high price elasticity—if a reduction in its price will greatly increase its sales and if an increase in its price will substantially reduce them— then there is direct substitution between closely competitive brands within the category. If A's price goes down, consumers will buy more of A and less of B and C. If A's price goes up, the opposite will happen.

Manufacturers naturally like to price high in order to maximize profit. To do this, they need to block the substitution of competitive brands. This is a prime role for consumer advertising because of its ability to publicize Brand A's functional excellence and to create and build the brand's added values in the minds of consumers. Advertising can be seen then as a device not only to boost demand but also to impede substitution, which means that it *reduces the price elasticity of demand for the brand advertised.*

The elasticity of demand is worth studying, and an American academic, Gerard J. Tellis, published in 1988 a summary of the price elasticities of 367 different brands.[6] The calculation was made for each brand by averaging the response of sales to changes in price on a number of occasions. Tellis's average figure was −1.76, which shows a vastly greater raw response of sales to reductions in price than to increases in advertising. (The phrase "raw response" is used deliberately because the effect of price reductions on the *profitability* of brands is a different story, described later in this chapter.)

Sales promotions are essentially devices to reduce temporarily the prices charged by manufacturers to the retail trade and the end consumer. The high average price elasticity provides a powerful reason why promotions are so popular with manufacturers. These organizations are, however, less conscious of what promotions cost them in profit foregone.

Tables 9.6 and 9.7 describe the sales increases generated respectively by a 5% and a 10% price reduction for four hypothetical brands, each of which has a different price elasticity clustered around Tellis's average.

TABLE 9.6 Effect of 5% Price Reduction on Sales

Effect	Brand FAA	Brand FAB	Brand FAC	Brand FAD
Price elasticity	−1.6	−1.8	−2.0	−2.2
Initial volume (million units)	100	100	100	100
Initial net sales value (in millions)	$100	$100	$100	$100
Volume from price reduction (million units)	108	109	110	111
Net sales value from price reduction (in millions)	$103	$104	$105	$105

TABLE 9.7 Effect of 10% Price Reduction on Sales

Effect	Brand FAA	Brand FAB	Brand FAC	Brand FAD
Price elasticity	−1.6	−1.8	−2.0	−2.2
Initial volume (million units)	100	100	100	100
Initial net sales value (in millions)	$100	$100	$100	$100
Volume from price reduction (million units)	116	118	120	122
Net sales value from price reduction (in millions)	$104	$106	$108	$110

As with advertising elasticity, we can only fully judge the effect of price reductions by estimating the influence of the price reduction on a manufacturer's profit because his costs will also go up when he sells more merchandise. Various alternatives are worked out in Tables 9.8 and 9.9. The cost estimates have been rounded to nearest whole numbers.

Tables 9.8 and 9.9 do not paint an optimistic picture of the value of price reductions. It is only at the lowest ratio of direct costs and at the highest levels of price elasticity that they break even or yield a small profit. The reason is that price reductions take a large bite out of a brand's NSV. Added to this, the substantial increase in volume sold has to be paid for in direct costs, perhaps also by an increase in indirect costs because the volume increase is so much larger than that brought about by an increase in advertising expenditure. (I have not factored this possibility into my calculations.)

Remember also that price reductions have only a temporary effect; there is generally no hope of a further, lagged effect to generate more revenue to bal-

TABLE 9.8 Profit and Loss From 5% Price Reduction

Effect	Brand FAA	Brand FAB	Brand FAC	Brand FAD
Price elasticity	−1.6	−1.8	−2.0	−2.2
Extra net sales value from price reduction (in millions)	+ $3	+ $4	+ $5	+ $5
Extra costs at different ratios of direct (in millions)				
40%	+ $3	+ $4	+ $4	+ $4
50%	+ $5	+ $5	+ $6	+ $6
60%	+ $6	+ $7	+ $7	+ $7

TABLE 9.9 Profit and Loss From 10% Price Reduction

Effect	Brand FAA	Brand FAB	Brand FAC	Brand FAD
Price elasticity	−1.6	−1.8	−2.0	−2.2
Extra net sales value from price reduction (in millions)	+ $4	+ $6	+ $8	+ $10
Extra costs at different ratios of direct (in millions)				
40%	+ $6	+ $7	+ $8	+ $9
50%	+ $8	+ $9	+ $10	+ $11
60%	+ $10	+ $11	+ $12	+ $13

ance the increase in cost. Price reductions also encourage competitive retaliation and often have a negative influence on consumers' image of the brand.

I am most concerned here with the long-term influence of a brand's advertising on its responsiveness to price changes. The most interesting type of response is to price *increases*.

Table 9.10 describes three brands which cover a rather extreme range of price elasticities. Each has a net sales value of $100 million and a 40% ratio of direct costs. As can be seen, a 5% price increase causes a slight reduction in NSV despite the increased price per unit. But direct costs are also slightly increased.

The important point about this analysis is that *the profit picture improves with reductions in the brand's price elasticity.* The reason is that brands with a low elasticity are not easily substituted. Following a price increase, they therefore hang on to their sales to a greater degree than is the case with brands with a high price elasticity.

TABLE 9.10 Price Increase and Profit (Price +5%; Direct Cost Ratio 40%)

Effect	Brand FAZ	Brand FAB	Brand FAD
Price elasticity	−1.4	−1.8	−2.2
Original net sales value (in millions)	$100	$100	$100
New net sales value (in millions)	$ 98	$ 96	$ 93
New direct and indirect cost (in millions)	$ 97	$ 96	$ 96
Change in net profit (in millions)	+ $1	No change	− $3

TABLE 9.11 Price Elasticity Compared With Advertising Expenditure for 18 Typical MMA* Brands

Brand	Average Annual Gross Rating Points	Price Elasticity
18 brands total	2,300	−1.2
9 brands with high advertising	3,400	−1.0
9 brands with low advertising	1,200	−1.4

*MMA = Media Marketing Assessments.

Successful advertising, by its ability to reinforce a brand's uniqueness in the minds of its users, impedes substitution and thereby reduces the brand's price elasticity. Data from 18 typical brands analyzed by MMA—data confirmed from other MMA databases—confirm that brands with high advertising expenditure have a lower price elasticity than brands that spend less (see Table 9.11).

We can therefore conclude that successful advertising, by its ability to reduce a brand's price elasticity, restricts the amount of substitution if the brand's price is increased, and this progressively enables the brand to profit from price increases despite the reduction in sales volume that results.[7]

Harmony out of Discord

The study of advertising elasticity and price elasticity in this chapter has led to the following five conclusions, all of which are confirmed by a number of analyses from earlier in this book:

TABLE 9.12* "Safe" Underinvestment: Share of Voice (SOV) Below Share of Market (SOM)

	Share of Market		"Safe" Underinvestment	
Case	% Points	Index	% Points	Index
Table 7.2 top group	42 (rounded)	100	−24	−57
Table 7.3	20	100	−5	−25
Table 7.4	17	100	−3	−18
Table 7.5	13	100	−3	−23

* Repeat of Table 7.6 from Chapter 7.

1. Advertising elasticity tends to be low. Despite this, advertising can often be profitable in the short term, although it produces a generally small return in sales. On the other hand, advertising is rarely profitable in the medium term—over the course of a year—although in the medium term it can also produce at least some increase in volume.

2. One of the important long-term outcomes of effective advertising is that it gradually increases its own elasticity. Advertising becomes, over time, increasingly responsive to the amount of money spent on it. A large strong brand—one that has benefited from the long-term effects of previous advertising—is more responsive to advertising than a small weak brand is. A large strong brand can therefore underspend on advertising, in contrast to a small weak brand, which must overspend.

   This point is confirmed in Table 9.12, which is a repeat of Table 7.6 from Chapter 7. This table summarizes the share of voice/share of market relationship between four separate groups of large brands. The SOV is consistently and safely below SOM; the brands analyzed managed to maintain and sometimes even boost their shares of market despite the significant degree to which they underspent on advertising.

3. The increased productivity of advertising for large strong brands is also confirmed by their greater average payback in response to television advertising than is the case with small weak brands. This point was discussed in detail in Chapter 6 and is confirmed by Table 9.13 (which appeared in the earlier chapter as Table 6.11).

4. An important manifestation of the long-term effect of advertising is that it reduces a brand's price elasticity because the advertising contributes to making the brand unique in the estimation of consumers and thereby impedes the ability of competitive brands to be substituted for the advertised brand if its price is increased. Over time, successful advertising brings about a gradual reduction in the brand's price elasticity.

TABLE 9.13* Large and Small Brands: Payback Differences (30 brands)

Share of Market	Number of Brands	% Average Share of Market	Average Television Productivity (cents per $)
Total	30	32.0	50.6
Larger than average	13	61.6	56.0
Smaller than average	17	9.4	46.5

* Repeat of Table 6.11 from Chapter 6.

TABLE 9.14* Marketplace Prices of Brands in 12 Product Categories, 1991: Indexes Compared With Category Averages

All brands	100
Largest 10 brands	114
Second-largest 10 brands	110
Remaining 58 advertised brands	99
64 unadvertised brands	97

* Repeat of Table 8.10 from Chapter 8.

5. Because large strong brands are less price-elastic than small weak ones, the manufacturers of big brands can control consumer price more efficiently. This means that, because large brands are to some extent protected from competitors (as explained in Paragraph 4 above), they can command a higher price than small brands can. This is manifestly a description of the real world, as can be seen in Table 9.14 (which had earlier appeared in Chapter 8 as Table 8.10).

Such harmonies as these run throughout the various chapters in this book. This is a point that becomes even more evident in Chapter 10.

Notes

1. Gert Assmus, John U. Farlet, and Donald R. Lehmann, "How Advertising Affects Sales: Meta-Analysis of Econometric Results," *Journal of Marketing Research,* February 1984, 65-74.

2. A figure chosen for ease of exposition. Only a massive brand would have a net sales value of $100 million in a month.

3. Evelyn Jenkins and Christopher Timms, "The Andrex Story—A Soft, Strong and Very Long-Term Success," in *Advertising Works—Volume 4; Papers From the Institute of Practitioners in Advertising (IPA) Advertising Effectiveness Awards,* ed. Charles Channon (London: Cassell, 1987), 183-187.

4. John Philip Jones, *Does It Pay to Advertise? Cases Illustrating Successful Brand Advertising* (New York: Simon & Schuster-Lexington Books, 1989), 249-259.

5. Ibid., 277-291.

6. Gerard J. Tellis, "The Price Elasticity of Selective Demand: A Meta-Analysis of Econometric Models of Sales," *Journal of Marketing Research,* November 1988, 331-341.

7. Interesting data on the effect of advertising in reducing price elasticity, and on the effect of promotions in increasing it were presented at the *asi* European Advertising Effectiveness Symposium in Copenhagen, Denmark, 2001. Jean-Bernard Kazmierczak and E. Craig Stacey, *Long-Term Effects—A New Approach.* asi@dial.pipex.com

10

Frozen Effects Versus Continuous Effects: Snapshots Versus Movies

---

Econometric analysis is able to quantify in round terms the effect on sales of individual doses of advertising.

Econometric analysis can quantify approximately the size of the medium-term effect of advertising. It does this by estimating the value of the sales during a year that can be directly attributed to the campaign.

The long-term effects of advertising take the form of an enrichment of the brand and a strengthening of its relationship with the consumer. There are at least six ways in which this enrichment can be evaluated. The most important of them is a measure specific to the advertising itself.

This extract from the Gatekeeper model is meant to convey my main objective in writing this book: to establish some degree of advertising accountability. Advertising accountability means measuring the extent to which the financial outlay on the advertising campaign can be offset by the value of the business directly generated in the short, medium, and long term.

Advertising analysts will notice one major difference between my approach and the one normally adopted for describing advertising effects. The customary way of studying such effects is to track, over time, the movements of various measures that directly or indirectly stem from advertising, the most important of them being a brand's sales. Short-term sales responses to advertising are seen as bumps on the trend line: long-term effects by a gradual rise in the line from southwest to northeast. In the subtitle to this chapter, such analyses are described as movies, as opposed to snapshots.

Tracking studies can be based on many more measures than sales and are normally very useful as ways of demonstrating the dynamics of a market; 21 different types of tracking study are described in Appendix A at the end of this book. Such studies can show clearly that an advertising campaign is working (or not working), and they can diagnose at least partially *how* it is working (or not). They are expository devices used mainly to help people see trends.

Tracking studies cannot, however, provide accountability. The notion of accountability is derived, as the name implies, from the practice of balancing the financial outlays and receipts from business or personal affairs. It is impossible to do this without establishing a finite period—a week, a month, a year—hence my use of the word snapshot, as opposed to movies, to describe the time frame for the analysis. We must, in fact, find a way of freezing advertising effects so that we can do our counting and balancing, using data relating to a defined period.

The periods I have selected for measurement are as follows:

- *Short term:* Generally one week but occasionally (for methodological reasons) one month
- *Medium term:* One year
- *Long term:* One year

Although the medium-term and long-term measurements use the same accounting period, the difference between them is that in the medium term we are measuring effects generated strictly within 12 months. On the other hand, the long-term effects embrace changes that have taken place over many previous years but are *measured from data that cover one year.* The medium-term effect is calculated by econometric techniques. The long-term effect is measured (as explained in Chapter 7) by applying a weighting to the medium-term measure, a weighting derived from the long-term effects of a brand's advertising.

People familiar with tracking studies will notice that many such studies are harmonious with what I have described as long-term effects. These harmonies are apparent from a number of the tracking studies described in Appendix A. *Inter alia,* Figures A.11 and A.12 cover penetration and purchase frequency (discussed in Chapter 8), and Figure A.13 is devoted to the share of voice/share of market relationship (the topic of Chapter 7).

I must, however, make one thing clear. Many tracking studies focus on the long term exclusively and disregard other effects. Some analysts go so far as to deny the very existence of short-term effects and look only to a gradual and progressive strengthening of the effectiveness of a brand's advertising, starting from a very low base. I am convinced—as I have stated explicitly in the Gatekeeper model—that advertising must generate a positive short-term effect that is repeated to produce a medium-term effect that is generally lower than the short-term one and that a medium-term effect is, in turn, a precondition for further incremental effects. Thus, the beneficial things that advertising can accomplish in the long term are predicated on its ability to sell the brand—in the first instance inside a week and in the second instance inside a year.

Six Measures of the Long-Term Effects of Advertising

Six measures of advertising's long-term effects are shown in Figure 10.1. The four measures on the outside of the diagram are described as the peripherals, and the two in the middle are described as the core advertising factors. The six measures are grouped in this way for an important reason. Although all six can be calibrated with reasonable precision, only the core advertising factors measure the advertising itself. They are, in other words, the only tools available to provide advertising accountability without the use of surrogate measures.

As mentioned repeatedly in this book, the long-term effects of advertising are manifested by a strengthening of the brand. It is easy to see this process in action in connection with the four peripherals in Figure 10.1:

- *Penetration:* Increasing penetration directly drives share of market (as described in Chapter 8). Penetration generates breadth of usage, and large brands are generally strong brands. Penetration is normally directly influenced by advertising, and this is a particularly important process during the early years of a brand's life.
- *Purchase frequency:* Brands with a high share of market have significantly above-average purchase frequency (again as described in Chapter 8). Purchase

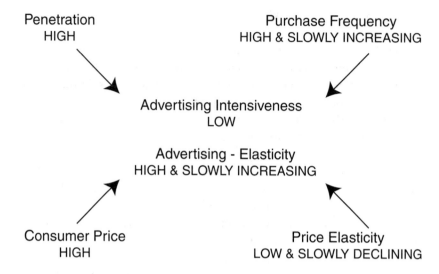

Figure 10.1. Long-Term Effects of Advertising

frequency provides depth and staying power to a brand. Advertising, working in combination with consumers' satisfaction with the functional performance of the brand, strongly influences purchase frequency. Purchase frequency is a centrally important dynamic for a mature brand.

- *Consumer price:* The largest brands in any category usually command the highest consumer prices (a topic discussed at the end of Chapter 8). High prices provide a double benefit to manufacturers. First, they signal high personal valuation of the brand on the part of consumers and therefore build a strong franchise. Advertising influences this. Second, high price generally means high profit. Another way of making this point is that manufacturers of large, strong brands are not compelled to undertake orgies of self-destructive sales promotions.

- *Price elasticity:* As discussed in Chapter 9, a long-term benefit of successful advertising is that it gradually engineers a reduction in a brand's price elasticity of demand. This makes it possible for a manufacturer to maintain sales volume when he increases price in order to boost his profit. One of the most important roles of advertising is to reduce substitution of other brands for the advertised brand if the price of the latter goes up, and this is what brings about the reduction in the price elasticity of the advertised brand.

I see the four peripherals as the most important indicators of a brand's health and growth. If the advertising is successful, its influence will inevitably be felt by these four measures. However, a number of readers will immediately think of something important that has been omitted from my list. Is not raw share of market the first and most obvious measure we should look at in appraising an advertising campaign? None of us needs to be reminded that advertising evaluation before the 1960s was based on this simple measure to the exclusion of everything else. It will also be noted that the majority of the excellent tracking studies described in Appendix A are based—in some cases exclusively—on SOM data.

Penetration, purchase frequency, consumer price, and price elasticity are all ultimately expressions of share of market. But because they are measures of consumer behavior, they are more relevant to evaluating advertising than SOM is on its own, as the latter can be influenced by stimuli other than advertising (e.g., retail distribution and out-of-stock). All four peripherals are based on studying the people to whom advertising is aimed. They therefore have the great merit of monitoring advertising directly rather than indirectly.

This brings us finally to the two core advertising factors, advertising-intensiveness and advertising elasticity. These are not linked to consumer behavior in as straightforward a fashion as the four peripherals are. But the idea, repeatedly emphasized in this book, that the long-term effects of advertising bring about a strengthening of the brand, means that effective advertising reinforces the four peripherals. And this is a process that can be efficiently and clearly measured through changes in the two core advertising factors.

The connection is quite logical. If the four peripherals are powerful, and as a result the brand has a strong marketing impetus, the advertising does not have to work particularly hard to do its job. This means a lower advertising-intensiveness and a higher advertising elasticity. On the other hand, if the four peripherals are weak, the advertising has a harder job to do—hence a higher advertising-intensiveness and a lower advertising elasticity. Because the core advertising factors are both measured in terms of the advertising itself, *they provide the key to accountability.*

Of the two core advertising factors, advertising elasticity is the more precise measure because it is on its own virtually a definition of advertising effectiveness. But the problem with using it, as we saw in Chapter 9, is the thinness of the empirical data. None is in fact available for publication, although the few unpublished examples are highly persuasive. An indirect way of measuring elasticity is with the techniques of the shifting demand curve and shifting response function, discussed in Appendix B. But these ingenious devices also suffer from the limitation in the amount of available empirical support.

We are left with advertising-intensiveness, which is anything but a poor man's alternative. It has the great advantage of being a simple device, and it is one that can be brought into play case by case with the use of relatively plentiful supporting data. The next section of this chapter shows how it has been employed with a number of real brands.

Advertising Accountability in Practice

I now return to the brands in the MMA database and incorporate advertising expenditure information alongside the econometric deconstruction data for each brand. Of the 35 brands featured in Chapter 6, the number has now shrunk to 17. With my usual caution in the use of statistics I concentrate on the brands for which full and comparable data are available and scrutinize each brand separately to eliminate outliers. The information for the 17 brands is presented in Table 10.1.

The data for these 17 brands are presented in the same form as in Table 7.7 in Chapter 7. The table is in two separate parts because of the large number of variables that is covered. Accountability is the concern of Part 2. The first key measure is the medium-term percentage payback (as described in Chapter 6). This is based on the estimate made by MMA of the cash return (in cents) for each dollar of television advertising investment over the course of the year.

I now go further by estimating the long-term effects of advertising that should be added to the medium-term effects. The method is as follows: Each medium-term payback figure is weighted according to the brand's Sales-Weighted Budget Index (SWBI). This index is calculated to represent how much the brand's share of voice is smaller or larger than its share of market (which is given the value of 100). SOV below SOM means relatively productive and economic advertising; SOV above SOM means relatively unproductive and uneconomic advertising. A low SOV means extra profit, and this is in essence the measure of the long-term result of effective advertising.

If the SWBI is below 100 (i.e., SOV below SOM), then the medium-term payback is inflated by multiplying the payback by 100/SWBI. This represents the addition of a strong long-term effect to the medium-term effect. On the other hand, if the SWBI is above 100 (i.e., SOV above SOM), then the medium-term payback is deflated. This means that the medium-term effect is actually reduced because the brand loses profit by having to overadvertise. Eight brands

TABLE 10.1 Medium-Term Plus Long-Term Effects of Advertising for 17 MMA* Brands, 1997

			Part 1	
Brand	*% TV Share of Voice*	*% Share of Market*	*TV Share of Voice Minus Share of Market, % Points*	*Sales-Weighted Budget Index*
22	13.8	65.2	−51.4	22
11	9.9	37.0	−27.1	27
7	9.4	33.2	−23.8	28
25	23.2	68.4	−45.2	34
18	8.4	13.9	−5.5	60
1	14.8	20.7	−5.9	71
16	49.3	60.0	−10.7	82
19	3.0	3.3	−0.3	91
10	13.8	12.8	+1.0	108
21	20.6	17.6	+3.0	117
5	28.8	24.2	+4.6	119
15	9.5	6.7	+2.8	142
27	3.0	2.0	+1.0	150
17	98.5	62.3	+36.2	158
26	28.8	17.2	+11.6	167
35	7.7	4.5	+3.2	171
30	3.1	1.6	+1.5	194

* MMA = Media Marketing Assessment.

			Part 2		
Brand	*(Medium-Term) TV Percentage Payback (cents per advertising $, rounded)*	*(Medium-Term TV Plus Long-Term) Weighted Percentage Payback (cents per advertising $)*	*TV Advertising Budget ($ million)*	*TV Advertising Deficit (cents per advertising $)*	*TV Absolute Advertising Deficit ($ million)*
22	93	Over 100	10.9	Nil	Nil
11	22	81	0.3	19	0.1
7	(60)	Over 100	(10.8)	Nil	Nil
25	72	Over 100	21.4	Nil	Nil
18	37	62	6.0	38	2.3
1	31	44	3.0	56	1.7
16	84	Over 100	14.4	Nil	Nil
19	53	58	2.2	42	1.9

(Continued)

Table 10.1   (Part 2 Continued)

Brand	(Medium-Term) TV Percentage Payback (cents per advertising $, rounded)	(Medium-Term TV Plus Long-Term) Weighted Percentage Payback (cents per advertising $)	TV Advertising Budget ($ million)	TV Advertising Deficit (cents per advertising $)	TV Absolute Advertising Deficit ($ million)
10	31	29	5.5	71	3.9
21	95	81	(11.4)	19	2.2
5	57	47	21.2	53	11.2
15	68	48	7.4	52	3.9
27	43	29	11.4	71	8.1
17	41	26	6.0	74	4.5
26	19	11	6.5	89	5.8
35	19	11	0.4	89	0.4
30	30	15	10.4	85	9.3

NOTE: Figures in parentheses represent averages for a number of years.

have a SWBI below 100, demonstrating positive long-term effects from advertising; 9 brands are above 100, demonstrating negative long-term effects.

With the brands in Table 10.1 that are seen to cover their advertising cost (brands numbered 22, 7, 25, and 16), I have not quantified the absolute size of the advertising surplus when the medium-term and long-term effects are added together.

Besides my usual care in the use of statistics, there is another reason for my avoiding this extrapolation. Although it is a matter of some importance that the advertising passes the payback threshold—that it turns red into black ink—the absolute differences between the sizes of the surpluses are rather small, remembering that the advertising expenditure as a percentage of net sales value for most brands of repeat-purchase packaged goods is only in the 6% bracket.

I am therefore not at all sure that, once we have passed the threshold, maximizing the positive advertising payback is a useful operational objective because it diverts attention from more important matters. In planning advertising, the job that needs by far the greatest attention is the broad strategy, in particular to plan campaigns that are properly balanced between short-term sales effects and long-term brand building, with the aim of boosting sales volume and profit in both the short and long term. This requires skill, experience, and commit-

TABLE 10.2 Medium-Term Plus Long-Term Advertising Effects: Summary of 17
MMA* Brands, 1997

Total number of brands	17
Number of brands showing	
Positive net return	4
Deficit under 50% of advertising budget	4
Deficit 50%-75% of advertising budget	6
Deficit over 75% of advertising budget	3

* MMA = Media Marketing Assessment.

ment of a high order. However, in this difficult task, I believe that it is liberating
to know that the advertising for the brand, particularly if it is a large one, will in
all likelihood be a no-cost investment. But it is irrelevant to attempt to "micro-
manage" an eventual surplus—of 20 cents or 30 cents or whatever—on the advertising dollar.

The skeleton of Table 10.1 is presented in Table 10.2, and the relationship for
each brand between its share of market and advertising deficit is illustrated as a
scatterplot in Figure 10.2.

No robust generalizations are possible from a sample as small as 17 brands.
However, from these and other brands I have known in detail during my professional career, I think that the following conclusions are fair:

- *Most important,* there are circumstances in which advertising *can* pay for itself
  when the medium-term and long-term effects are added to one another.
- The number of brands whose advertising pays for itself represents a substantial
  minority, one-quarter of our small sample.
- A further substantial minority of brands runs advertising that pays for more than
  half its cost, a further one-quarter of our small sample.
- The brands that benefit from high advertising productivity are mostly the larger
  ones (SOM of 20% or more), but there are exceptions. The regression in Figure
  10.2 points clearly in this direction, although the correlation itself is relatively
  weak.
- In my personal experience, the small number of minor brands that show an advertising surplus tend to be those with a specialist franchise: a relatively small group
  of users who are loyal to the brand.

These are all important findings, although an even more significant conclusion is that *the statistical methods are now available to measure advertising's*

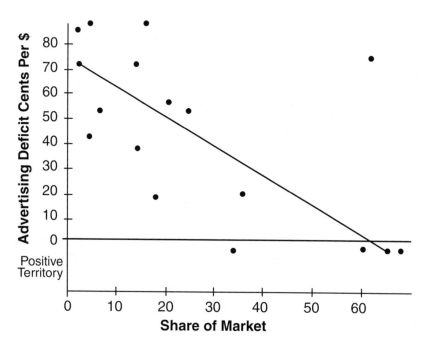

Figure 10.2. Scatterplot of Relationship Between Share of Market and Advertising Deficit for 17 MMA* Brands
* MMA = Media Marketing Assessment.

medium-term and long-term productivity for specific brands. These are a real addition to advertisers' battery of analytical tools. Calculating the medium-term effect is complex and difficult. However, once this has been done, estimating the incremental long-term effects is a surprisingly simple procedure.

These conclusions form a suitable ending to the main text of this book. But as a confirmation of my most important conclusion, that advertising is capable of paying its own way, I describe briefly two real and identified brands, whose sales performances have been rigorously analyzed and also shown to provide surpluses on their advertising account. The two examples are British and published by the Institute of Practitioners in Advertising (IPA), the professional association of British advertising agencies, whose exemplary work in pioneering objective advertising evaluation is also illustrated in the case studies discussed in Appendix A. The campaigns I describe are from two major British advertisers: Ford Motor Company and Alliance and Leicester Building Society, a mortgage lender.

Two Campaigns That Pay Their Way

Ford's Galaxy

Soon after its launch, Ford's Galaxy became the market leader in what is described in Great Britain as the "People Movers" automobile segment. These are van-type passenger vehicles with a large seating capacity.[1]

The A:S ratio in the car business is low because even large advertising budgets are very much smaller than the net sales value of the vehicles sold. Thus, if advertising succeeds in generating even a small percentage increase in sales volume, this is likely to translate into a large sales *value,* a geared effect that is likely to produce a positive return on the advertising investment. With the Galaxy, this return was dramatic.

The Galaxy was launched in Summer 1995, and within three months of its launch had achieved 40% of volume sales in its segment. Taking account of many other factors influencing sales, and also comparing Galaxy's British performance with what happened in other European countries, the advertising agency estimated that during the marque's first year, the advertising campaign on its own accounted for extra sales of 9,000 Galaxy cars, representing incremental gross revenue of £131 million (US$216 million).

This gross revenue was conservatively estimated to generate £33 million (US$54 million) of contribution to overhead after paying for the direct costs of the extra vehicles sold. This estimated contribution should be compared with the cost of the advertising campaign—£7 million (US$12 million)—thus yielding a surplus far greater in both absolute and proportionate terms than in any of the examples discussed so far in this book.

Five other examples published in the IPA series of case studies also come from the automotive field, and these all show a surplus on the advertising account, although in all cases a smaller one than that produced by the Galaxy. The surplus from the Galaxy campaign was remarkable, although one should remember that it was almost certainly eroded over time as a consequence of the normal onset of diminishing returns.

Alliance and Leicester

In Great Britain, building societies are old established financial organizations that attract mass savings, and they use the funds to make long-term loans to individuals to buy real estate.[2] They are traditionally managed in a highly conservative fashion. Various mergers have taken place in the industry over the past three decades, and Alliance and Leicester (A&L), an amalgamation of two separate firms, became in the mid-1980s the sixth largest building society measured by total assets (i.e., mortgage loans outstanding).

A new advertising campaign that began in 1987 emphasized the probity, reliability, and straightforward and conservative nature of A&L and did so in a surprisingly original and involving way. The communication was concerned essentially with the psychological associations of the organization in the minds of depositors and borrowers, since functional differences are not important: Building societies all use similar types of contract and offer and charge approximately the same rates of interest. The campaign had both an immediate and a long-term effect. These effects were evaluated in terms of business generated and also by diagnostic tracking of the brand and its advertising campaign among consumers.

A complex econometric evaluation produced an estimate that the additional business directly generated by the advertising campaign amounted over a 5-year period to £656 million (US$1.08 billion) in deposits from members of the public. In addition, over the same period a projection was made of long-term advertising effects amounting to a further £554 million (US$910 million). This was calculated by comparing the actual trend in the business from the new campaign with the much less positive trend from the campaign that had preceded it.

The analysis therefore estimated that a large increment—approximately £1.2 billion (US$2 billion) of deposits—stemmed directly or indirectly from the new advertising campaign. (But although this is a large sum in absolute terms, it represents less than 3% of A&L's total business). In turn, this extra business was estimated to produce a gross profit of £93 million (US$153 million) over the 5-year period, at an aggregate cost of £22 million (US$36 million) in advertising. This suggests a surplus of large dimensions.

A&L, in common with manufacturers of cars and other high-ticket items, is a commercial enterprise that operates with low advertising-to-sales ratios and generates large sales values, so that even a modest percentage sales response produces large incremental revenue. There is therefore a strong likelihood that the advertising expenses will be comfortably covered by extra revenue. But even bearing this in mind, the A&L campaign did particularly well.

Conclusions

These two cases will boost the natural optimism of advertising practitioners. However, because of the special characteristics of the businesses—the low A:S ratios and the large value of the sales/deposits—they are untypical, and the range of brands in Table 10.1 provides a better guide to what can usually be expected. The estimates in Table 10.1 are derived from the field of repeat-purchase packaged goods, which is characterized by A:S ratios that account for a more perceptible proportionate chunk of receipts than is the case with cars and financial services.

It must also be borne in mind that, although the majority of advertisers will still run their advertising operations by making a net investment, producing as little as 10 to 50 cents on the dollar, advertising still usually works to *maintain a brand's sales level.* The sales of most major brands will generate significant scale economies. These will invariably keep costs and prices low, a process that continuously stimulates consumer demand and so keeps the wheels of business turning. For this reason, for most businesses, advertising has an important role at the heart of their operations. But for a special few brands that can now be identified, the advertising itself also makes money.

Notes

1. John Howkins, "Ford Galaxy: Building Brand Value for Ford," in *Advertising Works: Volume 10. Cases From the IPA Advertising Effectiveness Awards,* ed. Nick Kendall (Henley-on-Thames, UK: NTC Publications, 1999), 401-422.

2. Will Collin, "Alliance and Leicester Building Society: Advertising Effectiveness, 1987-1991," in *Advertising Works: Volume 7. Cases From the IPA Advertising Effectiveness Awards,* ed. Chris Baker (Henley-on-Thames, UK: NTC Publications, 1993), 359-382.

Appendix A:
Tracking Studies

The traditional way to examine the effects of advertising is to follow continuously the progress of a brand's sales alongside different variables that are directly or indirectly connected with them (e.g., advertising, consumer price, retail distribution, and seasonality). This tracking is carried out using techniques that vary widely in their sophistication and purity (i.e., their ability to isolate the influence of advertising from the many other stimuli that affect the sales of a brand).

The marketing literature is full of tracking studies, and this appendix is devoted to examining their range. It features exclusively examples taken from a single collection, one that represents the most solid corpus of case-study material on advertising available anywhere. This body of cases has been built up over the past two decades by the Institute of Practitioners in Advertising (IPA) from studies submitted by the British marketing and advertising communities for the annual IPA Advertising Effectiveness Awards.

More than 600 cases are now available in electronic form,[1] and the best of these have been brought together and published in 11 substantial hardback volumes (a new one comes out every second year). In view of the range and analytical rigor of the IPA collection, it is difficult to understand why these British cases are not more widely studied in the United States.

The 21 examples featured in this appendix were chosen from the IPA cases published since 1990. All 21 were chosen as being typical, although the number of different tracking studies that *can* be carried out is very large indeed. My selections are illustrations of the techniques, and the facts of the individual cases are touched on only briefly.

There are two basic types of tracking study. First, what I call simple studies show the progress over time of a single variable or a number of separate (generally unconnected) variables affecting a brand. Second, complex or multivariate studies examine a number of separate influences on a brand's marketplace performance, but they aim to compare the effects of these influences and to evaluate their relative importance. This is a difficult procedure, but it can enable the role of advertising, in particular, to be isolated. The technique requires high-order mathematics, and the most common method, multivariate regression, is what gave this type of tracking its name.

Virtually all the IPA studies feature simple tracking. A substantial minority also use multivariate tracking, and these are of particular interest because they represent analyses at the state of the art.

Simple Studies

When advertising is successful and succeeds by working directly, it is generally possible to detect a close relationship between the advertising and the consumer action that it prompts. Figure A.1 shows the progress of a campaign to persuade the Scottish public to stop smoking. The television campaign is indicated by the vertical bars, and the numbers of telephone calls requesting help to quit smoking are shown by the continuous line. The connection between the two variables is not invariably precise, but the cause-and-effect relationship is quite clear.[2]

In this diagram (as in most of the others in this appendix), the two variables are totally different in nature from one another, but the scales used for comparing them are chosen to emphasize the tightness of the fit between the two. This is an arbitrary but generally legitimate procedure, although on occasion it can exaggerate the closeness of the relationship and therefore mislead by implying visually a stronger connection between cause and effect than actually exists.

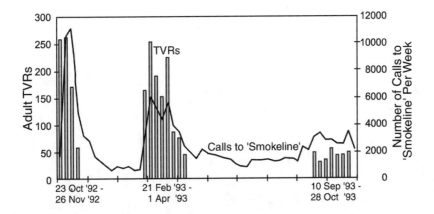

Figure A.1. Health Education Board for Scotland Antismoking Television
Advertising and Television Inquiries

Figure A.2 introduces two variables in addition to advertising: sales tracked
for heavy and light television viewers separately. The brand in question is
Nescafé Gold Blend, whose campaign used a series of commercials featuring a
man and a woman who became romantically involved when one of them borrowed a jar of Gold Blend from the other (a campaign that was also used by
Nestlé in the United States). The objective of the advertising was to stimulate
interest in the stories in the commercials with the aim of boosting interest in the
brand's starring role. The heavier television viewers, who would have seen
more of the advertisements, would therefore have been likely to buy more Gold
Blend than light viewers would. Figure A.2 shows this hypothesis to be valid.[3]

Figures A.1 and A.2 have described ongoing campaigns. A close relationship between advertising and sales can often also be established in successful
new brand introductions, but it should also be remembered that these are rather
rare. Figure A.3 shows what happened when Häagen-Dazs ice cream was introduced into the United Kingdom. The response of sales to the periods of intro-
ductory advertising was quite direct.[4]

The examples so far have illustrated the immediate, short-term effect of advertising. However, in Figure A.2, the sequential short-term effects are super-
imposed on an upward trend in the consumption of Gold Blend by heavy television viewers. Tracking studies are extensively used for the explicit purpose of
demonstrating long-term trends. Figure A.4 shows a 4-year sales trend con-

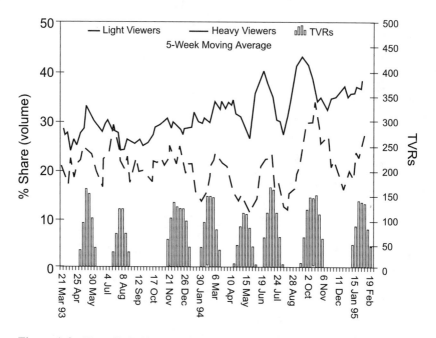

Figure A.2. Nescafé Gold Blend Television Advertising and Share of Market by Heavy and Light Television Viewers

nected with a new advertising campaign for Stella Artois, an expensive brand of imported beer (represented by the heavy line at the top of the chart). Note that the sales of the other five brands are quite flat over a period of 6 years, thus emphasizing the significance of Stella Artois's performance.[5]

Figure A.5 demonstrates a slightly more subtle point. It tracks the worldwide sales of diamond jewelry, which are ultimately controlled by the international cartel De Beers. Over a 5-year period, sales of diamond jewelry, measured by individual rings, brooches, and other pieces, declined slightly. However, the dollar value of sales significantly increased.[6] This was partly a result of the advertising campaign run by De Beers, and the cognitive effects of this are shown in Table A.1, discussed later in this appendix.

One of the best ways of tracking long-term movements is to use moving totals or moving averages. A moving total for a year (although it can be done for any period) starts with the total for the first 12 months—for example, January through December 1999. The next figure is arrived at by adding January 2000

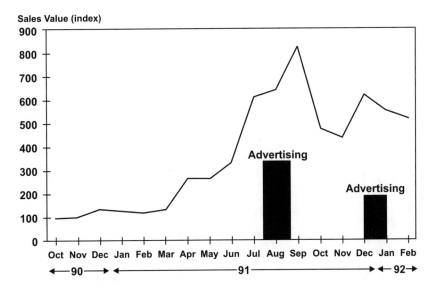

Figure A.3. Introduction of Häagen-Dazs Ice Cream in Television Advertising and Value of Retail Sales

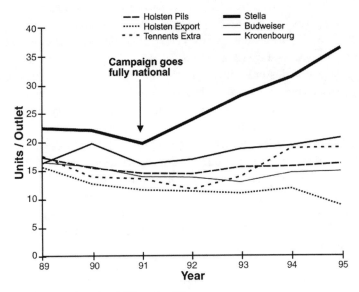

Figure A.4. Sales Trends of 6 Brands of Beer

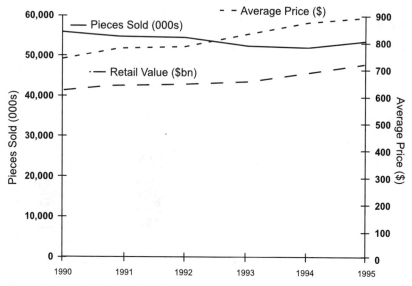

Figure A.5. Worldwide Sales of Diamond Jewelry

and subtracting January 1999. We next add February 2000 and subtract February 1999, and so the progression continues. A moving average for a month (again, any period can be chosen) is arrived at by taking the first year's total and dividing it by 12, then adding January 2000 and subtracting January 1999 and dividing the new total by 12, and so on.

The object of this procedure is to smooth short-term movements, particularly seasonal ups and downs, and concentrate them as the resultant trend line. In Figure A.6, this process is shown in action for two major brands of chocolate confectionery, Roses and Quality Street.[7]

Figures A.1 through A.6 relate advertising to sales. Tracking studies are also employed very widely to show how advertising influences nonbehavioral variables—in particular, various measures of cognitive effect:

- *Advertising awareness,* that is, whether the campaign can be recalled by the public either spontaneously or by being prompted (sometimes both)
- *Brand awareness,* measured either spontaneously or by being prompted (also sometimes both)
- *Brand associations,* that is, whether the brand is associated in the consumer's mind with certain specific functional features and nonfunctional attributes

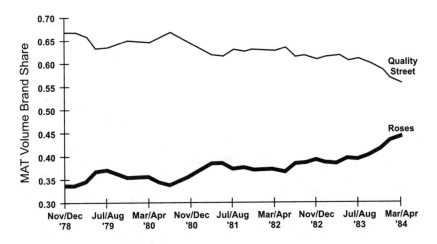

Figure A.6. Moving Annual Totals for Brand Shares of Roses and Quality Street

Figure A.7 illustrates the launch of an extremely successful new brand of mobile telephone with the unusual name "Orange." Spontaneous brand awareness of Orange (shown in the heavy line) is seen to be increasing strongly and largely without interruption, a rise obviously associated with the periods of advertising (indicated by the horizontal lines enclosed within arrowheads). Orange's strong upward trend contrasts with the unchanging awareness levels of each of the 5 competitive brands.[8]

Figure A.8, also devoted to Orange and its competitors, examines a series of brand associations embodied in three separate phases: "sets the standard for the future," "leads the way in new technology," and "is dynamic." How much consumers agree with these phrases is given an averaged score for each brand. The rapid growth in the average score for Orange is again compared with the flat or declining scores for leading competitive brands. The periods of advertising for Orange are indicated by the horizontal lines, as in Figure A.7, and again the relationship is clear.[9]

The Orange research is concerned with the launch of a new brand, and with such successful launches the measures can show strong increases. With existing brands, cognitive measures are usually extremely stable. Figure A.9 tracks the average of a number of consumer attitude measures relating to 6 leading marques of car. Note that the left vertical scale only covers the top range of variations, but even with this rather exaggerated presentation of the data, consumer

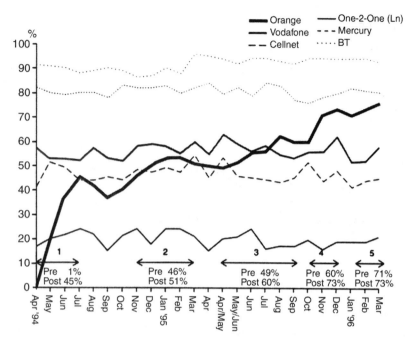

Figure A.7. Spontaneous Awareness of Brand-Name Orange Related to Periods of Advertising

attitudes change very little over a period of 5 years.[10] (This stability echoes the trends in Figures A.7 and A.8 for the existing brands that were on the market before Orange.)[10]

Long-term cognitive tracking can provide confirmation that an advertising campaign is having a progressive effect as planned. In other words, it can provide valuable post hoc diagnostic information. Figure A.10 describes the continuous tracking of consumer awareness of advertising for the Meat & Livestock Commission, whose advertising campaign was aimed at raising the public profile of beef. Figure A.10 shows that the advertising campaign that ran between 1990 and 1993 was remembered by a steady proportion of people, although there was a good deal of short-term volatility in the awareness figures.

With a new campaign introduced in 1994, the average level of awareness jumped up to a higher plateau, which was maintained for the next 4 years, albeit with a similar pattern of up-and-down movements to the earlier period. The advertising campaigns ran over the whole 8 years relatively continuously, and

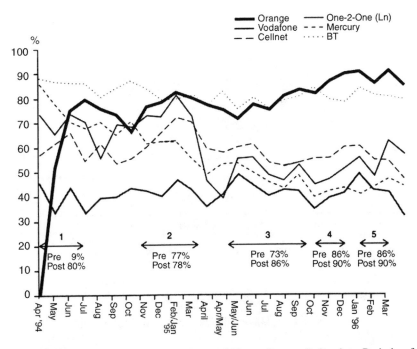

Figure A.8. Image Associations of Brand-Name Orange Related to Periods of Advertising

there does not appear to have been a higher level of expenditure during the last 4 years than during the earlier period. The new campaign was therefore clearly more memorable.[11]

Image attributes can change gradually over time. Table A.1 shows such changes in consumer perceptions of diamond jewelry.[12] Note the overall similarity between the trends in both the United States and Great Britain. In both countries, diamonds maintained a high rating for "worth the expense" while showing perceptible improvements in the other measures. The increasing strength of consumers' personal valuation of diamond jewelry therefore helps explain the increasing dollar value of sales, seen in Figure A.5.

One of the most useful types of tracking study is one that relates a brand's advertising not only to its market share but also to its penetration. Figure A.11 tracks these data for Unilever's remarkable brand of margarine "I Can't Believe It's Not Butter," a brand that had been marketed first in the United States with similar success. Figure A.11 shows the development of the brand's SOM from

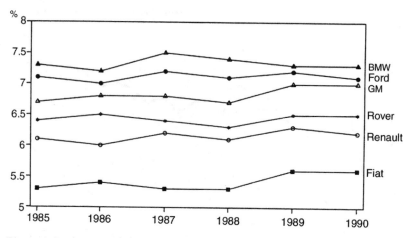

Figure A.9. Image Associations of 6 Leading Automobile Marques

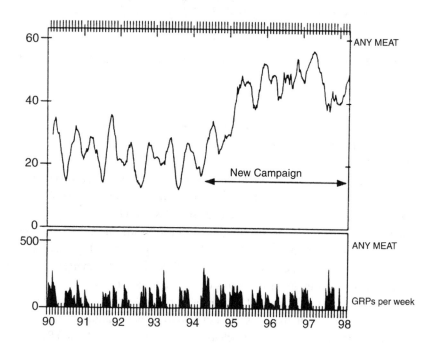

Figure A.10. Meat & Livestock Commission Advertising Campaign: Claimed Advertising Awareness

TABLE A.1   Image Perceptions of Diamond Jewelry: United States and Great
Britain (in percentages)

Percentage of People Agreeing:	*1991*	*1992*	*1993*	*1994*	*1995*
United States					
"Expression of love"	69	70	70	76	81
"Diamonds are more beautiful than any other stone"	53	56	55	59	58
"Best way of marking an important occasion in one's life"	52	52	47	55	61
"Worth the expense"	65	60	61	65	65
Great Britain					
"Ultimate gift of love"	59	61	61	67	64
"Best way of marking an important occasion in one's life"	54	51	52	55	79
"King of all precious stones"	61	56	63	63	65
"Worth the expense"	66	67	65	67	67

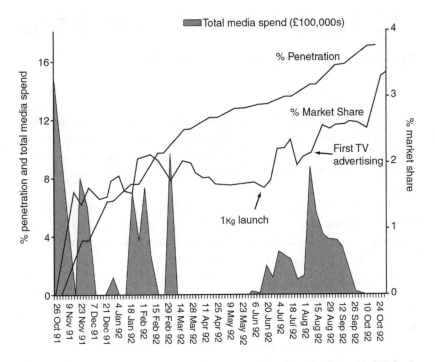

Figure A.11. Share of Market, Penetration, and Advertising for Launch of "I Can't
Believe It's Not Butter"

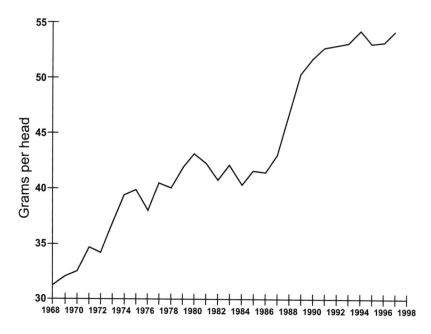

Figure A.12. Growth in Per Capita Consumption of Marmite

the time of its launch: a generally upward progression despite interruptions. The growth of penetration is steady. This pinpoints clearly that the main task for the brand would now be to boost purchase frequency in order to enable sales growth to keep up with penetration growth.[13] This case underlines the lessons in Chapter 8.

A similar analysis can be used to explain the success of Marmite, an old-established strong-tasting savory yeast extract that is spread on bread and toast, particularly at breakfast. (The Australians eat enormous quantities of a similar brand called Vegemite.) Despite Marmite's long history, advertising success-fully boosted the brand's sales. And as can be seen in Figure A.12, this success was due to a relatively steady increase in the brand's purchase frequency. Dur-ing the years 1985–1997, the brand's household penetration rose by 12%, but the per capita consumption (roughly equivalent to purchase frequency) went up by 35%.[14] This is another confirmation of the conclusions in Chapter 8.

The last example of simple tracking shows a rare method but one that pro-vides an insight into how advertising productivity can grow. The procedure is

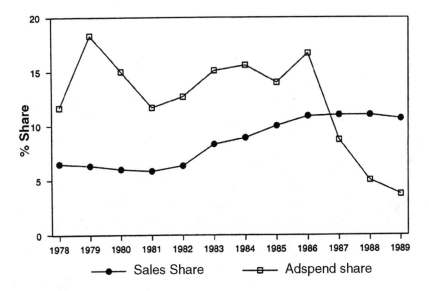

Figure A.13. Share of Voice and Share of Market for Stella Artois

based on a brand's share of voice/share of market relationship, the topic of Chapter 7 of this book. Figure A.13 plots the changes year by year in the SOV and SOM for Stella Artois, the brand of beer examined in Figure A.4. The sharp drop in the brand's SOV (described in Great Britain as Adspend Share) during the period when its SOM was holding steady and its volume sales were increasing significantly, is the clearest possible illustration of the increasing productivity of Stella Artois's advertising.[15]

Complex or Multivariate Studies

The IPA case studies include a substantial minority that employ multivariate regression to deconstruct the sales of a brand, in particular to isolate the influence of advertising on those sales. As discussed in Chapter 6, this procedure is often called model building, the model in question describing and quantifying the size of the various inputs that determine a brand's sales. I selected six cases to illustrate the methods used, and these are all exceptionally important. (Readers

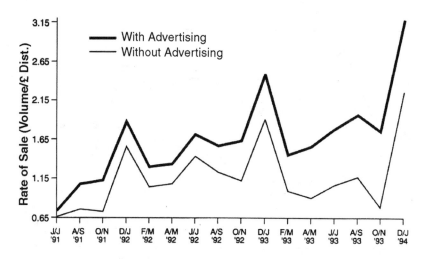

Figure A.14. Rate of Sale With and Without Advertising for Boddington's Beer in Cans

will also remember that I discussed in Chapter 10 the estimates of advertising profitability made in two further IPA cases: those for the Ford Galaxy and the Alliance & Leicester Building Society, a mortgage lender. These examples are based on the sensitive interpretation of considerable statistical data.)

In all these studies, the measurement is made by sophisticated statistical analysis, and the simple diagrams explaining the findings should not mislead the reader into thinking that the analyses are in any way facile.

Figure A.14 presents in a straightforward way the incremental effects of advertising. The brand in question is Boddington's, a beer with great market strength in the north of England and one that is advertised with considerable finesse. In Figure A.14, the volume sales of Boddington's in cans are indexed to maintain confidentiality and are calculated to show sales for each percentage point of weighted distribution (thus factoring out of the calculation any changes in the distribution itself). Figure A.14 shows the modeled rate of sale, over time, *with* advertising and *without* advertising. The difference between the two trend lines is clear, and the gap between them is seen to widen after a year and a half of the advertising campaign.[16] This is visual evidence of a long-term effect.

Figure A.15 illustrates the progress of Cadbury's Boost, a filled chocolate bar directly competitive with the Mars bar so familiar to American chocolate consumers. Figure A.15 tracks the sales of Boost *with* and *without* advertising

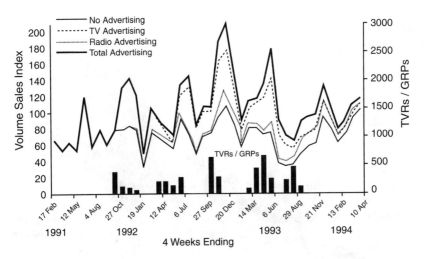

Figure A.15. Sales and Advertising, by Medium, for Boost Chocolate Bar

(the top and bottom lines on the chart). It shows in addition the contributions to sales made separately by television and radio advertising. Both have a significant effect, but the contribution of television was, as would be expected, greater than radio.[17]

Figure A.16 presents the data in a similar way as done by Figures A.14 and A.15, but this time, the brand's sales are deconstructed to measure the separate contributions of (a) advertising, (b) the brand's distribution, and (c) general economic growth in the economy. The brand is Johnson & Johnson's Clean & Clear medicated skin lotion, and the period covered was when the brand was effectively launched. (Clean & Clear had been available in stores during the preceding 2 years but had not been successfully promoted.) Figure A.16 demonstrates the relative sales performances of two commercials, "Girls Talking" and "Real Girls," which were run sequentially. They both had a measurable effect in the marketplace, but the second generated considerably more sales than the first, although the diagram does not answer the question whether the superior performance of "Real Girls" may have been at least partly due to synergy with the improved brand distribution and better economic conditions that were happening when this commercial was run.[18]

Figure A.17 tracks the sales *with* and *without* advertising for Knorr stock cubes. "Moira" and "Hen Night" are the names of the two commercials used during the period covered. The deconstructed effect of the advertising on sales

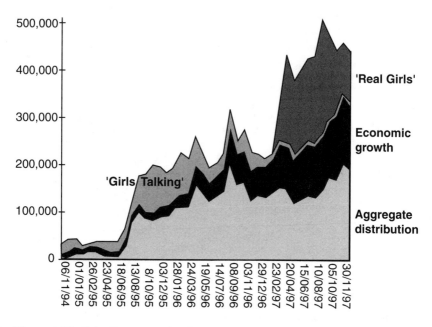

Figure A.16. Sales Deconstruction for Clean & Clear

appears to have been modest, but it was nevertheless significant.[19] Most important, the case study makes it clear that the effect of the advertising did not stop, but it also had a delayed effect:

> —Each burst produces a sales effect with a very long "tail" (to the extent that there is no point during any year when advertising is having no effect on sales).

> —Sales are always above the level preceding the last burst, when the subsequent burst of advertising takes place.[20]

Statistical modeling is often applied to brands with the specific intention of factoring in the delayed effect of previous advertising. In such models, advertising is generally assumed to decay at a fixed rate, and the (declining) residual effect, often known as Adstock, provides a base onto which additional shorter-term effects should be added.[21] However, the procedure is not free from controversy. It raises two problems. The first is that lagged effects may be relatively common but are more usually modeled than observed. (With Knorr they *are*

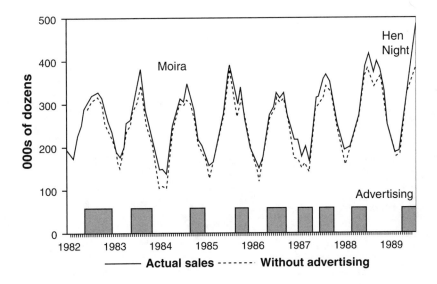

Figure A.17. Sales of Knorr Stock Cubes Related to Television Advertising

observed, which is one of the reasons why the Knorr case is so interesting.) Also, in many observed examples they appear to be absent; the effect of advertising appears to stop completely. The second problem is that the procedure does not make totally clear whether the delayed effect of advertising is the result of the advertising itself in the form of memory traces or whether it is the result of positive behavioral changes, especially improvements in penetration and purchase frequency triggered by the earlier advertising.

Figure A.18 uses a totally different tracking technique. The brand is again Marmite, described in Figure A.12. In Figure A.18, the advertising expenditures for each year for 30 years are shown on the one diagram, plotted against Marmite's sales during the same year.[22] There is a reasonably good correlation between the two variables, although the analysis does not completely establish the direction of causality. Does higher advertising always cause higher sales? Or do higher sales encourage the manufacturer to put more money into advertising toward the end of the year, in order to reinforce success? This is a perpetual dilemma for students of advertising effects, since the majority of advertisers still base their budgets directly or indirectly on their achieved or anticipated sales.

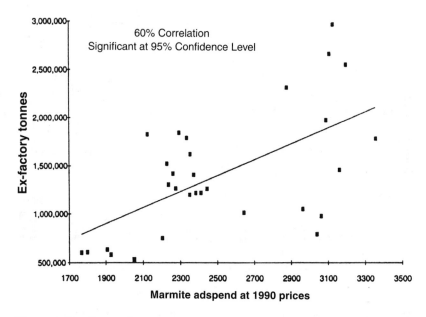

Figure A.18. Scatterplot of Advertising Expenditure and Sales, 1969–1998, for Marmite

The final example of complex tracking employs an unusual and very imaginative technique. It is based on the demand curve, an analytical device derived from microeconomics. A demand curve plots at any particular time the sales associated with different prices for a brand. Almost invariably, high price is associated with low-volume sales, and low price is associated with high-volume sales. Figure A.19 describes Audi, a high-end European automobile.[23] The analysis is based on the average price of *used* cars. Any improvement (i.e., increase) in price is seen to result from an enhancement of buyers' personal attitudes to Audi. This means, in effect, an endemic strengthening of the brand, something to which the advertising undoubtedly contributed. In Figure A.19, the supply curve, measuring volume of supply at each price level, is the dotted line rising from southwest to northeast. There are two demand curves, descending from northwest to southeast. The equilibrium level of price and sales on the first demand curve is plotted at D1.

During the 6-month period March–September 1995, the resale value of Audi increased by about 10%. By comparison, the average for competitive marques

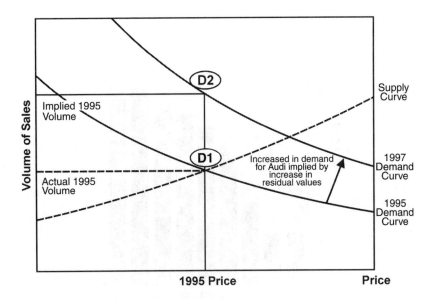

Figure A.19. Shifting Demand Curve for Audi

did not change at all. Audi's price increase, which represents buyers' higher personal valuation of the marque—an outcome influenced by the advertising—can reasonably be applied as a notional price increase for *new* Audi cars. (The enhanced value of the brand applies equally to used and new vehicles.) This higher valuation can be interpreted either as a higher price for an existing volume of sales or a higher volume of sales for an existing price. The latter hypothesis is represented in Figure A.19 by a shift to the right in Audi's demand curve. The difference between the points plotted at D1 and D2 represents the probable extra number of cars sold as a result of the boost in demand that took place between March and September 1995.

The influence of advertising is seen therefore as taking place in the following sequence: (a) an enhanced valuation of the brand by consumers—the result of successful advertising; (b) boosted demand; and finally, (c) a national increase in the volume of sales.

Demonstrating how advertising increases consumer demand by means of a shift in the curve to the right is not unknown in the literature of advertising. A similar example was published in 1986, based on market experience during the 1970s.[24] This relates to a brand on which I myself worked at J. Walter

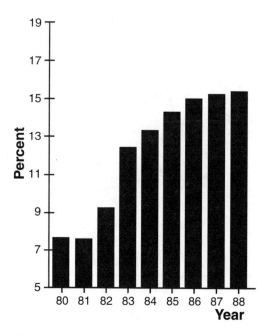

Figure A.20. Stella Artois Market Share, 1980–1988

Thompson and which is briefly described in Appendix B as the Corlett Shift. This is also the device employed by the Simon-Arndt Hypothesis, also described in Appendix B.

A Coda—and a Warning

The most common—and the most dangerous—use of trend lines is to project them into the future without too much serious thought about what this means. Such projection is often carried out in the most naïve fashion, by drawing a straight line connecting the past to the future. Even when the projection is made in a more subtle way, the procedure can result in disastrous outcomes.

Consider Figure A.20, which describes the year-by-year market share of Stella Artois, the brand of beer examined in Figures A.4 and A.13. Figure A.20 shows the progress of the brand during the years 1980–1988.

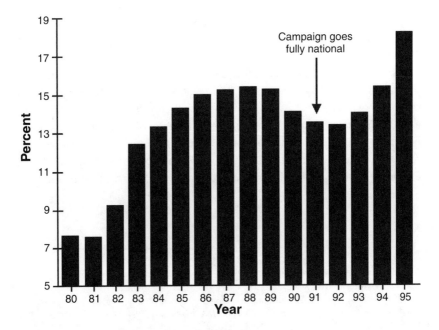

Figure A.21. Stella Artois Market Share, 1980–1995

Most observers, amateur and professional alike, would understand the point that Stella Artois's market share was increasing during this period, although at a declining rate. They would therefore immediately be tempted to extrapolate the trend into future years by suggesting a very gradual rise and eventually a flattening of the vertical bars.

The actual progress of the brand showed a very different picture, as is evident in Figure A.21.[25]

The important point made by this simple example is that statistics do not have a life of their own. They are nothing more than numbers that economically and precisely describe underlying patterns. If the statistics change—in particular, if they move consistently in one direction represented by a trend line—they are measuring underlying forces, and it does not mean that these will also continue to change in the same direction during the next 5 years or even next year. If we wish to forecast the future—something we always try to do when we are planning marketing activities—we must not look at any trend line, but we should examine *the underlying forces that are expressed by the statistics embodied in a trend line.*

The fallacy of extrapolating trends is apparent to a most distressing degree in all fields of human endeavor. During the closely fought presidential election of 2000, it was obvious to statisticians that the main issue dividing the two candidates was their alternative plans for spending a budget surplus of utopian proportions that was arrived at by straight-line projections of the long-term fiscal outcomes of an especially strong American economy during the years immediately leading up to the election. Even by the time this book is published, it will be interesting to measure the outturn of these projections one year down the road and, as a result, to judge the financial prudence of the administration's election promises. As I write these words I am overcome by skepticism.

Notes

1. Archives held by the World Advertising Research Centre (e-mail address: enquiries@ warc.com). Website: www.warc.com

2. Charlie Robertson, "Health Education Board for Scotland: Smoking. Sticks and Carrots," in *Advertising Works: Volume 8. Papers From the IPA Advertising Effectiveness Awards,* ed. Chris Baker (Henley-on-Thames, UK: NTC Publications, 1995), 401-418.

3. Colin Flint, "Love Over Gold: The Untold Story of TV's Greatest Romance," in *Advertising Works: Volume 9. Papers From the IPA Advertising Effectiveness Awards,* ed. Gary Duckworth (Henley-on-Thames, UK: NTC Publications, 1997), 387-403.

4. Nick Kendall, "Häagen-Dazs: Dedicated to Pleasure, Dedicated to Advertising," in *Advertising Works: Volume 7. Papers From the IPA Advertising Effectiveness Awards,* ed. Chris Baker (Henley-on-Thames, UK: NTC Publications, 1993), 191-216.

5. Jon Howard, Andy Palmer, and George Bryant, "Seven Years in Provence: How a Change in Strategy Helped Stella Artois Retain Market Dominance," in *Advertising Works: Volume 9,* 429-457.

6. Merry Baskin, "De Beers: Hard Times. Selling Diamonds in a Recession," Ibid., 307-345.

7. Liz Watts and Cindy Gallop, "Cadbury's Roses: 'Thank You Very Much,' " in *Advertising Works: Volume 8,* 81-101.

8. Charles Vallance, "Orange: How Two Years of Advertising Created Twelve Years of Value," in *Advertising Works: Volume 9,* 5-28.

9. Ibid.

10. Gavin Macdonald and Antony Buck, "The Volkswagen Golf, 1984-1990," in *Advertising Works: Volume 7,* 75-99.

11. Sarah Carter and Sam Dias, "Meat & Livestock Commission: Pulling Round the Red Meat Market," in *Advertising Works: Volume 10. Papers From the IPA Advertising Effectiveness Awards,* ed. Nick Kendall (Henley-on-Thames, UK: NTC Publications, 1999), 283-315.

12. Baskin, "De Beers," in *Advertising Works: Volume 9.*

13. Jacqueline Feasey, "I Can't Believe It's Not Butter! From Extraordinary Launch to Long-Term Success," in *Advertising Works: Volume 9,* 459-472.

14. Lucy Jameson and Les Binet, "Marmite: How 'The Growing Up Spread' Just Carried On Growing," in *Advertising Works: Volume 10,* 127-160.

15. Howard, Palmer, and Bryant, "Seven Years in Provence," in *Advertising Works: Volume 9*.

16. Guy Murphy, "Boddington's—'By 'eck,' " in *Advertising Works: Volume 8*, 129-160.

17. Derek Robson, "Cadbury's Boost: 'Why Work and Rest When You Can Play?,' " in *Advertising Works: Volume 8*, 279-307.

18. Polly Evelegh and Sam Dias, "Johnson's Clean & Clear: Global Advertising in a Local Market," in *Advertising Works: Volume 10*, 363-399.

19. Sarah Carter, "Knorr Stock Cubes: How Thinking 'Local' Helped Corn Products Corporation (CPC) Develop Advertising Which Toppled the Brand Leader," in *Advertising Works: Volume 6. Papers From the IPA Advertising Effectiveness Awards*, ed. Paul Feldwick (Henley-on-Thames, UK: NTC Publications, 1991), 141-167.

20. Ibid., 163.

21. Lagged effects are discussed widely in the literature of advertising evaluation. They are most clearly described in Simon Broadbent, *The Leo Burnett Book of Advertising* (London: Business Books, 1984), 88-98. See also Chapter 6, Note 8.

22. Jameson and Binet, "Marmite," in *Advertising Works: Volume 10*.

23. Richard Exon, "Audi: Members Only. How Advertising Helped Audi Join the Prestige Car Club," in *Advertising Works: Volume 10*, 321-347.

24. John Philip Jones, *What's in a Name? Advertising and the Concept of Brands* (New York: Simon & Schuster-Lexington Books, 1986), 95-96.

25. Howard, Palmer, and Bryant, "Seven Years in Provence," in *Advertising Works: Volume 9*.

Appendix B:
Alternative Systems for
Measuring Long-Term Effects

This appendix is devoted to describing two further methods of evaluating the long-term effects of advertising. These are partly in the world of theory and partly in the world of practice. If they were to be applied to the measurement of long-term effects in a wide range of specific cases, they would fulfil their potential as important inductive techniques. The first is an extension of the share of voice/share of market relationship discussed in Chapter 7; the second leans on expository devices developed in the field of microeconomic analysis, namely, shifting curves.

Changes in Share of Voice

The discussion of share of voice in Chapter 7 has been based on data for up to 5 years, and the averages for share of voice and share of market have been calculated in a similar way to make the comparison. The average SOV is assumed to

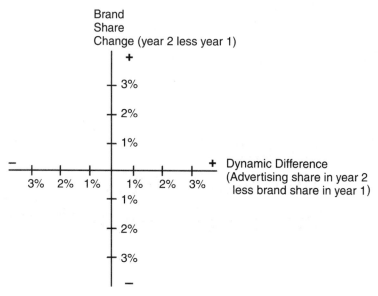

Figure B.1. Structure of Dynamic Difference/Marketing Advertising Pattern

be relatively stable and the extent to which it can continuously and safely run below SOM is an expression of the strength of the brand—a strength to which advertising has contributed in its long-term role.

However, what happens if a brand's SOV is increased or decreased as part of a plan either to boost sales or to increase profit? This possibility has been widely explored, and it was examined with the use of simple mathematics at least 40 years ago by British statistician Michael Moroney, who worked for Unilever, and by American market researcher James O. Peckham, Sr., of A. C. Nielsen. These two experienced analysts were working totally independently but came to the same conclusion. The Moroney method was called Dynamic Difference,[1] and the Peckham term for the same system was Marketing Advertising Pattern (MAP).[2]

The system is set out diagrammatically in Figure B.1. Year-on-year changes in SOV are plotted in percentage points on the horizontal axis. (These are calculated as SOV in Year 2 minus SOM in Year 1. The assumption is, of course, that the normal stable category-average relationship is SOV = SOM.) Year-on-year changes in share of market are plotted on the vertical axis. (These are calculated as SOM in Year 2 minus SOM in Year 1.)

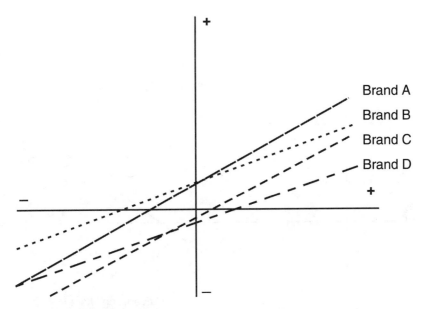

Figure B.2. Dynamic Difference/Marketing Advertising Pattern Lines for Four Hypothetical Brands

As can be inferred from Figure B.1, a positive effect from advertising will lead to a regression that ascends from southwest to northeast. If the relationship between changes in SOV and changes in SOM is found to be relatively consistent over a number of years, a line can be drawn connecting the observation points. This line is different for different brands, as can be seen in the hypothetical examples in Figure B.2. The steeper the line (e.g., Brand A), the more responsive the brand is to changes in advertising investment, up or down.

Each observation in Dynamic Difference/MAP really measures changes in the medium-term effect of advertising. However, when we can plot a regression line derived from a number of years of data, then the slope of the line can be interpreted as a measure of the long-term effect.

There is however a serious problem with Dynamic Difference/MAP. During the 1960s, it was possible to construct lines that fit in about 70% of cases. At that time there was less volatility in most brands' advertising than there is today, when a different campaign is introduced for most brands every 2 or 3 years. In addition, the large and increasing volume of sales promotions today tends to cloud the advertising expenditure/sales relationship. These factors mean that

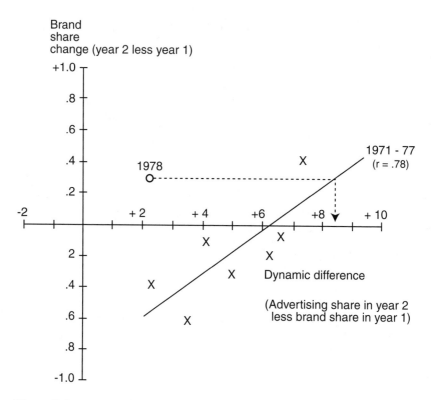

Figure B.3. Elliott Extension: Dynamic Difference for Kellogg's Rice Krispies in Great Britain

stable Dynamic Difference/MAP regressions are now relatively rare, although when they do exist they are capable of providing a good measure of advertising's long-term effect, a measure akin to year-on-year changes in a brand's advertising elasticity. (Advertising elasticity is discussed in Chapter 9.)

There is another interesting aspect to Dynamic Difference/MAP. If a regression *can* be established for a brand, it is possible *to quantify the productivity of a successful new campaign* that has produced an effect outside the regression line. Figure B.3 demonstrates this device in action with a historical example. I call this special case the Elliott Extension, named after Jeremy Elliott of J. Walter Thompson, London, who first published it.[3]

Before the exposure of a new campaign in 1978, Kellogg's Rice Krispies had an established Dynamic Difference/MAP line constructed from 7 years of data (indicated by the crosses on the diagram). The 1978 campaign—based on an extremely powerful advertising idea—received advertising support of 2 percentage points SOV above the brand's SOM of the preceding year. The campaign's performance is shown by its market share improvement of 2 percentage points.

This sales improvement was far better than the previous regression suggested. According to the earlier response of sales to changes in advertising, an improvement of 2 percentage points in SOM would have incurred an expenditure in advertising of more than 8 percentage points of SOV above the previous year's SOM. Elliott's analysis shows that the productivity of the new campaign in comparison with the old one can be calculated as a dollar value—the difference between an overinvestment of 8 percentage points and 2 percentage points. In this particular example, it meant about a million dollars at 1978 prices, a sum representing the enhanced value of sales from the more effective advertising.

Dynamic Difference/MAP and the Elliott Extension of this are simple statistical devices. For most brands, the statistical data are readily available. Despite the fact that the first of these artifacts will only operate on infrequent occasions, and the second more rarely still, they are both capable of uncovering hidden underlying relationships.

Two Shifting Curves

Corlett Shift

Microeconomic analysis is usually based on simple geometry. A demand curve, which plots volume bought against price charged, almost invariably descends from northwest to southeast, representing the commonsense idea that a high price equates to small quantities being sold but that a low price will stimulate large sales.

Tom Corlett, of J. Walter Thompson, London, managed to demonstrate the long-term effects of advertising through a simple shift in the demand curve, but he had to collect a significant amount of data for the brand he used for his exposition.

Corlett's starting point was to build a demand curve. He chose a major British brand in a reasonably large packaged goods market. This calculation was

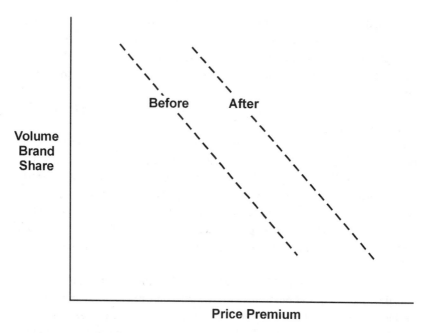

Figure B.4. Corlett Shift

possible because the brand is sold at various price premiums above other brands in different regions, with resultant differences in the brand's market share, so that a range of data could be provided for a time period of defined length.

The price was expressed as the premium over other brands, thus eliminating the effects of inflation. This also means that what is measured on one axis (the price of one brand compared with others in the market) is entirely consistent with what is measured on the other axis (the sales of one brand compared with others).

The second stage in Corlett's work was the construction of a similar demand curve for a later period after the exposure of advertising. The campaign in question had earlier been judged highly successful on the basis of all available objective measures: ex-factory sales, market share, attitudinal and other qualitative research, and popularity polls. But the best demonstration of the campaign's success is Corlett's analysis of the brand after the campaign's exposure because his demand curve had moved quite significantly to the right, as shown in Figure B.4.

This clearly showed that, after the advertising, (a) at a given price premium, the brand could now command a quantifiably larger brand share; and (b) at a given brand share, the brand could now command a quantifiably greater price premium.

This made it possible quite simply to make estimates of marginal sales revenue added by the campaign. These estimates could also be compared with the cost of the campaign so as to indicate its marginal profitability to the manufacturer.[4]

Simon-Arndt Hypothesis

Two academics, American Julian Simon and Norwegian Johan Arndt, addressed the perplexing problem of the strong underlying tendency to short-term diminishing returns (as discussed in Chapter 5) and also the strong underlying tendency to long-term economies of scale for certain brands. Increasing returns and scale economies are different concepts, but in certain circumstances they can be related: The latter can contribute to the former. How can we explain this apparent contradiction between short-term diminishing returns and what looks like long-term increasing returns?

The most plausible explanation is that the scale economies associated with successful brands apply to *all aspects* of those brands, stemming as they do from their functional and nonfunctional values and also from such things as distributional ubiquity and high usage.

An elegant explanation of this phenomenon appears in Simon and Arndt's analysis of Lambin's review of 107 European brands and his findings that larger brands have advertising economies. Lambin noted, "for large brands, the inverse relationship between the advertising-sales ratio and market share."[5]

When Simon and Arndt came to consider this widespread phenomenon, they rightly concentrated on the *overall* scale economies associated with the larger brands:

> It is reasonable and likely that firm E has a much more extensive distribution network and a larger sales force than firm A. That would explain *both* why firm E has a higher response function *and* why it advertises more in total than does firm A. And, depending on the particular slopes of the functions, the advertising-sales ratio could well be lower for the larger firm for this reason alone.[6]

Although Simon and Arndt were thinking in terms of the firm rather than the brand, they had clearly grasped the essential point, and their diagrammatic

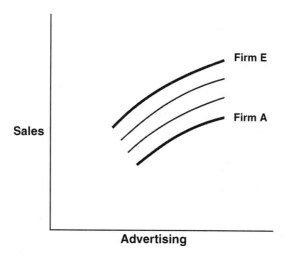

Figure B.5. Simon-Arndt Hypothesis

expression of this point in Figure B.5 explains the position of the larger brand with its scale economies.

The authors show the possibility of a *family* of advertising response curves. Here the position of the large firm with scale economies (Firm E) would, of course, be higher than that of the small one without the scale economies (Firm A). From this analysis, it is obvious why a given incremental dose of advertising has a greater effect for Firm E. The position of the two curves relative to one another is not a reflection of the advertising alone but of the relative strengths of the firms overall to which advertising has naturally made and continues to make a contribution.

The short-term response function is driven by advertising directly. The fact that this curve has shifted to a more productive location—a long-range outcome—is the partial and indirect but unmistakable outcome of the advertising. This is a true long-term effect.

Notes

1. John Philip Jones, *What's in a Name? Advertising and the Concept of Brands* (New York: Simon & Schuster-Lexington Books, 1986), 87-92.

2. James O. Peckham, Sr., *The Wheel of Marketing,* 2nd edition (privately published 1981, but available from A. C. Nielsen), 108-130.

3. Jeremy Elliott, "Kellogg's Rice Krispies: The Effect of a New Creative Execution," in *Advertising Works: Volume 1. Papers From the Institute of Practitioners in Advertising (IPA) Effectiveness Awards,* ed. Simon Broadbent (London: Holt, Rinehart & Winston, 1981), 86-87.

4. Tom Corlett, "How to Make Sense of Market Analysis," *Campaign,* May 26, 1978. Also discussed in Jones, *What's in a Name?,* 95-96.

5. J. J. Lambin, *Advertising, Competition and Market Conduct in Oligopoly Over Time* (New York: American Elsevier, 1976), 127-132.

6. Julian L. Simon and Johan Arndt, "The Shape of the Advertising Response Function," *Journal of Advertising Research,* August 1980, 22. Also discussed in Jones, *What's in a Name?,* 203-204.

Index

About the Author

John Philip Jones was born in Wales in 1930 and graduated in economics from Cambridge University (B.A. with Honors; M.A.). From 1953 to 1980, he worked in the advertising agency field. This experience included 25 years with J. Walter Thompson—as a market research executive in London (1953-55), advertising account executive in London (1957-65), account supervisor and head of television in Amsterdam (1965-67), account director and head of client service in Scandinavia, based in Copenhagen (1967-72), and account director in London (1972-80).

He worked with a wide variety of advertising clients and was most concerned with major brands of packaged goods (which in his research he titles Beta brands). His responsibilities included many brands marketed by Unilever, Chesebrough-Pond's (before its acquisition by Unilever), Beecham, Gillette, Nestlé, Pan American, Pepsi-Cola, Quaker Oats, and Scott Paper. He was international account director on Lux, the largest selling bar soap in the world, from 1972 to 1980.

He was extensively involved with advertising education both within and outside the agency. He conducted his final agency seminar in January 1981 before becoming a full-time educator in the Newhouse School of Public Communications at Syracuse University, where he is a tenured full professor and was Chair of the Advertising Department in the Newhouse School for seven years. He has taught a wide range of advertising classes at both the graduate and undergraduate levels.

For three years, he edited the university's interdisciplinary journal of ideas, *Syracuse Scholar.* He was a member of the Mellon Foundation project group, which spent two years exploring the connection between liberal and professional education and published its findings in the book *Contesting the Boundaries* (1988).

He has published widely in the professional press, with articles appearing in *Admap, Commercial Communications, Economist: Media & Marketing Europe, Harvard Business Review, International Journal of Advertising, Journal of Advertising Research, Journal of Marketing Communications, Marketing & Research Today, Marketing Management, Market Leader,* and many other publications, including journals in Australia, Great Britain, the Czech Republic, Germany, India, the Netherlands, Scandinavia, and Switzerland. He has also contributed pieces to the *New York Times* and other publications.

His books *What's in a Name? Advertising and the Concept of Brands* (1986), *Does It Pay to Advertise? Cases Illustrating Successful Brand Advertising* (1989), *How Much Is Enough? Getting the Most From Your Advertising Dollar* (1992), and *When Ads Work: New Proof That Advertising Triggers Sales* (1995) are widely used in the advertising profession in the United States and overseas and have been translated into German, Spanish, Japanese, Korean, Chinese, Portuguese, Turkish, and Arabic.

He was editor and part-author of five major handbooks, published by Sage in 1998, 1999, and 2000. The 2000-page collection deals with all major aspects of advertising practice.

He has developed measurement devices based on robust quantitative research. These include STAS (Short-Term Advertising Strength) and AIC (Advertising-Intensiveness Curve), which are used in professional practice and described in his books. He is a consultant to many leading consumer goods companies and advertising agencies in the United States and abroad. He also regularly addresses major professional conferences.

In 1991, the American Advertising Federation named him Distinguished Advertising Educator of the Year. In 1996, he received a major award from Cowles Business Media and the American Association of Advertising Agencies for leadership in the media field. He received the Telmar Award in 1997 for extending the concept of STAS from television to print media. In 2001, he was awarded the Syracuse University Chancellor's Citation for Exceptional Academic Achievement.

Every year, he presents his work to professional and academic audiences worldwide. He is Adjunct Professor at the Royal Melbourne Institute of Technology, Australia, where he teaches each May.